Wayne Cheselka

Foreword

Pastor Wayne Cheselka serves as Director of Driven by the Spirit Motorcycle Ministry and Outreach Pastor at Midland Valley Community Church of the Nazarene in Clearwater, SC. He also serves as a member of the Executive Counsel for the Nazarene Motorcycle Fellowship.

Wayne retired from the US Army after 20 years of active service and he again recently retired as a Senior Engineering Consultant, where he served as a support contractor for the U.S. Army at Fort Gordon, GA.

Wayne has been married to his wife Joy for 23 years. They call North Augusta, SC home and have one adult son, Bryan and one grandson, Levi.

Wayne answered the call to start the motorcycle ministry in 2004 and the call into ministry in 2007. He was Ordained in July 2016 after completing his course of study through Northwest Nazarene University.

Wayne enjoys leading bible studies and speaking at various biker events. He also enjoys spending time with his family, riding motorcycles, traveling, camping, writing and entertaining. He is looking forward to serving God and continuing his call to minister to those outside the church as well as disciple those inside the church.

January 1

"I urge, then, first of all, that petitions, prayers, intercession and thanksgiving be made for all people..." (1 Timothy 2:1)

Sometimes God puts special people in your life. God has blessed me by putting people in my path that just make me a better person. When I think of such people, I can't help but remember Scott and Trish. I met them in Laconia, NH during bike week. They were camped beside us and we immediately hit it off. Scott had an infectious smile and Trish was a tender old soul. We shared stories and even a tear or two.

I hated to see them pack up and go. I liked the conversations we had, but as they departed, I felt a twinge of regret.

You see, I had the opportunity to share Jesus with them. We talked about things like hope, mercy, grace and love. We talked about a peace and understanding that can only come from knowing Jesus Christ as our personal Savior. We talked about how, through a relationship with Jesus, we can live a life free from guilt of our past. I saw their eyes change; they got it, they understood. Now I don't know if they made any life changing decisions that day or the days after, but it affected me in several ways.

First, I was humbled to be allowed to share with them the things of Jesus. To be used by God to help others come to know Jesus is one of the greatest feelings to have. I loved sharing with them and I tried to use my life experiences to give them comfort and hope.

But the other way this affected me was that I missed an opportunity. You see, I failed to pray for and with them. As they drove away, a feeling of regret came over me; one that, to this day, I still carry.

They heard about Jesus, they had that glimmer of hope in their eyes, yet they didn't receive one of the greatest gifts we can share with others, and that is the gift of intercessory prayer.

Paul urges us to pray for others, to lift up their needs, desires, and lives to God. We say it all the time, "I'll pray for you" but do we? I missed the one opportunity I had to pray with that sweet couple and to this day I regret it. I never want to miss a chance like that again.

So, when I say I'll pray for you, know that I do. But if we are face to face and you ask for prayer and I don't pray right then, stop me and ask me to. I never want to miss another opportunity to lift up others to my God. Praying for others is a privilege we should never take lightly.

1

January 2

"Your word is a lamp to my feet and a light for my path." (Psalm 119:105)

While serving in the Army overseas, a letter from home was a treat. My dad and I were close. I missed him bad, so a letter from him was very special. As soon as I had his letter in hand, I would waste no time reading each and every word. My father's letter to me became the most important thing.

Psalm 119 is the longest chapter in the bible. Of 176 verses, 172 refer to God's Word. The Psalmist stressed the importance of God's Word to guide and direct us in our daily walk with Him. God's Word is vital if we want to live as overcomers of this world.

It is one thing to believe in God, but another to allow that belief to transform our lives. God's Word is meant for just that. It teaches right from wrong, Godly behaviors verses worldly behaviors. It keeps us focused on God's ways and helps us to steer clear of worldly ways. So reading that letter is crucial.

Imagine, if you would, how my dad would have felt if I would have received his letter and instead of reading it, I placed it on a shelf for later. Imagine how hurt he would have been if he knew that it held no importance to me. Now imagine how God may feel if we don't place priority on His letter to us.

God wrote the bible as a letter to His children. Within that letter contains His heart for us, His teachings, and His path for our life. Make consuming it a priority....

January 3

"Friends come and friends go, but a true friend sticks by you like family."
(Proverbs 18:24 MSG)

My little dog had an eye condition that caused her to lose sight in one eye. It was painful and part of the treatment consisted of drops several times a day. She hated those drops and tried to avoid us when she would see the little medicine bottles. But as soon as the drops were applied, she was over being mad at us and continued to show her love for us.

Her eye worsened and it had to be surgically removed. She didn't want to go to the vet, and I know the procedure was painful, yet minus one eye, she still loves on us like before.

We all need friends like that. Friends that even during the difficult or painful times, they still love us. Once I heard that everyone needs 9:00 a.m. friends and a few 3:00 a.m. friends. 9:00 a.m. friends like to hang out, have fun, yet aren't really devoted to the friendship once trouble hits. They can take you or leave you. We all have plenty of those kinds of friends.

What we really need are the 3:00 a.m. friends. These are friends you call at 3:00 a.m. when you are broke down, in the hospital or can't sleep. The 3:00 a.m. friend will answer the phone, come and get you or talk you down off the ledge.

These friends are rare and special. They love you no matter what or when. They are there for you through thick and thin. You can count on them when you need them.

I encourage you to find one or more 3:00 a.m. friends and treat them right. Be there for them as they are for you. And if you find yourself having trouble finding such a friend, remember that Jesus is a friend that is always there for you. He never tires of hearing from you and when you call He answers and comes, no matter what time of day or night.

3

January 4

"Just as man is destined to die once, and after that to face judgment, so Christ was sacrificed once to take away the sins of many people; and he will appear a second time, not to bear sin, but to bring salvation to those who are waiting for him." (Hebrews 9:27-28)

My little dog Ziggy sits outside by the back door anxiously waiting to be let into the house. She sits patiently for the most part, but every now and again she will let out a "Yelp" trying to get my attention. I love to watch her once I open the door because she rushes in and lets me know how excited she is to see me.

As I read our focus verse, I can't help but ask myself, am I waiting with as much anxiousness for Jesus as my little dog waits for me? What do I do to get His attention? Does He know how much I want to be in His presence?

The New Covenant Jesus gave us is that He will return one day. On that day Jesus will open the gates of Heaven and let the true believers, those who look for His return, into His presence for eternity. The wait will be over.

My little dog gets so excited when she comes into the house. She runs in circles and stands on her hind legs, looking for her treat. Not sure about you, but I think I will be so excited to get into heaven, I may run in circles as well. I look forward to my reward in heaven, but the thing I look forward to the most is, being in the presence of God.

So God, I know you can hear me, so I am letting you know now, I am waiting... Yelp... Yelp.... Yelp....

January 5

"I am the way and the truth and the life, no one comes to the Father except through me." (John 14:5)

There I stood after walking two miles up hill, staring at a tiny little sign made of wood with the words "Mt. Pisgah" carved into it. I thought for a brief second, then turned and followed the arrow that pointed the way. I was off to what I hoped was the top of Mt. Pisgah, some 5721 feet above sea level. I had already walked from 4235 feet to this point, what was 1486 more feet?

As I walked, a thought came to mind. I had set on a path that was very ill defined, narrow, rocky and steep. I was on a path to what I hoped was the destination I had imagined and never once questioned it. How is it that I didn't question this path? Was I sure it would take me where I wanted to go? How many others have trusted that tiny little sign and taken this same path?

Why is it people seldom question a path that is uncertain or marked with a small handmade sign, but question the path God puts before us? Neither path is at times well defined. Both could lead me to places "we" may not want to go. We question God's path, but trust the rocky steep climb to the top of a mountain.

We are faced with decisions every day in this life. We are given paths to follow and we must decide if it is the right one or not. One such path is the path to eternal life in Heaven. Our focus verse defines the path before us and what we must decide is if we will take it or not.

There are several paths one can take, a narrow one to heaven or a wide one to destruction. (Matthew 7:13-14) The path Jesus sets before us is a narrow path, and only a "few" will follow it. Those that take the right path will be led straight to heaven. Those that decide not to follow, the "many" will be left to face the alternative, hell. So, the next time you are faced with a decision on whether to follow Jesus' path, which will you pick?

January 6

"Jonah was a sign to the Ninevites..." (Luke 11:30)

"...they repented at the preaching of Jonah..." (Luke 11:32)

I get a chuckle when I am reminded of the story of Jonah. I think of how he ran from God, boarded a boat, and ran the opposite direction because he didn't want to do what God wanted him to do. He was thrown off that boat, swallowed by a big fish, spit up by that same fish and in the end did what God wanted him to do anyway. My mind plays out this cartoon of Jonah going through all that and I laugh at how funny that story would be on film.

Then I am snapped back to reality and my own life comes to mind. I too ran from God. I argued with God, I hid, went in the opposite direction, was swallowed up by the world, and did everything I could to keep as far from God as possible. And in the end, here I sit; doing God's will or at least trying to.

I often wonder what the Ninevites thought when they first saw Jonah? After three days in the belly of a fish, he must have been a sight, smelly and covered with fish goo. Did they focus on his exterior, or did they focus on his message? Well, we know the answer. Jonah 3:3-5 tells us that Jonah obeyed God, went to Nineveh and the people believed. They saw God through him and were convinced that they needed what he had.

The people saw God in Jonah and his preaching; they saw change from within. Remember Jonah hated the Ninevites, yet he was given a new heart, he humbled himself and obeyed God. What resulted was a whole group of people saved because of that obedience. Jonah 3:10 tells us that when God saw what Jonah had done *"He had compassion and did not bring upon them the destruction He had threatened."* God had mercy on Nineveh because of Jonah's obedience.

What about you? Are you a living testament to the power of the gospel? Can people see you and say, "...not sure what it is, but the change is definite, something is going on with them..."

It is something I am aware of in my life. I want people to see me and know there is change, know something is different and know that something much greater than me is at work within me. I want to be a sign to others that God changes and saves. How about you?

January 7

"Whatever you do, work at it with all your heart, as working for the Lord..."
(Colossians 3:23)

I am a very energetic person. I run wide open all day long. I don't sit much, nor do I stop when things need doing. I am a doer and I love to stay busy. But when I go to lie down, I am out pretty quick and I sleep very sound. I read a story today that sounds pretty much like me.

A young man asked a farmer for a job as a farmhand. "What can you do?" inquired the farmer. "I can do whatever has to be done, and I can sleep when the wind blows," replied the applicant. Although mystified by the phrase "I can sleep when the wind blows," the farmer did not press the question but hired the young man.

Some nights later, a violent storm awoke the farmer. He got up and tried unsuccessfully to arouse the farmhand. With considerable annoyance, he then went out himself to see if all was well. He found the barn locked, the chicken coop properly closed up, a wagonload of hay covered with a tarpaulin securely battened down, and all else safely secured. Then the farmer realized what his new farmhand meant when he said, "I can sleep when the wind blows." (Author unknown)

That young man knew what needed to be done and he did it, then he slept peacefully through the storm. This is a good lesson for us. Do the right thing, do it well and then rest. When you do what you know to be right, you rest much easier and you can weather any storm. My father used to say, "A job worth doing is worth doing right." I agree and I think that can be applied to every aspect of our lives.

As a Christ follower, this applies to our walk with Jesus. If we walk daily as Jesus instructs and modeled, we can be confident that we will weather any storm in life. Oh they will still come, but getting through it is much easier when you prepare beforehand. Just like the farmhand, when we do what is needed before we sleep, our sleep is uninterrupted. The same is said about our lives, when we live our lives as we should, our lives are less likely to be thrown into turmoil and chaos, but when they are, we can rest knowing that God is in control.

January 8

"Bad company corrupts good character." (1 Corinthians 15:34)

A 12 year old boy asks his mom to take him and his friends to a movie. He explains to his mom that she must escort them in because the movie has "a little bad in it". He tells her all his other friends have seen it and it is a must see movie, even though it has a little bad in it.

Mom agrees and even offers to make brownies for the boys before they go. Sometime later she calls them to the kitchen; it's filled with the aroma of fresh baked brownies. Before they dive into them, mom said that they were special brownies. While she was mixing the batter, she went out in the yard and got a little dog poo and added it to the mix. She assured them that it was just "a little bit of bad", but that they were okay to eat. The boys, grossed out yelled "we can't eat these; they have bad stuff in them!" In which mom replied, "exactly, and you aren't going to that movie either." (Author unknown)

How much "bad" is acceptable in your life? Do you go along with the notion that as long as it doesn't hurt you or others it's okay? This world revolves around that mentality.

We learn in scripture that those who profess to believe in Jesus must be set apart from the world. We don't do the things this world seems to accept as normal.

I heard a term the other day that describe many who profess to be Jesus believers. It's called "fashionable Christianity". The thought behind this term is that you are a "Christian" when it suits you or the situation. Yet you give up a piece of that belief when it doesn't quite fit the things you want to do.

But that goes against the grain of being a Christ follower. We learn in scripture that when we come to believe, we must be "born again", become a new person, one birthed from within, filled with the Holy Spirit. We leave all our old ways behind and take on the image of Jesus Himself. Not being Him, but living as Jesus modeled.

So what about you? Do you accept a little bad in your life? Is it okay to keep some of the old, and only have a little of the new? Or are you totally sold out and living as Christ would want you to? Our passage above tells us that bad corrupts good. So to me, that means we must leave the bad out in order to live the good life Jesus wants us to live. Think about it!

January 9

"'For I know the plans I have for you,' declares the LORD, 'plans to prosper you and not to harm you, plans to give you hope and a future.'" (Jeremiah 29:11)

I often wonder if I disappointed my parents. Most parents have an idea of what they want their children to become when they grow up. Mine never mentioned it, but I often wondered if they would have wanted me to be something other than what I have become.

When my son was young I had this notion he would go to college and be successful. I thought of him as a doctor or a lawyer. But his idea of a career path took him in a different direction. He does have a very good career and I am very proud of him.

Our focus verse tells us that God has a plan for our lives. God has a plan for each of our lives, but often we take a wrong turn somewhere. Satan has a plan as well. He wants us to go down that wrong road, make that mistake. He loves it when we disappoint God. He wants you to be ruined, destroyed, lost, suffering, tempted, miserable, bitter, frustrated, and fallen. He wants our friendships, marriages, ministries, family life, and reputations to be destroyed. He wants the total opposite for our life than what God wants.

God doesn't really care what career path we take. What He does want is for us to prosper and live rich and full lives. We can fight the enemy if we follow a few simple precautions. First, don't take one step towards any temptation from the enemy. Once you do, he releases his plan on your life, causing ruin, devastation and turmoil. Second, to avoid the enemy we must draw closer to God and His plan for our life. If we continue to seek God's will for our life, and gain a closer relationship with Him, He will unleash victory in our lives.

We can't be in God's plans and the enemy's plans at the same time. By seeking God's plan, the further away the enemy's plan gets. God's path is perfect and by following that path, we can receive the full blessings that He desires for us. So, whose plan are you following?

"But the plans of the LORD stand firm forever, the purposes of his heart through all generations." (Psalm 33:11)

January 10

"This, then, is how you should pray...your will be done." (Matthew 6:9-10)

I have been walking with God for some time now. I have to admit, I still don't always get everything right. For example, take my prayer life; it is at a minimum at best. I know how important it is, but taking the time to do it right is hard.

I love to talk. I can spend hours talking to my friends and wife. Yet when it comes to talking to God, I get shy or have little to say. Is it because I think He already knows it, so why speak it? Or am I afraid to ask because it may sound selfish? Or is it both of the above?

When it comes to prayer, this is what Jesus taught His disciples. Yet in Mark 11:24 we learn that Jesus said *"whatever you ask for in prayer, believe that you have received it, and it will be yours."* Sounds confusing? Ask for God's will yet also ask for whatever I want? So, how should one pray?

Consider this: if God's will is perfect; if He loves us even more than we love ourselves; if He knows everything about us and everything about our future; if He crafted us Himself; if He is powerful, able to do beyond what we can even ask or think; if He desires to bless us with the best; if His desires for us are infinitely better than our requests for ourselves; then why would we ever ask anything other than His will?

Prayer is a conversation between us and God. It is a two way conversation between friends. He wants to pour out His will on our lives and He wants us to ask Him for our desires. He wants the two to be one and the same. But are they in our prayer life?

Are we only praying for our needs, wants and desires or are we asking God to give us what He wants for us? Are we really interested in His better judgment for our life or is our prayer life filled with a grocery list of things we want?

Try praying "His will" for your life and have faith that it is greater than anything you could ask for. I bet your life will be blessed beyond your comprehension.

January 11

"Jesus tells us that HE is *"...the way and the truth and the life."* (John 14:6)

Ever had an "aha" moment? A time when you see something for what it really is? Well, I did this morning and I believe it may change my life. Let me explain...

Have you ever thought about your life and who is a part of it? My wife is a part of my life. She relies on me to provide, love and care for her. My son is a part of my life. His very existence relied on me for his birth. As a child he relied on me to feed, clothe and care for him.

Up until this morning I would have said Jesus was a part of my life. But then came the "aha" moment. Is Jesus really a part of my life? Is that really the way to think about Jesus? To think about Him in that way puts the emphasis on me.

As I read my bible, I realize that the emphasis should be on HIM. My life relies on Him, not the other way around. I rely on His provision, His care and His love. I am alive because of HIM. HE is the reason for my life.

So my "aha" moment is that Jesus isn't a part of my life, I am a part of HIS. HE is the priority, my creator and Savior. Our focus verse tells us that Jesus is the source of life itself, physical, spiritual and eternal.

So, ask yourself, are you a part of Jesus' life? If not, change your priorities today and become a part of Jesus' life, and then share your "aha" moment.

January 12

"Why do you call me, 'Lord, Lord,' and do not do what I say?" (Luke 6:46)

Have you ever been to a pistol range? The desired outcome is to hit a target. When you miss the target, you try to figure out what went wrong? In life we have a similar problem. We know what we should do, what is required of us, but sometimes we miss the target. In the Spiritual realm that is called sin. Sin is missing the mark set by God.

Sin separates us from God and that separation causes our defenses to weaken. A weakened defense makes it easier to continue in sin, causing even further separation from God. The cycle of sin and separation continues until we view this behavior, attitude or way of life as normal.

When we compromise any area of our beliefs, when we go against what we know to be right, we are in danger of sending our eternal souls to Hell. God won't allow sin into His presence, so by allowing sin in our life, we risk eternal damnation and separation from God.

God gives us opportunities to repent, to turn away from the ways of sin. But too often we become comfortable in sin and are unwilling to change. Some even continue in their sin and refuse to change. People who live without Jesus in their lives have a difficult time recognizing their sin and the effects of it on their life. What we see as sinful, they see as normal behavior.

People that claim to follow Jesus are no different. Many make little effort to apply the teachings of Jesus to their lives. They ask Jesus to save them, but don't want Him to transform them. In our focus verse Jesus asks us why.

We find exceptions to His commands. He tells us *"Go into the world"* (Mark 16:15) and we say "not there"; He tells us *"Love your enemies"* (Matthew 5:44) and we say "not them"; He says *"anyone who doesn't give up everything"* (Luke 14:33) and we say "not that". All these commands are the target, but often we miss what we should be aiming at.

Only Jesus can create true change; only His grace can reveal and remove sin. Jesus can transform us from the inside. If we allow Him and follow His teachings, we can change. Change is uncomfortable. We must be willing to allow Him to change us, to help us overcome and to break the cycle of sin. Let us never become so accustomed to sin that missing the target is acceptable, always aim for the bull's eye.

January 13

"Do not be anxious about anything, but in every situation, by prayer and petition, with thanksgiving, present your requests to God. And the peace of God, which transcends all understanding, will guard your hearts and your minds in Christ Jesus." (Phil 4: 6-7)

I love working with my hands and they do take a beating. A close look at my hands and you will always see scars and scabs. The problem I have is that I am always opening up an old wound.

Old wounds take time to heal. And sometimes the wounds of the heart are the hardest to heal. They can be reopened when you least expect it and can cause you great pain. This happens to me as well, and I struggle as to how to handle it.

Those wounds that can't be fixed with a Band-Aid need special attention. Sometimes I need to talk to someone for help. I can call on my friend Dennis, but I know what he will say. He will tell me to "build a bridge and get over it." I can call my friend and wife Joy, but her advice won't be much better. She will tell me to "suck it up buttercup."

We all want to talk about the old wounds when they reopen. We want to vent, rant and rave, but Jesus tells us in our focus verse not to worry, just give it to Him. He is the only one who can give us peace in this situation. I am not saying my friends' advice isn't good, but the reassurance from Jesus helps to soothe my soul. So, the next time one of those old wounds reopens, just let Jesus handle it. He will make it all better.

January 14

"Then He (Jesus) said to them all: "Whoever wants to be my disciple must deny themselves and take up their cross daily and follow me." (Luke 9:23)

"Often we say to Jesus, 'I don't mind you making some changes in my life', but Jesus wants to turn your life upside down. We say, 'I don't mind a little touch up work', but Jesus wants complete renovation. We're thinking tune-up, He's thinking overhaul. We think a little decorating, why not, but Jesus wants a complete remodel." ("Not a Fan" Kyle Idleman)

The word "follow" means to come or go after; proceed behind, to be in pursuit of; to go in the direction of; be guided by; to accept the guidance, command, or leadership of; to imitate; to obey.

To be a fully devoted follower of Jesus, as He desires, we must put aside ourselves and do so in the full sense of the word. This implies that we must be led by Him, obey His teachings, and live life as He expects us to live.

Jesus isn't interested in "enthusiastic admirers." He wants disciples that are all in. Following Jesus is an all or nothing lifestyle. Don't take my word for it; read Matthew 19:16-22. Jesus wants followers that let nothing stand in their way of His fullness.

He wants followers that will go where He wants them to go, do what He wants them to do and be what He wants them to be. Jesus wants followers that have an all or nothing mindset. Are you all in?

14

January 15

"...join with me in suffering for the gospel, by the power of God." (2 Timothy 1:8)

While traveling, I couldn't help but notice how many large trucks and SUV's there are on the road. Many of these are equipped with 4 wheel drive and sit pretty high up in the air. What do people use these for now days? None of them showed any signs of ever being off road and most didn't even have a speck of dirt on them.

These vehicles are designed to go through mud and dirt and climb the sides of mountains, yet very few ever see anything but pavement. In fact, most will never be seen off road. The owners are afraid of getting them scratched or dirty. In fact, some owners will brag about the capabilities, yet when asked, they may say "Are you serious, do you know how much I spent on that thing?" So they never use the vehicle for its intended purpose, what it is actually designed for.

Well you guessed it; I can turn this into something spiritual. How about you? You who believe in Christ Jesus are equipped to get dirty, go into the world, climb mountains so to speak, but do you? We talk about our beliefs, but how often do we put them into practice? You know, be the hands and feet of Jesus in this dirty world?

You who believe are called to get dirty, feed the homeless, give to the poor, lift up our neighbors and get out of our comfort zones. We are called to use our talents, the stuff God equips us with to reach the lost, clothe the less fortunate and to get into the trenches for Jesus. But how many actually do?

If you believe in Jesus, let His power that is within you get you out into the world and go get dirty. If you have ever been 4-wheeling you know how much fun it is. Once you get dirty for Jesus, you will see how fun it is, see the blessing you receive and you will want to do it over and over again. So it is time to get dirty! Enjoy it and watch how many lives you can impact.

15

January 16

"And we know that in all things God works for the good of those who love him, who have been called according to his purpose." (Romans 8:28)

Ever received bad news? Well I have been there when families are told a loved one is dying. I have been there when a loved one is taken off life support. I have seen people lose their jobs, homes and marriages.

Not everything is going to work out the way we want. Sometimes in life we are disappointed, bad news arrives, a tragedy happens. We may never be able to explain it, but we must understand that it does happen.

How we believe determines how we move forward. Those who have their hope in Jesus know there are better days to come. But sometimes that just isn't enough.

The thing that should keep us going is the knowledge that God is in charge and things work for His purpose and His will. The will we may not understand, but is perfect none the less.

Our focus verse tells us that "*In* all things", not "all things," but "*In* all things", God works, meaning He is always present, for the good, His ultimate good and His purpose, for those who love him.

So take hope and trust in His plan. Stand firm in the faith that He sees the big picture. And remember, this life is not the end; it is only the beginning!

January 17

"I tell you, my friends, do not be afraid of those who kill the body and after that can do no more. But I will show you whom you should fear: Fear him who, after your body has been killed, has authority to throw you into hell. Yes, I tell you, fear him." (Luke 12:4-5)

When I was younger I liked being a part of the crowd. In the military, where I served 20 years, you were always with a group. You hung out together, worked together, and even bunked together a lot of the time. Being liked and fitting in is important in settings like that.

What about you? Do you ever feel like you have to fit in to be liked? The world expects us to conform to their standards. Being different isn't very popular. Often people try to blend in out of fear of ridicule and persecution because of what they believe.

Our focus verse tells us to fear no one other than God. We must fulfill God's purpose and live according to His character, regardless of opposition or criticism. The world doesn't understand the ways of God, but as a believer, you do.

Whose opinion matters to you? Some try to work God into their obligations and schedules. But nowhere in the bible do we read that this is how it should be.

God often puts us in situations that test us. He can even allow people and events to seem too big to handle. Other people may try to influence us, contrary to God's will. What will our response be?

God's power can help us overcome any trial, temptation or intimidator. By relying on His strength we can overcome anything. When we live according to His will and purpose, nothing can stand against us.

January 18

"'As surely as I live,' says the Lord, 'every knee will bow before me; every tongue will confess to God.' So then, each of us will give an account of himself to God." (Romans 14:11-12)

While in the Bahamas, I purchased a few cigars for my son. He enjoys one every now and then and since it was close to his birthday I thought, why not? As we came to the end of our trip I filled out the customs form and did the right thing and claimed the cigars. As we went through customs I was asked about them. I told the agent I had picked them up on one of the islands. His response was "Follow me." I was led to a glass room and told to wait.

There comes a time in your life when your actions and deeds will be under investigation. The bible tells us that a time will come when we all must face God and stand in judgment for how we have lived our lives.

As our focus verse says, "Every knee will bow" and we all must "give an account" of the things we do in this life. God holds the final decision of our fate, and that decision stands for eternity.

I faced another agent who asked more questions, inspected the "contraband" and eventually let me go. His judgment determined my fate. Because I was honest and did the right thing, I was merely detained and then given freedom.

How we live our lives matters more than one may think. It's more than just getting by day after day; it determines our eternal fate and where we spend that eternity. So for those who believe in Jesus, and live a life in step with Him, that judgment will result in the response "well done good and faithful servant....

Come and share your master's happiness!" God is pleased when His children do the right thing...

January 19

"I can do everything through Him who gives me strength." (Philippians 4:13)

Do you ever wonder why God uses certain people? I, for instance, am the least likely to have been called to be a pastor. I feel I am unqualified for the job, yet God thought otherwise. Sometimes what we see isn't what God sees.

One night at a men's meeting we discussed Gideon and thought him to be an unlikely hero as well. In the book of Judges we are told the story of Gideon. He was a man who hid in a winepress thrashing wheat to keep it from being stolen.

An angel of the Lord appeared to him and called him a "mighty warrior". Gideon was confused. He was from the weakest clan in Manasseh and he was the least in his family, so why would this angel, sent from God, call him a "mighty warrior"?

Because God was able to see him for what he was and for what he could become. God saw potential, if he followed God on the adventure that was about to open up for him.

As we read the story, we find out that once Gideon knew it was God calling him, he obeyed and became the hero, just like God knew he would. How did this happen?

When God calls and we obey, God can do anything through us. God will empower us, use us for His glory and give us the strength to defeat the very things that cause us pain and suffering. We have no idea where God will take us or what He will do through us, but we do know scripture assures us we don't go alone.

The Holy Spirit is our equipper, our encourager and our guide. He will give us the courage to fight the enemy, even when we don't feel like the hero. What are you battling today? When faced with an obstacle that seems too big for you, remember, God "gives me strength."

January 20

"Do not leave Jerusalem, but wait for the gift my Father promised, which you have heard me speak about." (Acts 1:4)

I had the privilege of spending an evening with my grandson. The evening included a haircut and dinner. Three year olds do not like getting haircuts. They don't want to sit still while someone plays with sharp, pointy things around their ears. So Dad promised a stop for a toy if he was good. Yes, he bribed them.

Telling a boy he is getting a toy means he will ask for it every five seconds. He anxiously awaited his new purchase and the wait was hard on all of us.

Our culture hates to wait. We live in an age of instant gratification. Our food is fast, checkout lanes are express and we often get frustrated when we are stuck behind anyone that is slower than we. Waiting is not fun.

I remember when Heinz ketchup had a commercial advertising the thickness of their product. They played a song called "Anticipation" while the ketchup slowly began to pour. They boasted of their slowness then, but not now. Now they have introduced the "squeeze" bottle, and now we get the same ketchup only quicker. We force it out instead of waiting for it.

We have forgotten that good things come to those who wait. In Jerusalem the disciples did just what Jesus had told them to do; they waited. They sat in the upper room and waited. They prayed and waited, then they waited some more. Finally, in God's perfect timing, He delivered the Holy Spirit upon them and their lives were transformed. The gift was worth the wait.

As Christ followers, we must cling to the promise that God is with us. We must learn that His timing is perfect and that in each and every situation of life, God will deliver that promise at just the right time. We can't lose hope in the waiting.

The grandson waited for the minute he arrived in the toy department. He picked out his toy and spent the rest of the evening enjoying his new treasure.

We too can enjoy our new treasure if we just learn to wait on God. It's when we get impatient that we miss out on what God has planned for us. So let's learn to wait patiently on God and then enjoy the blessings that come with the wait.

January 21

"But seek first his kingdom and his righteousness, and all these things will be given to you as well. Therefore do not worry about tomorrow, for tomorrow will worry about itself. Each day has enough trouble of its own." (Matthew 6:33-34)

To be totally honest, the social media craze is getting pretty boring to me. Every time I scroll through it, I see the same posts from days and weeks ago being recycled. I see videos of craziness and I see false stories take life. And it doesn't take long to see more and more drama than a soap opera.

With each "newest thing", I see people get so wrapped up in it and I see how much stress it seems to cause them. Anxiety is epidemic in our country, or at least on social media.

Just about anything can cause undue stress. We can worry that we don't have enough. Then we can stress about security; about keeping all of our stuff safe. These days, people are worried about what they have and what they don't have, about what they did and what they didn't do, about the past and about the future. And if that isn't enough, a single issue, like the newest thing on social media, can fill their minds with enough worries to last a life time.

Instead of being anxious, we are told by Jesus to trust, and to turn everything over to him. If we put Him at the center of our lives, He will give us everything we need, now and in the future. So if we do that, we have no need to worry.

What consumes your thoughts? What fills your mind and keeps you awake at night? Is it a relationship, money, or the latest "thing" on social media? Maybe you're worrying so much about those things because that holds the highest importance for you.

We should put nothing above God. So replace all those thoughts with Christ and let him take care of all that. He can reorder our life, all we have to do is take a deep breath and relax. By the way, personal contact is much better than social media...just saying.....

21

January 22

"On the third day Abraham looked up and saw the place in the distance. He said to his servants, "Stay here with the donkey while I and the boy go over there. We will worship..." (Genesis 22:4-5)

I love our praise and worship time in our church. We not only have some amazing talent in singers and musicians, but there is something about the way it leads me into a time with God. It goes beyond the mere entertainment value.

For me, worship sets the stage for me to hear from God. I love to hear the music, to sing and to praise our God. It is so nice to come into God's house and sing to the one I love.

But I ask you, is that all there is to worship? I have to say that is part of it, but I think there is more. There is something about worship that goes beyond what we hear, to what we begin to feel when we allow the worship to penetrate our very souls.

Let's stretch our minds a little and get a clearer picture of what worship really is, according to scripture. Our focus verse comes after Abraham took his son Isaac to a mountain, with all intentions to sacrifice him. Why, because God told him to do so.

So why did Abraham say *"We will worship"*? Wiersbe, a famous writer, wrote "worship is the believer's response of all that they are - mind, emotions, will, body – to what God is and says and does."

Worship is more than singing and raising our hands in praise. It is sacrifice, obedience, and living according to God's will, no matter what.

22

January 23

"Enter through the narrow gate. For wide is the gate and broad is the road that leads to destruction, and many enter through it. But small is the gate and narrow the road that leads to life, and only a few find it." (Matthew 7:13-14)

I like going to Lowe's. I can spend an entire day in that place. I look at tools, lumber, light fixtures, etc., even though I don't need any of it. I am tempted to buy a lot of things, but normally I only come out with what I went in for. It is a tough battle, but I fight the temptation to take the entire store home.

This world offers so much and if we aren't careful, we can become bogged down with so many worldly things that we forget the important things. In a world filled with so many temptations and distractions, how can we continue to live a life as God commands us to? How can we stay on that narrow path and enter through that narrow gate? It is so hard and life throws so much at us that we can sway from that path.

We must remember that we aren't the only ones that are tempted. Jesus was tempted as well. He suffered and felt the sting of this world all around Him. He knew what it was like to live in a world filled with corruption, bitterness, hurt, temptation and destruction.

Yet He overcame. He overcame Satan by a life of obedience to the Father, a life holy and pure. He was and still is the living example that we should use to model our lives after. He overcame. So can we?

He turned to what He knew best. He clung to God's promises and scripture to overcome the great pressure of Satan; we can do the same. We must endure, stay true to our faith and God's promise of eternal life with Him, and overcome the temptations of this world. We can resist, we can turn from the worldly ways of life and we can receive the greatest reward ever offered to mankind. Be an overcomer.

January 24

"Therefore keep watch, because you do not know on what day your Lord will come." (Matthew 24:42)

Our son is staying with us temporarily. He works night shifts and comes home in the early morning hours. Our little dog, Ziggy, loves our son and each morning she sits in my lap with her eyes glued to the front door. She watches and waits for him to walk through it, and when he does, she gets so excited.

We are told in scripture to live our life in anticipation of Jesus' return. We are told to keep a watchful eye out, and be prepared. We are told He is coming back, but we just don't know when.

So, as I watched Ziggy this morning I had to ask myself, "Do I anticipate the coming of Jesus as much as she does our son?" Do I look forward to Jesus' return, and most importantly, am I excited about His pending arrival?

When we become followers of Jesus, we should prepare ourselves for a moment's notice of Jesus' return and our leaving this world for heaven. That means our life must be in order, our spiritual affairs up to date and our hearts right with God. We must live each day pleasing in His sight, obeying His call, direction and example in order to be ready for His return. We must live our life in a manner that guarantees our entrance into heaven.

Ziggy gets so excited when our son walks through the door that she shakes all over. She wants his attention; she wants to be near him. How about you? Do you get excited thinking about Jesus coming back? Are you watching? Are you ready? I am....

January 25

"...if anyone is in Christ, he is a new creation; the old is gone, the new has come!" (2 Corinthians 5:17)

As hard as it may be to believe, I was a real hell raiser in my "other" life. I lived so different from the person I am today that most "Christians" would not even have liked me. I made some decisions that have come back to haunt me. I lived for myself, until one day I knew enough was enough. I am not ashamed of who I used to be, but am so glad that I am who I am today. My life has been radically changed and I never want to go back to the old lifestyle.

When I gave my life to Jesus Christ, I started to live out our focus verse. My life was transformed and the old habits, behaviors and actions started to fall away. I became a different guy.

Often I hear people talk about their "relationship" with Jesus yet they continue to live as if they are still the old creations. Their behaviors are the same as the world; they do the same things, say the same things, and yet they will tell you they believe. This is contrary to the above mentioned scripture. If you are truly a believer and follower of Jesus Christ, there must be change.

Matthew 22:37 tells us to *"Love the Lord your God with all your heart and with all your soul and with all your mind."* If you do this, then how can you continue to live as if nothing has changed?

Think about it this way; before you entered into a relationship with your boyfriend, girlfriend, husband or wife you may have dated around. But once you became committed to that one person, your heart, mind and soul became occupied with them. You stopped dating (or at least I hope you did) and you became committed to that person and your life changed.

The same applies with Jesus. Once we accept His mercy, grace and love, our lives should be transformed. We should start to live our life pleasing to Him and that means the old must go away and the new (attitudes, behaviors, thoughts, actions) must be replaced with those that are like Jesus'.

So, if you claim to believe in Jesus and call yourself a Christian, are you really changed or are you still playing the field? Jesus calls us to be like Him and He empowers us to live our lives as the new people He calls us to be. Are you ready to shed the old and put on the new? It is never too late. I am living proof that people can change...

January 26

"I am the vine; you are the branches. If you remain in me and I in you, you will bear much fruit; apart from me you can do nothing." (John 15:5)

In life, we will encounter many things that can ruin a day. Rarely does a day work out quite as we expect. Life is unpredictable. If we are faced with something bad and we allow it to mess up our day, who wins?

Most people who ride motorcycles know that rain and bikes don't mix. Visibility is limited and the road becomes slick. Road hazards, like road oil and standing water, are abundant and affect the handling of a bike. Getting caught in a rain storm creates hazards beyond our control.

Life is no different. Things pop up, hazards come, and life can sometimes spin out of control. How we handle these situations can be the difference between a good or bad outcome.

Case in point, yesterday while riding I was in the middle of just such a storm. Visibility was less than comfortable, it was foggy, the roads were slick and traffic was heavy. Lightning started to flash ahead of me. So what did I do? I had two options, to continue and allow the situation to get worse, or pull over and take myself out of the situation. I chose the latter.

Jesus taught about the dangers of this world and how to avoid them. He told us He was the answer; we must rely on Him for strength, power, protection and provision.

When we find ourselves in situations that aren't favorable, He is the answer. By remaining connected to Him, He protects us and will bring us through so His glory can be revealed. For me, I asked Him for protection and a clear path and in a couple minutes the lightning and thunder passed over, the fog lifted and the rain subsided enough for me to proceed. In less than two miles the road cleared, although a lot of rain had fallen, and the pavement was dry.

When we recognize a hazard and put our faith and trust in Him, He will clear the path for us and His glory. Say what you want, but I know this to be fact, it has been revealed to me many times.

Do you want to see the sky clear, the path get easy, and blessings poured out? Believe, obey, and remain in Him. Read and follow His word, have faith that He can move mountains, calm the storms and part the seas, even today!

January 27

"If you love me, you will obey what I command." (John 14:15)

When my son was growing up, I taught him several important things. I taught him manners, respect and most importantly, authority. As he grew up, if he was told to do something, he did it. Today, if he says he will do something, he does it. At his job, his co-workers and his supervisors know that if he is told to do something, he does it. He understands that authority is important.

As a young father I watch him now with his own son. He is teaching him the same things. He has manners, shows respect and knows that when dad says something, he is expected to listen and obey.

That is what Jesus is saying in our focus verse. Jesus was talking to His disciples and basically it all comes down to this, if you say you love Jesus, you will do whatever it is He says, no questions asked. We know Jesus would never tell us to do anything that is wrong, immoral or illegal. We know Jesus has our best interests at heart. We know that Jesus wants us to succeed and would never cause us harm.

To say we love Jesus yet live a life contrary is not love, it is a lie. If my son, or his son, were to say they love their father and do the opposite, they are assured of one thing, discipline. They will suffer the consequences of their actions.

Ask yourself this question. Does my life represent the blessing of Jesus because of my obedience, or the consequences of my disobedience? If your answer is the latter, then change is necessary. Think hard, and make the proper adjustments, Jesus wants to reward, but He only rewards those who obey.

January 28

"...they all rushed at him, dragged him out of the city and began to stone him. Meanwhile, the witnesses laid their clothes at the feet of a young man named Saul." (Acts 7:57-58)

As Stephen is being stoned, one of the people involved was Saul. Saul, who became Paul, was changed by God to become one of the most profound leaders of Christianity. He brought the Gospel to the nations and wrote the majority of the books of the New Testament, He was also one of those present at the stoning of Stephen. That is amazing! God used a man like Saul, a hater of Christ followers, a murderer and a persecutor of the Gospel, to be the leader of the early church. Get your mind around that for a minute.

How do we comprehend a God that can use the likes of Saul/Paul in this manner? One reason is that God can use anyone and any circumstance for His glory. Think about this, with all that Stephen was going through at that moment in time, he never imagined that one of those stoning him would become a person like Paul. It was impossible for him to see that at that particular time.

We are no different than Stephen. When things are coming at us and it seems that nothing else can go wrong, and yet it does, we can't see any good of it at that time. We have to take God's word that there is a blessing there somewhere, but we may not see it right away. We have to take time to think and comprehend that there is a higher reason for what we are going through, a higher purpose, a blessing and glory. What you are facing may even be a part of the problem, just as Saul was.

But rest assured that the very things you may be facing in life can be changed by God to reveal His glory. So we have to rejoice in our problem, situation or crisis and know that God is in charge and *"in all things God works for the good of those who love him, who have been called according to his purpose."* (Romans 8:28)

28

January 29

"Therefore, since we are surrounded by such a great cloud of witnesses, let us throw off everything that hinders and the sin that so easily entangles, and let us run with perseverance the race marked out for us." (Hebrews 12:1)

I used to travel a lot for my job. One of the things travelers concern themselves with is whether their luggage will get to the destination or not. Many times I have arrived without my luggage arriving with me. I have waited as long as two days to get my luggage. When I arrive at my destination without a change of clothes and no tooth brush, I find it is hard to live without those things.

Baggage is a part of our journey. Our life is a journey and we tend to collect baggage as we live it. There are things in life that we find hard to live without, and we tend to hang onto them with all our might. But I have good news! There is no baggage allowed in heaven. There is no baggage claim and no fear of lost baggage; because we have to get rid of it before we get there.

If you are a believer then you are on a journey. During our "prior" life we accumulated some baggage along the way. When we come to salvation, we have to get rid of that baggage. We have to unload the baggage of sin, the baggage of our old identity, our old wounds, our failures, regrets, idols and who we were. We learn in Ephesians 4:22-24 *"You were taught, with regard to your former way of life, to put off your old self..." "...to be made new in the attitude of your minds; and to put on the new self..."* We have to leave all that baggage behind, because we, and everything about us, should be new. By letting go of the baggage, we lighten the load.

January 30

"After fasting forty days and forty night..."(Matthew 4:2)

As I turned the key of my old truck my heart sank. The engine barely turned.- It was obvious that the battery was drained and it had very little life. It had just enough power to bring the engine to life, but would it do it again? I was relieved it started, yet I knew that the battery was dead and was in need of either a recharge or replacement.

I decided to go where I normally buy all my batteries. It was time to replace the old lifeless battery with a new one. I searched my memory banks for how long it had been since this battery has had any maintenance or how old it was – 3, 4, maybe 5 years? Either way, it was time to do something about it or I would find myself stranded.

With time to kill I pondered this and thought of my own spiritual life. How much of a charge does it have? When was the last time I did some maintenance on my relationship with God? Do I need to replace the old things with new ones? Interesting concept, but one I think is very real.

I find myself running around, constantly on the go. I am always busy doing this and that, jumping from one task to the other. I am constantly on the go and seldom take time to do a recharge. I had the thought: how long will it be before I find myself hard to get started, or will I eventually find my spiritual life lifeless, stranded?

Jesus modeled the concept of taking time to recharge and rest. In our focus verse He fasted before the tempter came. Fully charged, He was able to overcome Satan. In Matthew 14 Jesus *"withdrew by boat privately to a solitary place."* Upon arriving, the crowds awaited Him. Because He was fully charged, He healed many.

We all need recharging, taking time to put new life in our souls and hearts. We all need time with Jesus to be refreshed and restored to the life He wants for us. Unless we stay connected to Him and pull power from Him, we will eventually drain ourselves and be left stranded. So how did you start your day? I encourage you to take time daily to get alone with Jesus and recharge your batteries.

January 31

"Jesus looked at them and said, 'With man this is impossible, but with God all things are possible.'" (Matthew 19:26)

When I joined the Army I considered myself in pretty good shape. I worked construction before enlisting. In the Army we were taught the concept of a "Battle Buddy", a team mate, someone to help us get through the course. We were to do nearly everything together.

Once we entered the obstacle course, we were told to rely on our battle buddy and we would get through the course a lot easier. As we took off through the course, we both thought, "we got this" and we each went solo. We cruised along until we came to the wall. It loomed over us, too tall to get over alone. As we stood looking up, we remembered what our Drill Instructor had told us about team work and relying on each other. Alone we would fail, but together we overcame that wall and the rest of the course.

We face obstacles in our life that are often too big to handle alone. Some are too big even for a human "battle buddy", so we must rely on a source of power that far exceeds anything on earth...and that would be God.

Jesus said *"'I am the way and the truth and the life. No one comes to the Father except through me'"* (John 16:6) and He means it. In order to get there, we need the help of Jesus, sometimes lifting us, sometimes carrying us, but always helping us. Our focus verse tells us that with man it is impossible, but with God, everything is possible. No wall is too tall, no valley is too deep, no problem too difficult for Him!

So the next time you are facing something too big for you to handle, call on the one true battle buddy that can help you through anything. Call on the one that can make everything possible, God, and watch what happens!

February 1

"Therefore be imitators of God, as beloved children, and live in love, as Christ loved us and gave himself up for us, a fragrant offering and sacrifice to God." (Ephesians 5:1-2 NRSV)

I have been a Christ follower for a while and know the bible teaches that we are to believe, repent, follow and receive the Holy Spirit. These things all seem pretty easy and, for the most part, we can do them without much effort.

I had to remind myself that it is more than believing in a person named Jesus. It is more than saying a simple prayer. It is more than living our life as we please with the assumption that when we die we are heaven bound.

A popular Christian song asks a question, "Which Jesus do you follow? Which Jesus do you serve? If Ephesians says to imitate Christ, then why do you look so much like the world?"

Based on this song and our focus verse, we are told to imitate Jesus. How do we do that? We must know who He is; what He stood for and how He lived His life. When I grew up I wanted to be like my dad. I watched how he walked, talked, worked and interacted with people. I have been told I am the spitting image of my father, and I attribute that to the fact I knew him well. So, in order to fully understand Jesus, we must have a relationship with Him; study His actions, words and deeds. Then, and only then, can we grasp how to imitate Him.

We can't be like Him until we are ready to live like Him, in word, deed and action; love like Him, unconditionally and totally. We can't live like Him until we are ready to die to self, like He did.

Jesus took up that cross and died for us, so to be like Him, we must take up our cross and die for Him. Think that over and ask yourself, do you want to be like Jesus?

February 2

"As the Father (God) has sent me, I am sending you." (John 20:21)

I have often been told I look like my father. In fact, as I was growing up my mother would tell me I was just like him. As I get older, some of my ways reveal that I am truly my father's son. I am developing some of his ways, attitudes and personality traits.

The bible teaches us that we were created in God's image. The bible also teaches us to be like Christ. As believers and followers of Jesus Christ we are to become like Christ in action, thought and deed. We can never be Jesus, but we can start to take on His personality, ways, and attitudes. It is what we are called to do. The very definition of Christian means to be Christ-like. So, as we grow in our faith, we should start to be like Christ, much like I am like my father.

John 20:19-23 tells us that after Jesus died, was buried and rose from the grave, He visited His disciples. He went to them and gave them clear instructions to be like Him. Our focus verse is telling us not only to be like Him, but to take on His mission and purpose.

Jesus came to this earth and clothed Himself in flesh to do several things. He lived an example of how we are to live if we are God's children. He lived to show us things like mercy, grace, and forgiveness. He lived to be a sacrifice for the sins of the world, so that we can break free from the worldly ways and live godly lives here on earth. He lived in order to teach us to be like Him.

He came from heavenly riches to earthly rags, from authority to obedience, from significance to rejection, from comfort to hardship, from glory to sacrifice, all for us. The reality of His coming was to teach us to go into this world and do exactly the same thing and live the same way.

Does your attitude match Jesus'? Do you take the mission of living as He lived and telling others about the Father as He did seriously? He intended to shine His light in the darkness through us. Are you willing to be like your Father, the one whose image you were created in? If you are, then live as He lived, go into the world and tell others, not through words, but by your very appearance, attitude, actions and deeds. Will others say you are starting to look like your Father? I pray they do.

February 3

"Be still, and know that I am God..." (Psalm 46:10)

Traveling can bring out the worse in people. I once traveled from Augusta, GA to Ft. Dix, NJ. I arrived in Charlotte, only to be told that my connecting flight was canceled due to bad weather. People can get very ugly when flights are rescheduled or cancelled.

As for me, God brought this passage of scripture to mind and I calmly went about trying to figure out what to do next. It wasn't the airport's fault, nor the ticketing or gate personnel's fault. They don't control the weather. I knew God was in control so I treated people as God would want me to, with a smile and in a polite manner.

How we respond to difficult or trying situations can clearly indicate we know who is in charge. Only God controls the weather and events of our lives. Things happen for a reason, even the weather and cancelled flights. When we get upset or panic we are actually saying we don't trust God to deal with a bad situation. When we try to fix things in our own power we are saying that we have more control over our life than God. I think not.

That day turned out to be a good day. I was warm, safe and comfortable. I had a roof over my head and food in my stomach. I was kept safe from the bad weather and protected from something that I may never know about. God redirected my steps and sent me home because that is where He wanted me. I was "still" and let God be God in my life and I thank Him for controlling the events of my life.

So the next time a bad situation comes up, think first before you respond. Is God teaching you something? Does God have a better plan? Take time to let God be God, then be prepared to be blessed.

February 4

"Be still before the LORD and wait patiently for him…" (Psalm 37:7)

Sitting on a porch early in the morning is, to me, one of life's simple pleasures. My morning is pretty complete with coffee in my hand, bible on my knee, and pen and paper to write on. I just sit and take it all in. I can sit and wait for God to speak.

But if I try I can hear the birds chirping. I can hear the drone of traffic and lawn mowers in the distance. If I listen closely, I can hear dogs barking and kids playing. If I am not careful, I can let all that noise ruin my quiet morning with God.

It seems like this world never stops or even slows down. People go 24/7 and there never seems to be a time when nothing is going on. Silence is hard to find.

With all the noise, hustle and bustle, how can one "be still"? With the world going every minute of the day, it is very hard to "be still before the Lord…" as our passage tells us to. But we know that in order to hear God's voice, silence is necessary.

So how do we get that silence? Unless we make an effort to find the right place and right time, we will never find it. But in order to hear from God, one must find a way. Seems like a staggering challenge.

But here is what I find works for me. I just take the time to be still in my own little area. I sit and remove the noise in my life, blocking out the noise in the distance. I stop and listen, letting my mind search for God and not the world. It is a learned task, but one that I have found benefits me well.

So take time to be still and listen for God's voice. Find the perfect place and time where you can have the quiet that is necessary. You will be surprised at what you will hear when you make the effort. God has never failed me yet, and I doubt He will fail you either.

February 5

"Do not be misled: "Bad company corrupts good character." (1 Corinthians 15:33)

My dad told me a long ago that if you lay with dogs sooner than later you will get fleas. That was his way of telling me the people I chose to hang out with were bad and they would ruin me if I continued to hang out with them. Well, I am much older now and tend to agree with him.

I have a friend that, some time ago, I thought was the picture of a Godly person. That friend was the person I wanted to be; constantly in tune with God, His calling on their life and a true worshipper of God, mind, body and soul. But then things changed.

The values they once held high began to diminish. Their worship dulled; the Godly behavior declined, and their way of life became in total opposition to the teachings of God. Fornication, drinking, tolerance, and compromise to name a few, had come into their lives. Their spiritual life had taken a nose dive. This person that I once looked up to is now the person I do not ever want to be.

This was all a result of the people they chose to associate with. The people in this person's life had values that were far less than the values they once held, and it began to have a slow fade effect. The good began to be replaced with the bad and the godly behaviors became that of the acceptable world.

The warning of our focus verse stands out in the world in which we live. In a world where everything is acceptable, allowable and permissible, good people can become bad. Satan will use every tool to make you think that you are okay, a little bad never hurts anything. Think again, a little bad can ruin the entire batch.

So stand firm in your faith. Each day make a decision to go against the world view and stand for God. Take a look at the life of Daniel and learn to be a person of principles, morals and ethics. Do the hard right over the easy wrong.

February 6

"When crowds of people came out for baptism because it was the popular thing to do, John exploded: 'Brood of snakes! What do you think you're doing slithering down here to the river? Do you think a little water on your snakeskins is going to deflect God's judgment? It's your life that must change, not your skin." (Luke 3:7-8 MSG)

Have you noticed that people often follow the most "popular" thing? No matter what it is, they will flock to it and everyone then becomes whatever it is.

In my teenage years, long hair, bell bottom pants and peace signs were in. I became a hippie, not because I was born one, but because it was cool. I looked and dressed the part, but honestly, I wasn't a hippie, I was more a beatnik.

This passage is talking about a similar concept. John the Baptist appeared on the scene with a new message of repentance. People flocked to hear him preach because he was radical, challenging, offensive and heart piercing. He spoke of new things and the people were curious to hear what he had to say. Until they heard the challenge; then they fell back on their family ties to Abraham and their heritage. They presumed they were safe because of who they were, or who they claimed to be.

There are many who believe in "faith by association". They believe if they hang out with saved people, or profess to believe, or even attend church once in a while, God will accept them. Many think that if they are a good person they automatically get to heaven. Well, it doesn't quite work that way.

Our acceptance into the family of God is based on our faith in Jesus Christ and an obedient attitude. A true follower of Jesus must "bear fruit". Ever watch a fruit tree change in the spring time? It starts out withered and dry, and then it produces buds, which changes to leaves, then it develop the fruit which is then picked and eaten.

In order to be a Christ follower we must be all in, every minute of every day and our lives must be transformed from what it used to be, to that new creation the bible talks about. If we truly are followers of Christ we should produce results in our lives and the lives of those around us.

So let's stop claiming, let's stop playing, and let's start living a life of obedience to the teachings and lessons of Jesus Christ and produce fruit that is pleasing to God's eye.

February 7

*"'Everything is permissible for me' - but not everything is beneficial.
'Everything is permissible for me' - but I will not be mastered by anything."*
(1 Corinthians 6:12-13)

"'Everything is permissible' - but not everything is beneficial. 'Everything is permissible' - but not everything is constructive." (1 Corinthians 10:23)

When we first moved into our new home, I planted a small Magnolia tree in our front yard. I had always admired those majestic, beautiful, blooming trees and thought it would be so nice to have one. As it grew larger, I started to second guess my decision. Oh yeah, it is pretty, but it sheds large hard leaves constantly. It drops dozens of prickly balls that take a toll on my mower, not to mention my feet. And the grass that I worked so hard to get to grow is dying because no sun can get to it. What started out as beautiful and pleasing to look at became ugly, messy and a nuisance.

Isn't this true in our lives? We see something we have to have, only to find out later it isn't what we thought it to be? We soon find that that thing of beauty turns out to be a beast in disguise.

The above passages tell us that not everything that is pretty, pleasing, and permissible is good. Something can bring visual pleasure but turn out to be destructive. Some things that you may want at first, can soon become an eyesore or harmful to you. They may start out good, but over time they create a mess in our life and may even start killing the things that were meant for good.

I pondered about that tree. What to do with it; keep it and put up with the mess it is making in my life or get rid of it for good. I knew it would be tough, but I came to realize it had to go. So yesterday, even in the scorching heat, I armed myself with a chain saw and down it went. As my wife and I cut, loaded and hauled that tree away, I felt a sense of accomplishment and a feeling of having control of my yard once again.

Sometimes in life we make mistakes. We all have messy things in our lives and we know we need to get rid of them. Taking that first step is hard. Ask God for help and for His strength to rid yourself of the mess. Arm yourself with the One that can help and you will feel the strength to continue, knowing your life will be so much better.

February 8

"I the LORD do not change." (Malachi 3:6)

My wife and I have a very special relationship. We love spending time together. We are best friends and we are pretty much inseparable. Our son calls us "weird". He says normal married people don't act like that. Well, if this is weird. I am guilty and loving it.

We do not like to be apart. I went away for two nights and the plan was that we were not to have contact at all. It was to be a time with no outside contact, no connectivity, and total isolation. To be honest, it was miserable not being able to talk to or text her. I counted down the time until I could see her again. Okay, I know, this is the part where you start to think I am weird.

We work hard at keeping this type of relationship. It takes effort. We believe if we don't, our relationship could fade and we could drift apart.

An old couple reminisced about the old days as they drove down the road. The wife said "Remember when we first started dating? I would sit beside you as you drove. Your arm would be around me and we would snuggle while we traveled? What happened?" The husband looked at his wife and said "We still have the same truck; I am still driving, who moved?"

Do you often feel like God is distant? Well, here is a news flash, God didn't move, you did. We move away by getting busy. We stop reading his Word, stop talking to him in prayer, except for maybe the quick blessing at meal time. We stop putting Scripture to work in our lives. And the icing on the cake, we start living under our power, going in our direction verses His.

I guess what I am saying is, if you feel distant from God and don't like it, do something about it. When I was away, I missed my wife. So I got up early, finished what I needed to get done and hit the road. My focus was getting back to her.

Focus today on getting back to God. Start today by stopping what you are doing and talk with Him. Read His Word, spend time praising His name. He waits, as our concerned and loving Father, for us to return to Him and to live close to Him again. And just as my wife met me with open and loving arms, He meets us the same way. So, what are you waiting for? Get moving....

February 9

"'Lord, if it's you,' Peter replied, 'tell me to come to you on the water.'
'Come,' he said. Then Peter got down out of the boat, walked on the water
and came toward Jesus. But when he saw the wind, he was afraid and,
beginning to sink, cried out, 'Lord, save me!'" (Matthew 14:28-30)

As hard as I tried, I often failed at things growing up. I loved to play football, but I wasn't very big, so I never made the team. I liked the drums, but failed at reading music, therefore, never made the band. My dad was an encourager. Each time I failed, He would remind me that "the only thing worse than failure is not trying at all." He was proud that I at least tried.

We humans are prone to focus on the failures of life. We tend to make them define us when, in reality, under the right conditions, failure isn't always a bad thing. Often the doorway to success is entered through the hallway of failure.

Our focus verse illustrates this point. We read it and focus on Peter sinking; his failure. But let's take a closer look, Peter did what no other man has done (other than Jesus) when he walked on water. He succeeded where others never even tried.

His success may have been short lived, but he learned where his strength came from. He learned that anything was possible when you focus on Jesus. He learned that when Jesus tells you something, and you obey, you can succeed. If he hadn't tried, he would have been like the other 11 in the boat.

So what is God calling you to do? Are you afraid to fail, so you won't try? Or do you have faith that Jesus is ready and willing to lend a hand and not let you sink? The choice isn't that hard, take that first step....

February 10

"A woman, a Samaritan, came to draw water. Jesus said, 'Would you give me a drink of water?'" "The Samaritan woman, taken aback, asked, 'How come you, a Jew, are asking me, a Samaritan woman, for a drink?'" (John 4:7, 9)

I started in ministry by ministering to bikers. I received my call on top of a motorcycle and have spent the last 14+ years going where most other Christians would never go. I have always believed that short of sin, I will do whatever it takes to win souls for Jesus.

Some people often put down churches that use radical ideas and methods to introduce people to the gospel. They think that Christians are supposed to stand at the door of their local church and people will come running. They disagree with anything that they feel "lures" people in or produce emotions that lead to conversions.

We should never water down the gospel, we should state the pure facts of the gospel, all the while preaching and teaching holiness. But I also believe we must find ways of reaching the lost and un-churched. We need to allow them the opportunities to hear the truth of Jesus Christ, even if it means being radically different.

Jesus taught us how to be radical in order to reach people and introduce them to the gospel. Let me give you a few examples: The woman at the well. What is more radical than a Jew in Samaria and talking to a woman? Yet there He was and He offers her salvation.

What about the healing of a leper? What is more radical than a clean Jewish man touching an unclean person? Jesus touched him to show others that the man was clean. What about the feeding of the five thousand? It's pretty radical to feed so many with so little.

I think Jesus' lessons teach us to be radical today in order to reach, teach and introduce people to His gospel. So, what radical things can you do in order to introduce someone to Jesus? Ride a motorcycle and share the gospel to a group most Christians ignore? Help feed the homeless? Go into the streets and under bridges to share the love of Christ? Be an example of Godliness in the work place?

Get out of your comfort zone, off of your sofa, out of the pew and share the Word of God with someone. Jesus didn't sit around and wait for them to come to Him. He went out, talked, prayed, healed, held revivals, and made relationships. Jesus was radically different and we, as Christ followers, are called to be like Him. So be like Christ, get radical!

41

February 11

"Just as Moses lifted up the snake in the desert, so the Son of Man must be lifted up, that everyone who believes in him may have eternal life." (John 3:14-15)

What would you do to save your life? Would you take experimental drugs? Would you travel to far off lands in hopes of finding a miracle treatment? Would you crawl through trenches or climb over people, all to save your life?

I heard a speaker say that the most quoted passage of scripture, John 3:16, was a passage, that if misread and misunderstood, could lead many to hell. The problem with this verse is the fact that the word "believe" is not fully understood.

One can "believe" in something without it impacting one's life. I personally think a lot of people "believe" intellectually that Jesus is real, yet they have never allowed that belief to impact their life or penetrate their heart. They know it in their mind, but it means nothing to their soul.

Our focus verses refer to Numbers 21. The wandering Israelites made God mad. Because of their constant grumbling and complaining, God sent snakes among them and people were dying. God told Moses to make a bronze snake and put it on a pole, and if anyone was bitten, all they had to do to save their life was to look at the pole.

I know that story seems crazy, but the people would do anything to save themselves. Remember what I asked up front, what would you do to save yourself? These people believed that by looking at the snake on a pole, they would live. So they did any and everything to get a look at the pole. It impacted their life, their future, their comfort level. They would run, crawl, climb, push and shove to get a look at what hung on that pole.

What about you? Do you "believe" that by putting your eyes on Jesus your life will be saved? Do you believe it to the point that you would do anything, go anywhere in order to save your life? Would you align your life and your actions with that truth? That is the meaning of the word "believe", it is an action, not a thought.

So I ask again, what will you do to save your life? Will you truly "believe" with all your heart, mind, body and soul? Will you go to extremes? Do you "believe" like it is a matter of life and death? I pray the answer is yes. When you understand the word "believe" like that, then John 3:16 becomes the greatest verse in the bible.

February 12

"For God so loved the world that he gave his one and only Son, that whoever believes in him shall not perish but have eternal life." (John 3:16)

Our focus verse is said to be the most famous verse in the bible. For most, it's the anthem for being saved. Believe and have eternal life! That is what the verse says.

But we often fail to realize that this verse is part of a conversation between Jesus and a man who worked for a religious organization. He spoke the religious language and participated in religious activities. Nicodemus thought he was in good standings with God, but Jesus tells him that isn't enough. Jesus says one must be "born again" in order to enter the kingdom of Heaven. In other words, Christ's kingdom can only be entered by those who have been changed.

Jesus is saying that it takes more than being good, it takes more than belief, it takes more than going through the motions, to share in the promise of eternal life. He tells us that He, Jesus, came to save the world, but He also tells us that it takes more than mere belief.

This world is dark and evil. The things of this world entice us, tempt us and lure us. They are pleasing and fun. But we must also remember that they are evil and not acceptable by God. In order to truly believe and receive, one must have new thoughts, attitudes and behaviors. Jesus said we must come into the light, live a new life filled with the goodness of Him.

Trust me when I say this, I have lived that dark lifestyle. While I was there I thought I had a good life, but something was always missing. I came to "know" Jesus and for a few years I "played" the part. I lived a John 3:16 life and thought I was good with God.

Then one day I realized I was missing something. I was missing a real relationship with God. I knew of Him, but I didn't know Him. I became fully committed to live my life for him as a "born again", totally sold out Christian. That is when my life went from empty to full. I went from darkness to light and I have never felt so alive.

God filled that void and now I feel more alive than ever. So, what are you waiting for? Go beyond John 3:16 and live a John 3:1-21 life! Being "born again" and living in the light is the way to go…to heaven that is!

February 13

"Then the LORD said to Joshua, 'Today I have rolled away the shame of your slavery in Egypt.'" (Joshua 5:9)

My father loved to tell me stories of his younger days. He once told me he had an old motorcycle and but he wasn't a very good rider. Once he started to date my mother it became obvious that the thing needed to go. You see, in order to get to my mom's house he had to cross a set of railroad tracks. Every time he went over them he would drop the bike. So one day he just left it there and set a match to it.

I have often wondered why he did such a thing. Why didn't he sell it? Why not trade it for something else? He told me that in order to keep from getting killed on it, or worse yet, hurting my mother, he had to rid himself of it permanently.

Our focus verse is what the Lord told Joshua just before the Israelites walked into the promise land. God delivered them in a day, yet they continued to act like slaves. It's hard to break the chains of old habits, and they had been slaves for 400 years. For them it took 40 years to break that habit, for my dad, it took the striking of a single match.

All of us struggle with something in our life that has the potential to harm us. There are sins and habits that keep us from receiving everything the Lord wants to give. There are sins that could affect our eternal state, yet for some, they are very difficult to get rid of.

All it takes is confessing and asking God to take it. But, like the Israelites, old habits can be hard to break. So, if we want to leave the past in the past, then bury it, burn it, walk away from it, and leave it for good. God can help with that. He can empower us to live a life without that "thing", and a life far more fulfilling.

February 14

"Blessed...are those who hear the word of God and obey it." (Luke 11:28)

My earlier life was far removed from Christianity. I was a different person. Then one day my life changed. I hit my knees and God entered in. Now I would like to say that was the exact moment my life was altered, but that isn't true either.

When I first gave my heart to God, I was saved, but I had some things in my life that I knew didn't belong. I often played around with the world while claiming to belong to God. I would follow God's teachings up to a point, and then when I realized it meant change, I would back off. And since I am being honest, my life wasn't all what God wanted it to be either.

I was confused and wondered what was missing. I believed. I read my bible a few times a week. I went to church on Sunday and gave money every time the plate came around. Isn't that enough?

Then something changed. I realized to get the fullness of God I had to go all in for God. If I wanted my life to be what God wanted my life to be, I needed to be fully devoted to God or my life would not be much different than it was before I was saved.

The bible teaches us that we must be obedient to God's will. That means we must submit (yes I used that word) to a power greater than ourselves. We must allow God to control us. It is one thing to say you believe, but a totally different thing to be all in.

When I finally came to that realization and started allowing Him to rule me, lead me, guide me, and teach me, my life exploded. Things have never been so good, life has never been richer.

Believers have two options: the way of the flesh (old self) or the way of the Spirit (the new self). It is a choice a believer must make. How do you want to live? God didn't birth us in order for us to continue to live in the strength of the flesh, He gives us a supernatural source that is readily available to us, that helps us make decisions, choices, use our talents and to minister to others.

We must learn to use the new, the Spirit of God, to empower us to live different lives. Christ chooses to be in our life rather than watch us struggle in our own strength, or should I say weakness. If we allow Him, He will demonstrate His presence. Let Him, you were born for this!

February 15

"Thomas said to him, 'Lord, we don't know where you are going, so how can we know the way?' Jesus answered, 'I am the way and the truth and the life. No one comes to the Father except through me.'" (John 14:5-6)

I lived at the National Training Center (NTC) outside of Barstow, CA and right in the middle of the Mojave Desert for four years. I recall the first time we drove the 37 miles from Barstow to NTC. We looked in amazement at the sites and beauty of the desert. We also noticed there was only one road in and out of the place we were going to call home.

One stretch of road, known as "10 mile stretch", went from one hill down through the desert floor and back up to another hill, exactly 10 miles from one hilltop to the other. You could see every inch of that two lane narrow road.

I heard stories of how one could get to the NTC via the desert, off road, but never actually met anyone who did it. Everyone knew if you wanted to get to the NTC, you had to take "10 mile stretch".

When the disciples asked Jesus how to get to God's house, He told them He was the only way. That may not be popular in today's society. We live in a world where people think there are many ways to get to heaven. Some think they can get there under their own merit, by being good or by saying certain things. But the reality is, Jesus is and will always be, the only way to God.

Just as that two lane road into the NTC seemed long and narrow, it was adequate to take those who lived and worked there in and out.

Jesus' way is wide enough for everyone, but one must believe and follow in order to get there. Instead of arguing and worrying about how narrow that may sound, we should be grateful that there is a way for us to get there.

Instead of wandering around trying to find that "other way in", we should just be focused on following the way we know will actually get us there. I never once in four years explored those other ways into the NTC. I just took the road I knew would lead me there.

So know this; Jesus provides the path to get to heaven and to God. It is the only way in. It is long and narrow, but it leads there nonetheless. Decide today to follow Jesus by believing in Him, knowing He speaks the truth and living a life bound for glory. Regardless to what world claims, the road to heaven is through Jesus and is yours for the taking.

February 16

"Love the Lord your God with all your heart and with all your soul and with all your mind and with all your strength." (Matthew 12:30)

I once had a Basset Hound that wouldn't play fetch at all. She would bring me her toy, watch me throw it, and then give me a look. She wouldn't make any effort to go get it.

My one eyed dog Ziggy likes to play fetch, but it only lasts for about three throws. She grows tired easily and takes her toy and plops down to chew on it.

Some years ago I was visiting a friend and was introduced to his dog. The dog dropped a pine cone at my feet. I was warned not to touch it, but I ignored the warning. What resulted was a tiring game of fetch. The dog would not stop.

These three dogs had a different perspective on what the game of fetch consist of. They remind me of the three types of "Christians" in this world. Each one unique and each one has a different idea of what Christianity is all about.

The first are Judases. They appear to be Christians, while in reality they are connivers, deceivers, and liars. They look the part; say all the right things, but their hearts just aren't in it.

The second start out well. They follow Jesus and then drop out and quit. They enjoy being part of something exciting, but when they realized they can't use Jesus for their own purposes, they get bored and leave.

The last just won't quit, can't quit, because their hearts have been captured by the love of God. They can't get enough and keep coming back for more.

What about you? Do you just go through the motions; or follow for a while and then quit; or are you excited each day about being with Jesus and keep coming back for more? I pray the latter....

February 17

"The eunuch asked Philip, 'Tell me, please, who is the prophet talking about, himself or someone else?' Then Philip began with that very passage of Scripture and told him the good news about Jesus. As they traveled along the road, they came to some water and the eunuch said, 'Look, here is water. Why shouldn't I be baptized?'" (Acts 8:34-36)

Deborah has given her heart to God. She has wanted to get baptized, but the time was never right. As she looked at the frozen Broad River in North Carolina, I could tell she had found the place. No matter how cold, this was the place and now was the time. So at 9:30am, she took about 6 steps into that freezing water, sat down and allowed me to baptize her in the name of the Father, the Son and the Holy Spirit.

John the Baptist was going around speaking of the coming of Jesus Christ. People were listening and believing. John's message was simple: confess and be baptized. As people were following that advice, they heard that another one would come. John was talking about Jesus.

Then Jesus appeared and wanted to be baptized by John. And as Jesus came out of the water, "heaven was opened, and he saw the Spirit of God descending like a dove and lighting on him. And a voice from heaven said, *"This is my Son, whom I love; with him I am well pleased."* (Matthew 3:16-17)

Those words spoken by God should fill each of us with power and assurance. When we accept Jesus as Lord and Savior, and are baptized, the Holy Spirit fills us and God's words to Jesus apply to us as well.

I can only imagine the pleasure on God's face when Deborah stepped into that water. I can tell you it was cold, but I don't think she felt a thing. As I asked her a few simple questions, she never once shivered. As I dipped her into that icy water, she came up with a look on her face as if she saw the "Spirit of God" Himself. At that moment in her heart, I think she heard God say "This is my daughter, whom I love; with her I am well pleased."

How about you? Have you heard those words from God? Have you taken that step of faith to accept Jesus as Lord and Savior? Our days are numbered and time is running out. Hesitation can cost us an eternity of regret. It is my prayer that each and every one of you reading this has or will accept Jesus and take those steps into the water and be filled with His Spirit.

February 18

"See what I've given you? Safe passage as you walk on snakes and scorpions, and protection from every assault of the Enemy. No one can put a hand on you." (Luke 10:19 MSG)

One of my favorite stories to tell is about day we encountered a larger than life obstacle. We were riding motorcycles in Yellowstone National Park when we suddenly came to a complete stop. Being the last bike of four, it took me a moment to realize just why we stopped.

I looked ahead to see a male buffalo lumbering right at us. He was in our lane and he wasn't changing lanes or stopping. I watched (and took photos) as he got closer to my friend, Dennis. He was much larger than the bike and Dennis, much stronger, and he wasn't slowing down. I initially thought, "This isn't going to work out too well." I said a quick prayer for safety asking God to protect us.

What happened next amazes me still. As the buffalo neared, just a few feet from the front of the bike, he simply changed lanes and proceeded to walk past us. He was close enough for me to reach out and touch him, although I didn't.

Wow, is all I could come up with. Did I just see that? Did I just come that close to a massive animal and survive? What I thought to be a dangerous, near death experience turned out to be a once in a lifetime encounter with one of God's creatures.

Sometimes in life we see things or hear things that may seem larger than life. They may at first seem to be what we think is a life threatening situation. They may seem to be something we aren't going to be able to avoid. But then, at the last moment, something changes the path of the oncoming doom and we are safe once again.

God can change the path of anything if you allow Him. How many times do we try to resolve problems or move obstacles that are bigger than us? We struggle and fight, and sometimes we succeed. But most of the time we fail. If we give those things to God and believe He can move mountains, we would be surprised at how things turn out.

So no matter the obstacle, I challenge you to pray about it and let God handle it. Give it to Him and then rest assured He heard you and He will handle it according to His will. What happens may surprise you. Or it may just become a story to tell others of how God's hand reached out and moved that thing in your path.

February 19

"If anyone would come after me, he must deny himself and take up his cross daily and follow me." (Luke 9:23)

Do you remember watching movies or TV shows where a certain kid was being bullied, beat down and made fun of? In every instance, sooner or later, that kid decided he or she wasn't taking it any longer and they stood up to the bully.

The key to defeating the bully was that someone had to take a stand and put their life where their convictions were. They had to stand up for what was right, against what was wrong.

The same is true in the lives of those that profess to be Christians. We all face bullies in our life. There are bullies that want to rule our lives and beat us down. I face them daily and so do you.

The bullies comes in the form of temptations, unwanted thoughts, bad habits, troubles, heartache, pain, suffering, sin, etc. Sometimes the bully gets to us. We feel like the bully is too strong, we want to give up, give in, and allow the bully to win. If we are going to take a stand against evil and the bullies in our lives, then we have to take that stand just as Jesus did.

Living a life as a Christian has a cost and we must pay that price. Whatever sacrifices, whatever price, whatever risk, whatever it means or takes, to do the right thing, we must take it. The will and authority of God is with the righteous, and no matter what, in the end, the righteous overcome. That is what the cross did.

February 20

"The angel of the LORD appeared to him in flames of fire from within a bush. Moses saw that though the bush was on fire it did not burn up. So Moses thought, 'I will go over and see this strange sight why the bush does not burn up.'" (Exodus 3:2–3)

I love a fire. I could watch the flames dance for hours. I get lost in my thoughts and my mind wonders. It is relaxing and soothing to sit in front of a fire, especially on a clear crisp night. Have you ever noticed that some wood seems to burn faster than others? Pine lasts only minutes, but a hard wood log seems to last for hours.

Moses, the famous deliverer, had one of the more unusual encounters with God found in Scripture. It's called "the burning bush," but really, that's a misnomer. If we read the story carefully, Moses' watches the fire for a while before he notices that the bush isn't actually being burned? The fact that the fire wasn't consuming the bush got Moses' attention eventually.

How long do you think Moses watched that bush burn before he noticed that strange fact? Let's just say ten minutes. Think about sitting and watching a bush on fire for ten minutes, and then realizing it isn't really burning. Why did it take him so long?

Maybe he was mesmerized by the dancing flames and he didn't actually notice the bush. Ever see something, yet miss what's really going on? Maybe he was too caught up in his own thinking and he just missed it. Maybe he was so relaxed in his surroundings he missed the sign.

So consider this, maybe God is trying to communicate with you, but you're so busy with a multitude of distractions that you aren't paying attention. If God dropped a "burning bush" in your path, would you even notice? God is always there, but sometimes we need to slow down to notice Him. Sometimes we need to look deep within, to actually see the things God wants to show us.

So today, ask God to open your eyes to His signs. What might He be showing you that you are missing? Look closely at everything around you; it may be right before your eyes.

February 21

"Jesus entered a village. A woman by the name of Martha welcomed him and made him feel quite at home. She had a sister, Mary, who sat before the Master, hanging on every word he said. But Martha was pulled away by all she had to do in the kitchen." (Luke 10:38-40 MSG)

I have noticed that everyone seems to be so busy lately. Often I wish there were 36 hours in a day instead of 24. That still may not be enough time to complete everything I have to do. When did life get like this?

The busy-ness of this world can distract us from what is important. Our families and friends take a back seat to careers, schedules and other things. Even our eternal state is at risk because we are so busy we don't have time for what is important.

Have you heard the story about the little boy who wants to know how much his father makes an hour at work? The story has the little boy asking repeatedly and finally the father asks him why is it so important. The little boy's reply should stop each of us in our tracks. The little boy wants to know so he can buy some time with his father.

As I pondered this I remembered the story of Mary and Martha in our focus verse. As I read this passage, it occurred to me, just as the little boy wanted time with the father, our Heavenly Father wants time with us.

Mary sat and listened at Jesus' feet. Martha was distracted by her busy-ness. Mary took time to hear and learn from Jesus; Martha was too busy with the "things" she felt more important. Mary had a one on one encounter with Jesus; Martha missed that opportunity and complained about it.

The reality to life is that Jesus prizes our companionship over our busy-ness. He would much rather we sit at His feet (be a Mary) verses being so busy (being a Martha) we can't attend church, read His word, talk and listen to Him. We can claim to be believers, Christians, but the proof is in the amount of time we spend with Him.

Matthew 7 gives us a strong warning about claims and even "doing" when it comes to eternity. We can claim to know Him but unless we take the time to get to know Him, and Him us, we risk Him saying to us on our final day *"I never knew you. Away from me, you evildoers!"* Jesus wants us to be Mary's in a Martha world.

February 22

"Therefore go and make disciples of all nations, baptizing them in the name of the Father and of the Son and of the Holy Spirit, and teaching them to obey everything I have commanded you. And surely I am with you always, to the very end of the age." (Matthew 28:19-20)

I am currently an outreach pastor. My job is to go outside the walls of the church to introduce people to Jesus. It is also part of my job to find ways to get the members of our church to do the same. We are called by Jesus to do just that. But not everyone is comfortable doing so.

How many times have you felt like evangelizing is for those called to be pastors? It is their job, not yours, to tell people about Jesus. That is why a church pays them a salary, isn't it?

Through an encounter with God, our lives are changed and we become new people. But there is something else that we should experience; it's the call, a commission, a task, a mission set forth by God. In our focus verses God commands us to DO, GO, SERVE and SHARE.

When Moses put his sandals back on after the *"holy ground and burning bush"* experience (Exodus 3), God instructed him to work toward freeing his people. When Isaiah saw God *"high and lifted up"* he cried out, *"Here am I; send me."* (Isaiah 6:8) After Saul was dazzled blind on the road to Damascus he shouldered a commission to win the Gentile world for Christ. (Acts 9:1-31)

Is that not our story also? When God came to us in saving grace, did He not call us to minister in His name? We are commanded into service by God. Let us prepare not only to see the light, receive His grace and mercy and to embrace an eternal life with Him, but also to accept the challenge of service.

53

February 23

"Here's another way to put it: You're here to be light, bringing out the God-colors in the world. God is not a secret to be kept. We're going public with this, as public as a city on a hill." (Matthew 5:14 MSG)

I had the privilege to see a dear friend take a big step in her life. In front of a large crowd, she testified to accepting the saving grace of Jesus Christ. She went public about her faith and would soon be baptized.

She stood shaking, telling of people in her life who were "calling cards" along the way to her decision. People, to include my wife and I, who helped her to see Jesus was real; people who helped her to see that He was calling her to Him. I can't do justice to her words, but she spoke of people and events that led her to her choice to follow Jesus.

For years we knew God was calling this lady. Over the years we grew to love this woman. What hit me the hardest was when she handed me a little wooden disc that I handed her a few years ago.

She kept that little "Round TUIT", as a reminder. She finally got "around to it" and answered the call and become a "new creation". She gave that token back to me, to help me remember this day. I will cherish that wooden disc for the rest of my life.

She also gave everyone in the room a card with the words "You are His 'Calling Card'". She said each person was a "Calling Card" for Jesus. She challenged everyone to be a calling card to those they meet.

Those of us who profess to believe and follow Jesus Christ have a responsibility to help others see Him and to help lead others to Him. We all have something special in our lives, the love and saving grace of a Savior, someone who paid a very high price for us. We have the greatest news and we aren't to keep it hidden. We are to share it far and wide.

So I ask you, who are you a "Calling Card" to? If someone were to testify today, would your name be included? It is not for the recognition, but for the glory of God. God delights when His people tell others of Him. So make God happy; tell someone today about the greatest news ever, the news about Jesus Christ.

February 24

"For I know the plans I have for you," declares the LORD, "plans to prosper you and not to harm you, plans to give you hope and a future." (Jeremiah 29:11)

Have you ever arrived at an intersection and wondered, which way do I go? I have. Road signs can confuse me at times. Busy intersections with many signs make me second guess and question which way I want to go. Sometimes we turn to others for direction, only to be led astray. We use GPS devices, smart phones and Google Maps to tell us which way to go.

Well, news flash, they can get you lost! Just this past week, we took the RV up to the mountains. I got off the interstate and entered one of those turnabouts, following the path the GPS told me to. Once I exited the turnabout, as I was directed, the GPS immediately started to "recalculate", plotting another route. Don't you hate that?

Life can be filled with change, and most of us don't like it. Just when we think we are on the right path, something or someone changes and our life is "recalculated" so to speak. God can change our path from time to time, taking us down unknown byways and highways. Change can be scary, especially when you aren't sure of the way.

Another news flash! His plan for you may not be your plan. And if you follow, you will find that in the process of redirection, we discover that our security comes not in our plan, but His.

Spiritual maturity comes in learning to depend on God to direct our path, even when He changes it. We should never fail to follow what God has planned for us. God's plan is the expression of His love. God always has our best interests at heart.

God will take us through things, even if it is something terrible, and will use it for a good overall purpose in our life. When God is at work, it can involve risks and changes and new ventures. We need to trust in God, not in ourselves or any other source. We need to find security in God, depend on God, because God's plan is prosperous and hope-filled, one that will work for His people's benefit. God desires that His people trust in His plan.

So, where is God directing you? Do you feel His gentle nudge; or His full blown "recalculation" in your life? Change is hard, redirection is hard, but the end result, when we follow God, is always worth it. So let Him lead, and sit back and enjoy the trip.

February 25

"Fix our eyes on Jesus, the author and perfecter of our faith..." Hebrews 12:2)

One of the many blessings I have is a beautiful grandson. Spending time with him is limited because of life, but I treasure the times I do get. One of my favorite memories of spending time with him is the time we went to the fair. He clung to me as we walked through the chaos. He was all eyes. He looked and pointed at all the lights. He was fascinated with the rides, even though he didn't want to get on a single one. He met people with smiles and waves. He was so excited.

As we walked, we came across a tank of sea lions. They performed tricks for the crowd. He became fixated on them. Suddenly he was lost to all the things around him. He was totally absorbed in those animals and the tricks they were performing. It was as if he tuned everything else out and ignored the world. All that was important to him at that moment was what he was focused on.

The world around us is filled with chaos. We can go through life with our eyes darting from one thing to the next, or we can focus on what is important. We can get so caught up in the chaos that we forget the important things in life.

I once read that even in ministry or working for the church, one can get so focused on the doing, they forget the reason why. We can do great things, but ignore the most important thing, God Himself.

I am guilty of that. When I started ministry I was so focused on doing that it took me from time alone with God. My studies lacked. My prayer time was nearly nonexistent. I suffered from it and things had to change.

Our focus verse reminds us what is important. We need to fix our gaze on Jesus and become so absorbed in Him, that we tune out the rest of this world. Then, He will take us to where He wants us to be and that place is far greater than anything else imaginable.

February 26

"…you do not even know what will happen tomorrow." (James 4:14)

As a biker and a pastor, I minister to bikers. Part of what I do is to minister to bikers and families who are dealing with injury or death from motorcycle accidents. It is hard to walk into a hospital waiting room and find the right words to share with a family.

Imagine the trouble finding words to share with a biker community after a biker is killed by one of our own. A biker, behind the wheel of a SUV, pulled into the path of a bike. That one small mistake changed the lives of two families forever.

The loss was tragic, but there was some solace. The biker who died loved Jesus Christ. Just like he made a decision to ride a motorcycle, he had made a decision to believe in Jesus. His decisions sealed his fate and his eternity.

The lessons to learn at a time like this are simple. First, life is short and there are no guarantees. Secondly, bad things happen without warning. We cannot predict when life will end, so we must be prepared at all times.

Lastly, the decisions we make have consequences. Some decisions have eternal consequences. Like the decision to believe in Jesus or not. This decision, along with how we live our life, determines our eternal home. We all must choose and we must choose wisely.

No one can bring back the biker who died. But we can use that event to evaluate our eternal fate should the same happen to us. The decisions we make beforehand can determine heaven or hell as our eternal resting place.

So I ask you…have you thought about it? Have you really evaluated your life and do you know without a shadow of a doubt where you will go if you were to meet the same fate as the biker? Let his life help us make lasting choices and I beg you to choose wisely and choose now.

February 27

"Their sins and lawless acts I will remember no more." (Hebrews 10:17)

My dog Ziggy is a good dog. She rarely causes me to discipline her, but when she is bad, she gets it. I have scolded her, even whipped her on occasions for something she has done. But, no matter how much punishment I give her, she never holds it against me.

In fact, she seems to love me more. I can whip her and moments later she is in my lap licking me on my nose. Those are called kisses and I love them. Oh, how I wish everyone, to include me, could be like her.

How often do we get upset with someone and hold a grudge? How often do we mouth the words of forgiveness, only to not forgive at all? I must be honest, I know a few people who shun me for something I did years ago, and I have apologized for, and I received their "forgiveness".

But here is a promise from Jesus; He forgives us our wrongdoings if we sincerely ask for forgiveness. Better yet, He is like Ziggy. He chooses to forget them, never to bring them back up or hold them against us. Wow, that is a promise I like.

What have you done in the past that needs forgiveness? Have you asked Jesus for forgiveness? Better yet, once He has forgiven you, have you forgiven yourself and forgotten the wrong?

Forgiveness requires effort. Jesus' promise is twofold, He offers us forgiveness and He offers us a memory dump. How can we do the same? We must choose to forgive and then move on. My good friend always says "build a bridge and get over it". Jesus offers us that bridge; we too should offer it to others.

February 28

"Run from anything that stimulates youthful lusts. Instead, pursue righteous living, faithfulness, love, and peace. Enjoy the companionship of those who call on the Lord with pure hearts." (2 Timothy 2:22 NLT)

From the moment you get up in the morning to the moment you lay your head down on your pillow at night, you will have made hundreds, maybe even thousands, of choices. That is why ordering at some restaurants is no easy task. The menu resembles a small telephone book. There are too many choices.

Life is filled with choices. There are some choices that don't mean a lot, while other choices mean a whole lot. And it comes down to this: we make our choices, and our choices make us. So if you want to grow spiritually, you will. And if you don't want to grow spiritually, you won't. Either you will go forward as a Christian, or you will go backward. Either you will progress, or you will regress. Either you will gain ground, or you will lose ground. And if you stand still, then you will lose ground.

The reason some Christians succeed while others fail miserably comes down to their choices. It is not the luck of the draw or something that happens randomly. It is because people make the right choice to do the right thing. There are choices that will impair our spiritual growth, and there are choices that will enhance it.

That is why we need to make a commitment to seek and to grow spiritually on a daily basis--not to just hold our ground, but to gain ground in our relationship with Christ. Let's commit ourselves to spiritual growth.

February 29

"If people want to follow me, they must give up the things they want. They must be willing even to give up their lives to follow me." (Matthew 16:24 NCV)

When I first came to know Jesus it seemed that every time I turned around, conviction would hit me. Don't do this, quit that, leave them alone...I would say something and knew the minute it left my lips it was wrong. God has a way of doing that.

When you decide to live a totally surrendered life, that decision will be tested. Sometimes it will mean doing inconvenient, unpopular, costly, or seemingly impossible tasks. It will often mean doing the opposite of what you feel like doing.

Paul's moment of surrender occurred on the Damascus road after he was knocked down by a blinding light. For others, less drastic methods are needed to get our attention. Regardless, surrendering is never just a one-time event. Paul said he had to *"die daily."* (1 Corinthians 15:31)

There is a moment of surrender and there is the practice of surrender. The practice of surrender requires perseverance. It is moment-by-moment and lasts a lifelong. You may have to re-surrender your life fifty times a day.

Think about it. By nature we are self-centered, greedy, and revengeful people. But as you walk with Jesus you can usually figure out what will please Him by doing the opposite of your natural inclination.

Bill Bright founder of Campus Crusade for Christ once said, "When I was a young man I made a contract with God. I literally wrote it out and signed my name at the bottom. It said *"From this day forward, I am a slave of Jesus Christ."*

Have you signed a contract like that with God? Or, are you still arguing and struggling with God over his right to do with your life as He pleases? Isn't it time to surrender - to God's grace, love, and wisdom.

March 1

"Surely the arm of the LORD is not too short to save, nor his ear too dull to hear. But your iniquities have separated you from your God; your sins have hidden his face from you, so that he will not hear." (Isaiah 59:1-2)

Have you ever asked someone for something only to be ignored? When I was little I had certain things that I had to do...they were called chores. The simple rule was, do them and all was good, don't do them, and, well, there were consequences to suffer.

My mother was a stickler for chores. She wanted them done and done in a timely manner. I remember once wanting to do something and every time I asked for permission, it was as if she didn't hear me. I tried everything to get her attention until I realized I hadn't done my chore. Once completed, she could magically hear again and I was allowed to do whatever it was.

When you ask God for something, what happens when it isn't answered? Who do you blame? To be honest, we usually blame God. We have to have someone to blame because we never want to admit we are at fault. But let's be real...sometimes we are to blame. Sometimes an error in judgment, a poor decision, a thoughtless mistake, or sin in our life keeps God from answering us.

Sometimes our wrongs stand in the way of answered prayers. We may be the reason our prayers are not being answered. God's "no" can be our own fault.

Our focus verse tells us God has the ability to answer every prayer, but our unrepentant sins or our disobedience keep God away. Some of those sins could be broken relationships, husbands or wives dishonoring their marriages, pride, selfishness, and an uncaring attitude. Ignoring the things we know to do, like those chores I neglected.

Have you considered that your sin can close the spigot of God's flow to answer your prayers? If you tolerate sin and disobedience in your life, don't waste your breath praying unless it's a prayer of confession. God wants to answer prayers, not of perfect people, but of repentant people.

March 2

"A lot of you are going to assume that you'll sit down to God's salvation banquet just because you've been hanging around the neighborhood all your lives. Well, one day you're going to be banging on the door, wanting to get in, but you'll find the door locked and the Master saying, Sorry, you're not on my guest list.'" (Luke 13:23-25 MSG)

Hang around the motorcycle community for a while and you will soon be able to recognize the real bikers from the wannabes. Wannabes think that just because they own a motorcycle and ride, and wear the right clothes, that makes them a biker. But I am here to tell you there is more to being a biker than that. A real biker knows what I am talking about.

In all forms of life there are those that are real and those that are wannabes. These people want to fit in and belong, yet they are far from the real thing. I am not bashing wannabes, because some may think that of me, but I am trying to make a point.

When trying to be someone or something else, you only fool yourself. If I were to try to be a musician, even though I know a lot about music, it wouldn't take long before I would be found out to be a wannabe. I can't read music, sing and or play a musical instrument. I just like to listen to music.

Many people think because they believe in Jesus and go to church occasionally that makes them saved. They look the part, they even know the language, but is that enough? Jesus says in our focus verse that some will be disappointed and not make it to heaven. He tells us that it is more than just believing.

Those words should rock us. We should take note that Jesus is saying that just because we sit at the table, we shouldn't assume we are going to eat. Going to church doesn't give us the key to the door. There is more to entering into the kingdom of God than just looking the part.

So what is the lesson here? Jesus' own words tell us to focus our total attention on our life with God. We need to stop being wannabes and take on the total lifestyle of being a Christ Follower. We need to walk in His ways, live according to His example and be set apart from the ways of this world. We need to shed the grave clothes of the dead person we were and take on the totally new creation God makes us when we become the real deal. We need to stop pretending and become who we say we are...real children of God.

March 3

"But I tell you who hear me: Love your enemies, do good to those who hate you, bless those who curse you, pray for those who mistreat you." "Then your reward will be great, and you will be sons of the Most High..." (Luke 627-28, 35)

"Did you hear of the city on the hill, said one old man to the other? It once shined bright, and it would be shining still, but they all started turning on each other. But one by one, they ran away with their made up minds to leave it all behind. And the light began to fade... Each one thought that they knew better, but they were different by design. Instead of standing strong together, they let their differences divide. And the world is searching still. And the Father's calling still, "Come home".

These are lyrics from a Casting Crown song "City on a Hill." As I listen to that song, I can't help but think how true it is of our world today. We are not the strong, united nation we once were. Our light isn't shining; we are divided politically, culturally and even socially.

But that is not how God intended it to be. He created us to be different, it was His design. Yet in our differences, His intention was for us to live in harmony. Our differences make us unique and interesting. Yet we focus on the differences in a different way, we let them divide us.

What would happen if we started focusing on the similarities? Like, we all live in the same country, we all want peace, we all want to live as equals, and we all want to prosper. What if we all extended the right hand of fellowship and loved our neighbor as the bible teaches.

When we love someone, in spite of their differences and in spite of what they say about us or do, it doesn't change them, it changes you. Your heart changes, the bitterness and the hatred go away. You feel better; you have less stress and less anxiety. Try it. It's hard to dislike someone you are truly praying for. Love wins every time.

I propose we all start among our own circle of friends, family and influence. Love each other in spite of what's said, done or the differences. Learn to use and mean phrases like "I'm sorry", "I forgive you", and "please forgive me". Learn to overlook the differences and concentrate on the similarities. Pray for others, pray for God to let you see others as He does. I bet that in a short time you will see others differently. You will begin to see the good in people and your heart towards them will change. Love is the greatest of all.....

March 4

"I will sprinkle clean water on you, and you will be clean; I will cleanse you from all your impurities and from all your idols. I will give you a new heart and put a new spirit in you; I will remove from you your heart of stone and give you a heart of flesh. And I will put my Spirit in you and move you to follow my decrees and be careful to keep my laws". (Ezekiel 36:25-27)

Today I took on the task of pressure washing my driveway. I knew it was dirty, but never expected to see that much filth and grime. Each pass of the pressure nozzle swept away more dirt, mold and filth, leaving behind a clean path of concrete. As I progressed, I looked back at the clean concrete and was amazed at how good it looked, only to turn around and see the filth ahead of me.

I couldn't help but think about my past life. Some of you may not know, but my life was a mess. I was filthy, living a life filled with sin, looking like that driveway that lay ahead of me. I needed cleaning; I knew that, but how? I had been dirty so long it was unimaginable to think I could be different.

Then it happened, I was introduced to someone that had the power to clean my stains and filth. I was introduced to someone who could take the old me and make me brand new. Someone willing to take the time and energy to clean me of all that and make me what I was originally created to be. That someone was Jesus.

We are told in scripture that the blood of Jesus washes away our sins. Psalm 51:1-2, 7 says *"Have mercy on me, O God, according to your unfailing love; according to your great compassion blot out my transgressions. Wash away all my iniquity and cleanse me from my sin. "Cleanse me with hyssop, and I will be clean; wash me, and I will be whiter than snow."* Jesus is the only one who can clean a person and make them what He created them to be.

This process takes time, much like my driveway, but the point is, it is happening. Jesus took away some serious stains, sins, like my foul mouth and urge for alcohol, and He set me on a path, one He chose for me. Oh, I still have some work to be done, and He is slowly cleansing those areas as well, but I am thankful for a Savior who doesn't leave us filthy. He will take on the task willingly, if we call on Him. So, what are you waiting for, there is dirt to wash away.

March 5

"But mark this: There will be terrible times in the last days..."
(2 Timothy 3:1)

I am going to date myself, but I grew up watching shows like "I Dream of Jeannie" and "I Love Lucy". The other day I happened on a rerun of "I Dream of Jeannie" and was drawn back to a time when things were far different than today. Jeannie wore a costume that didn't even show her belly button and the language was clean and suitable for everyone.

The difference between that show and the stuff on TV today is staggering. Just last night, I happened to turn to a channel that airs one of today's hit shows. In a matter of minutes I heard a crude attempt at comedy where the actors made sexist comments about women, used words that I couldn't believe were on a major network and the content of the show could or should have been rated at least PG 13. It amazes me the things that people today think are normal.

We live in a world where values and morals are low and it seems to be okay. We live in a world today where anything goes and it's acceptable. We live in a world today where promiscuity, foul language, and crude behavior is the norm and no one seems to bat an eye. We live in a world today that was foretold thousands of years ago.

Paul wrote about these things back in the 1st century after Jesus' death. Paul wrote about godlessness and how the world would eventually become. So when I read 2 Timothy 3:1-5, I can't help but think we must be in our last days before Jesus comes back.

For those of us who are Christ followers, we must take a serious look at the world around us. We must remember that we are in this world, but not of this world. There is a huge difference. We must align ourselves to the things of God and not this world in order to receive the things God has in store for us. So, be watchful, ever vigilant of the things we take in and accept. Only Godly behavior is rewarded by the God in which we claim.

March 6

"Everyone who does evil hates the light, and will not come into the light for fear that his deeds will be exposed." (John 3:20)

My first Army duty station was Ft. Hood, TX. I moved there not knowing much about the place and with little money in my pocket. I rented an apartment and moved my family in. It looked great, came with furniture and was clean. The first day in the apartment went well. But when I got up early the next morning to go to work and turned on the lights, things moved. Yes, things scampered across the floor and the counters.

I called the landlord and he came to check it out. What he found were cockroaches. Those are some nasty critters. We had to stay a night in a hotel while he fumigated the place.

How many of you have ever seen a moth? It is the opposite; they are attracted to the light and fly towards it. Turn your porch light on in the summer and they buzz around it all night long.

Moths can handle the light, but obviously cockroaches can't. Jesus says people act in the same manner when God's light shines. The pure in heart run towards the light; those unclean run away. Look at our world. Those who have things to hide or go against everything moral or ethical behave like cockroaches. Those who want a better life have a fondness to God's light.

Light draws a clear line between those who love and follow Jesus and those who oppose Him. His light reveals the true condition of the heart. It either draws or drives away. What about you, in which direction are you running?

March 7

"'Come, follow me,' Jesus said, 'and I will send you out to fish for people.'
At once they left their nets and followed him." (Matthew 4:19-20)

"As Jesus went on from there, He saw a man called Matthew, sitting in the
tax collector's booth; and He said to him, 'Follow Me!' And he got up and
followed Him." (Matthew 9:9)

Have you ever met someone who you knew a long time ago and the first thing you notice is that they have changed? The new person is so far different that they are almost unrecognizable. Well, I have been told that is me. I was a wild one in my earlier days. But now, I walk with Jesus and the old life is gone, thank God.

We read about this change in many passages of the bible. Matthew tells a story of Jesus' simple request to ordinary men and their responses. In chapter 4, as Jesus walked by the shore He saw two sets of brothers, Peter and Andrew and James and John, doing what they did every day, fish. Then in chapter 9 he walks past a tax collector, sitting in a booth taking people's money.

In both cases, Jesus simply said "follow Me". He never said "give up that habit...." or "clean your act up and then..." He just says leave that every day, ordinary life and come follow Me! Amazingly, they did.

As we read the story of those who followed Jesus, we learn that once they accepted that invitation to follow, nothing about their life stayed the same. Their outlook, attitude, motivation, spirit and focus changed. They left the same old thing for something new, exciting and adventurous. The invitation may have been simple, but the life they lived afterwards was far from simple.

We also read that their response to the invitation was immediate. They didn't take time to consider the cost, what they would lose, how their life would change, they just went along. They heard the simply invitation and took off in wild abandonment, seeking a new life with new challenges and outcomes. The old life of ordinary thrown to the curb and the new life willingly accepted.

What we can also read is how their changed life impacted them and others. People who truly follow Jesus can't help but change. So what about you...have you committed to following Jesus and allowing Him to change you? Try it; you just may like what you become.

March 8

"Be still before the LORD and wait patiently for Him..." (Psalm 37:7)

Do you ever feel like you can't see God? Do you think God's purpose for you is unclear? Well, I have. Lately I have been reflecting on what God wants of me or what He wants me to do. I keep asking and seeking as I am told in Matthew 7:7, but I am still unclear. I have found myself looking with no clear picture in sight.

Have you ever sat on the banks of a lake and looked at the surface? If the water is still the reflection is clear. With a smooth surface the water reflects the sky, the trees, and everything as if it were a mirror image. But throw a stone in the water and see what happens. The stone creates ripples and the mirror image is distorted.

The same can be said about mud in the lake. As long as the mud is settled on the bottom, the water is clear and one can see through it. But stir the mud and the water clouds. As long as the mud is in motion there is no clear vision.

The same applies to our soul. If our soul is not still there is no clear vision. When we try to do things our way, or get restless waiting on God, we stir the waters of our soul and things get distorted or cloudy. We try to see but there is nothing clear. What are we to do?

As followers of the Lord, we know we live to fulfill His direction, purpose and will. We are His vessels and are to be used for His good. But when we feel He is distant or quiet we often grow impatient, restless. But scripture tells us we must wait and rest. We must allow our soul to settle, and then His vision for our life will be clear.

Sometimes that is the hardest thing for us to do. Waiting is something I know I am not good at, but if I want to be used by God I must learn to rest and be still. I must allow the waters of my soul to be still, let the silt settle and allow that image to become clear. The picture He paints is far greater than anything I could ever create, so the wait will be worthwhile.

March 9

"Brother will betray brother to death and a father his child; children will rebel against their parents and have them put to death. All men will hate you because of me, but he who stands firm to the end will be saved." (Matthew 10:21-22)

We all have shortcomings. At times our lives aren't exactly as we want them to be or where we think they should be. There is a gap between the life we are living and the life we want to live.

The same is true in our spiritual lives. Often there is a gap between the lives we are living and the life we are called to be living, the life we know God wants us to be living. There may even be a gap between the person others think we are and the person we really are.

Our focus verse tells us that we will not be favored by people if we live a life for Christ. We know up front that we may not be the favorite person on the block, but the promise makes standing firm worthwhile.

We, as humans, tend to make compromises between how God tells us to live and how we really live because we're afraid of what others may think or that we won't fit in. We often compromise the Word of God because it's too hard to live the Christian life as God commands. It's too hard to live the life that we know God wants us to live because it doesn't fit into a "main stream American" way of life. We compromise our beliefs, morals, ethics and Christian values to fit in, blend, and get along. The word compromise means: "agreement reached by adjustment of conflicting or opposing claims, principles; to make a dishonorable or shameful concession."

Living a life contrary to God's command is risky and has eternal consequences. So I say to you, be done with compromise and live the life that God wants you to live. Take God at His word and latch onto the promise, "…he who stands firm to the end will be saved." You may not be popular, you may be excluded from things because of your way of life or your stance on issues, but you will live a victorious life with Christ and share the eternal reward that is awaiting you! Stop compromising…

March 10

"No one can serve two masters, for either he will hate the one and love the other, or he will be devoted to the one and despise the other. You cannot serve God and money." (Matthew 6:24)

The world in which we live in has grown very evil. Persecution is all around us. In one article I read of the brutal things being done to people of faith, yet they are standing firm in their faith and allegiance in Jesus. A true example of what faith is all about.

But here in the civilized USA, things are a little different. I saw an article about a football player, one professing to believe in Jesus Christ, and how he reacted to opposition about his belief. As he approached the podium for an interview, someone in the NFL sees his t-shirt and objects. It reads "Know Jesus, Know Peace". He is told he can't wear that shirt. He is told to turn it inside out or be fined. This man who made a choice to wear the shirt, also made the choice to turn it inside out. Was this a compromise of what he professes to believe in?

Was his decision money driven? For a guy who makes millions a year to play a game, was he that concerned about a few thousand dollars fine? Our focus verse tells us that we can't serve both God and the world. Does money matter more than a confession of faith?

But is it about more than money? The bible also tells us that "When trouble or persecution comes because of the word, they quickly fall away." (Mark 4:17) Did this ball player fear persecution and compromise his belief in order to fit in? Did he fear trouble coming his way so he took the easy way out? We may never know, but it gives me a clear example of how some view their so called belief. And what does Jesus think of his decision? I don't think Jesus is very happy when we compromise what we believe in.

I, for one, am very disappointed in the decisions of this ball player. In a sport that doesn't believe in compromise, win at all cost, he folded. He sent clear a picture of his belief, one I never want to portray.

In the face of persecution, I pray I can be like Stephen in Acts 6:15. As he was seized and brought before the officials, we are told "his face was like the face of an angel." I believe he smiled at them and the light of the Lord was shining through him. Nothing they could do to him could take the joy of God from him and he stood for his faith, even to the death. Never compromise.

March 11

"This is how the birth of Jesus Christ came about: His mother Mary was pledged to be married to Joseph, but before they came together, she was found to be with child through the Holy Spirit." (Matthew 1:18)

Joseph had waited for the day he would take Mary as his wife. Like most of us, I bet he anxiously anticipated that day, maybe even dreamed of it. Then he received the bad news. The woman he waited for is now pregnant with someone else's baby. What would you have done? How would you have reacted?

Bad news comes and how we react or respond can make all the difference. I recall one late night I received some bad news and I responded badly. I didn't think, I just replied and I hurt the other person's feelings. The result of my response severed a friendship. I have apologized, but that friendship is over, all because I responded badly. I didn't take time to consider the outcome.

Joseph took time to "consider" his reaction to the bad news before he acted. When he did, and because we are told Joseph was a righteous man one can only assume he prayed first, look what happened, "an angel of the Lord appeared to him" and spoke truth to him. His response was in line with God's plan and the rest is history.

The lesson here is twofold. First, we have two ways to respond to a situation. We can just go with our first thought and do as I did, or we can take time to consider our response and how it may affect everyone involved. Joseph thought things through before reacting and as it turns out, great things come to those who wait on the Lord. As for me, I lost a friend.

The second lesson is when we take every situation to God first, He will help us see the big picture. So before we react, we should "consider" how our response will change the outcome.

We should take time to call on God for help before we respond and we then respond out of love, not haste. I received that lesson the hard way; so I pray from this point on, I consider before responding.

March 12

"Teacher, I will follow you wherever you go." (Matthew 8:19)

Nike Air tennis shoes were the shoes my son wanted. All his friends had them and he wanted a pair real bad. I looked at them, but to be honest, on a soldier's salary at the time, I just couldn't afford them. I knew he needed a new pair of shoes, but I was not willing to pay that much for a pair of tennis shoes he would wear out in a couple months.

So I took him to the store and told him to pick out what he wanted. Naturally he went straight to the Nikes. He begged me to buy them for him. I made a deal with him. I would pay the amount I was willing to pay for any other pair of shoes, if he would use his allowance to pay the rest.

Jesus was traveling through the country teaching and preaching the ways of the Father. In Matthew 8 we read about several who claim they wanted to follow Jesus, yet may not have counted the cost of that commitment. Jesus challenged them to count the cost of a life of commitment to following Him.

That cost consists of self-denial, rejection, and the reality that this place we call earth is not our home. That cost is accepting that this world cannot provide us with true comfort or rest. That cost is that we are foreigners in a strange land.

What cost are we willing to pay to follow Jesus? Are we willing to stand out in a crowd and not conform to the things of this world? Are we willing to pay the cost of being ridiculed, rejected, and talked about? Are we willing to pay the cost of living a life as Jesus modeled, even if it looks nothing like everyone else?

My son decided that day that he wasn't willing to spend his hard earned money on those overpriced shoes. He went with the ones that met his need, even though he knew that he would look different than his friends. He chose to make the right decision, even at a cost.

So what about you? Do you want to follow Jesus and His ways? Do you want a better life, one that is filled with forgiveness, love, mercy, grace and hope? If you do, what price are you willing to pay? Are you willing to make a decision to follow Jesus even if the cost is great, knowing the reward is far greater than anything this world has to offer? My prayer is that your answer is yes. I pray the cost of following Jesus is a cost you are willing to pay.

March 13

"But don't begin until you count the cost. For who would begin construction of a building without first calculating the cost to see if there is enough money to finish it?" (Luke 14:28 NLT)

I have some friends that are big into sports. You know it is game day by what they wear...hats, shirts, jackets, etc. Some are so extreme they have season tickets and travel great distances to see a game. They have bought in, no matter the cost. And win or lose, they are all in.

There is also a cost to following Jesus, but I would also add there is a greater cost in not following Him. Whatever you give up to follow Christ will be more than made up to you in this life and certainly in the life to come.

Jesus said, *"And if you do not carry your own cross and follow me, you cannot be my disciple. But don't begin until you count the cost. For who would begin construction of a building without first calculating the cost to see if there is enough money to finish it?"* (Luke 14:27-28). In other words, "Don't do this on the impulse of a moment. Count the cost."

Yet some people who set out to follow Christ haven't counted the cost. Sort of like couples who rush into marriage. Once you have made a marriage commitment, it is a lifelong commitment. And if you are not willing to make it, then do everyone a favor and stay single. Count the cost.

The Bible records the story of someone who saw Jesus walk by and blurted out, *"I will follow you wherever you go."* Jesus had not called this person to follow Him; he just volunteered. So Jesus said, *"Foxes have dens to live in, and birds have nests, but the Son of Man has no place even to lay his head"* (Luke 9:58). Loose paraphrase: "Buddy, I am not headed to the Jerusalem Ritz-Carlton. It is a rough life. I am headed to the cross. Are you sure about that?"

Sometimes in the impulse of the moment, someone will say, "I will follow Jesus," but they don't follow through on that commitment. They didn't count the cost.

We must realize that being a true disciple of Jesus is not easy. Therefore, we must count the cost.

73

March 14

"Do not get drunk on wine, which leads to debauchery. Instead, be filled with the Spirit." (Ephesians 5:18)

When something is going on around you that you don't want to hear, what do you do? When you are watching TV and your wife or husband is vacuuming, you typically turn up the volume of the TV to drown out the noise of the vacuum. In order to drown out a particular sound, you have to produce another sound louder than the one you don't want to hear.

The same principle can be applied to your life. When you are having a problem and you complain about it, you are just turning up the volume of it. You are doing nothing to get rid of the noise. You have to fight the problem by drowning that problem out. You drown the problem out by turning to God. You fight hatred by drowning it with love, you fight sin by drowning it with righteousness, and you fight evil by drowning it with good. Get the picture?

How do you fight Satan? It's not by dwelling or focusing on him. You fight sin, temptation and gloom by not dwelling on them. Instead of dwelling on what's wrong, you drown it out by not focusing or dwelling on what you intend to drown out.

You solve a problem by lifting your eyes off the problem and lift them to the answer. Stop listening to the enemy and start drowning him out with the presence and the joyful noise of the praise of God. Crank up the volume of God and drown out all the other noise.

March 15

"God created man in his own image...." (Genesis 1:27)

I like to make things. Put me in my workshop, give me a stack of wood, and I am happy. My latest creations are cigar box guitars. Not sure why, since I don't even play them. But they are fun to build and I like how each one is basically the same, yet they each have their own characteristics.

In our focus verse we are told we were created *"in His own image."* God took dust and the air from His lungs and created us yet when we look around we see people of different sizes, shapes, colors, etc. No two are alike. In fact we each are *"wonderfully made"* according to Psalm 139:14.

We each have unique characteristics, special talents and gifts. We may look different, but deep down we each have the image of God within us. Ever wonder what that means?

I believe it means we resemble God in certain ways. We have intellect, a moral nature, the power to communicate with others, and emotions, just like God. There is no physical likeness here, but within us are the characteristics of God. Man is a worshiper, a communicator, and a creator. We are the crown of God's creation.

With all that said, God created us to be alike, yet different. Based on the Word of God all lives matter, because we were made in His image. No one group is better than the other, because we were all created in His image.

I believe we should live in harmony with one another despite our differences. Each guitar may look different, yet each has the same parts. It's time we as people think the same way about each other.

March 16

"Give us each day our daily bread." (Luke 11:3)

I talked with a friend last night about her recent mission trip. She told of how miserable the conditions were. She told of the constant, unrelenting heat, no air conditioning, no cold water and very little sleep. She said at one point she thought she would die.

Even though she was explaining about what sounded like a nightmare, she had excitement in her voice. She told me she had to rely totally on God to get her through the ordeal. She talked of how close she drew to God and how He brought her through it all. She told me her relationship with God went to a totally different level, all because of her reliance on God, and His provisions for her life.

When the Israelites left Egypt, they went for a long journey in the desert. There had no food, they got hungry, and God provided. Manna rained down during the night and when they got up all they had to do was gather enough to last them the day. That was God's instructions. The only exception was on the day before the Sabbath they were to gather enough to last two days. Anything more would rot and be worthless.

Each day they had to rely on God's promise that more would fall. God said in Exodus 16:4 *"In this way I will test them and see whether they will follow my instructions."* That is the true test; do we really believe God will provide for us?

Saving is not an option when it comes to the things of God. We aren't talking groceries, we are talking heavenly bread, and it's only given daily. Each day we have to go to the Father in heaven and ask for His help, His protection, His guidance. Each day we must trust that He hears our prayers, He knows our needs and He will answer them in His perfect way.

That is the only way to get through tough times. We must rely on Him, but we must have that relationship with Him to begin with. And relationships must be maintained. God understands people, He created us. He knows if He gives us enough to last a week or month, we won't come to Him until we run out. What type of relationship is that?

How many of you would be content with one "I love you" a year from your spouse or kids? My bet is, none of you. God isn't either. He wants us to want Him enough to come to Him daily. Give it a try; you may be surprised at the outcome.

March 17

"...You are old, and your sons do not walk in your ways; now appoint a king to lead us, such as all the other nations have.' But when they said, 'Give us a king to lead us,' this displeased Samuel; so he prayed to the LORD." (1 Samuel 8:5-6)

As I was reading 1 Samuel 8 this morning, I couldn't help but let my mind wander to all the recent political posts and news. Everyone has an opinion on who will make the perfect leader for our country. As I read this chapter I couldn't help but understand how true scripture is.

Ever heard the phrase "Be careful of what you ask for"? Well the people of Israel, God's chosen people had a King (God) yet they wanted a human king to rule them. You see, it was (and still is) God's intention that He Himself should be the King of Israel (and those of us who believe, follow and obey). His people were to be holy, and not like any other nation on earth. But they didn't want to be different; they wanted to conform to the world.

Samuel was grieved by such a request, but God told him to do as they said. After all, they had not rejected the prophet, but had rejected God Himself. Yet before Samuel appointed the king he forewarned them as to the behavior of the king they would get. In brief, the king would enrich himself by impoverishing the people. Sound familiar? He would take a tenth of the harvest for himself and his attendants. Heard of taxes? He would make them slaves to him and those who serve him. Again, sound familiar?

But what shocks me the most is what Samuel closed with. *"When that day comes, you will cry out for relief from the king you have chosen, and the LORD will not answer you in that day."*

As a Christ follower we must understand that no political party, candidate, man or woman can change that in which has been written. This world will destroy itself...the bible tells us so. But those of us who cling to the promises of God are not of this world and God will rescue us.

Hang on to that hope, not some self-serving candidate that makes promises he or she never intend to keep. Cling to the only promise that will be kept, the promise of Jesus that He will return for His people. He is my hope for a better future!

March 18

"For since the creation of the world God's invisible qualities—his eternal power and divine nature—have been clearly seen, being understood from what has been made, so that men are without excuse." (Romans 1:20)

Years ago the Supreme Court decided that the Ten Commandments not be allowed in public places. This country took prayer and the bible out of our schools. This country has declared that there is no absolute standard to which the government and state must answer to, no higher authority that it is held accountable to. Where does it end?

The countries that have recognized nothing higher than themselves have descended into the path of dehumanization and destruction. The Soviet Union declared that there was no God and nothing higher than itself. There was no accountability and it wound up murdering millions of its own citizens. Communist China declared the same and ended up slaughtering even more of its citizens. What will happen here?

When there is no accountability to God, then the state or country becomes its own God and eventually anyone can become god. But as believers we must be an example of one that recognizes the reality of the one true God. We must stand firm to His word and honor His truth. We will all answer to God one day, but His people, those professing to be His followers answer to Him today and every day.

So, even though this world may be crumbling, we must remember that we are only here for a short time. This is a temporary place. James 4:14 says *"You are a mist that appears for a little while and then vanishes."* It is my prayer that when you vanish from this place, then you will hear *"Well done my good and faithful servant"* and end up in Heaven with the one true authority, God!

March 19

"Who of you by worrying can add a single hour to his life? Since you cannot do this very little thing, why do you worry about the rest?" (Luke 12:25-26)

While visiting Devil's Tower we took a stroll around its base. What a magnificent work of God's hand. It was like nothing we had ever seen. As we walked around the Tower it started to rain, first a light drizzle but then it turned into a downpour. We found a small cave in the base of the Tower to slip into to get out of the storm. It didn't take long for that shower to turn into something far greater. We literally caught "hail" on Devil's Tower.

How often does life go from bliss to a storm? Things pop up, storms come and life has a way of dealing out some "hail" from time to time. It comes unexpected, in the most inopportune times, and it can take us by surprise. But how we respond is up to us.

Jesus tells us that worry isn't good and it does nothing to change anything. We know this but not worrying comes hard. We want to not worry, but it is a human reaction to a difficult situation. But if we trust Jesus and know that He is our protector and provider, we should rest assured that He is in control.

That day on the Tower, crouched in that tiny cave, we had a decision to make, worry about how we were going to survive, or allow Jesus to protect us and enjoy the moment. We enjoyed the moment. We caught tiny balls of hail, we laughed, we watched as the hail bounced off the rocks and we marveled at the splendor of God's glory. Soon the storm left and we were able to continue our journey and tell others of our experience, as well as our protection provided by the Father who loves us.

Do you really trust Jesus to protect you? Do you value His plan for your life even when storms come and go? If the answer is yes, then you have recognized Jesus as Lord in the way He desires and is pleased with you. Trust your life in Jesus' hands.

Are you in a storm? Are things not quite what they should be? You have a choice to make, trust Jesus to bring you through it or worry about it and do nothing to change the situation. By putting your life in His hands, and allowing His will to guide your life, even in the midst of a storm, He will bring you out of that storm with a story to tell and a smile on your face every time you tell it.

March 20

"Do you not know that the wicked will not inherit the kingdom of God? Do not be deceived: Neither the sexually immoral nor idolaters nor adulterers nor male prostitutes nor homosexual offenders nor thieves nor the greedy nor drunkards nor slanderers nor swindlers will inherit the kingdom of God. And that is what some of you were. But you were washed, you were sanctified, you were justified in the name of the Lord Jesus Christ and by the Spirit of our God." (1 Corinthians 6:9-11)

While at the grocery store, my wife asked me to pick up cilantro for a dish she was making. I went to a bin marked "Cilantro" and picked a bundle up. As my wife prepared the dish, she mentioned it didn't have much smell or taste. Several days later she went to use some more of it and noticed the band around the bundle said "Parsley". No wonder it didn't taste like cilantro, it wasn't.

Things aren't always what they appear to be. Oh they may look like the real thing, they may even be in the right place, but that doesn't mean it is what it appears to be. People are no different. Being who we profess is critical, not to others, but to the one who will eventually judge us.

Our focus verse tells us two things. One, Paul is writing to the church in Corinth and is warning them to be careful as to who they are, because those who continue to practice the sins of the world will never enter heaven. That should make each and every one of us look at ourselves in a mirror and ask, "Am I who I say I am?"

Second, Paul writes that those who truly believe and decide to live their lives for Jesus "were" sinners, but have been set apart by Jesus Christ. Those people are different; they strive to live holy lives as Jesus modeled. He is saying that people who practice such sins are not Christians.

So the lesson is, if we are going to hang out in the "cilantro bin", we should be "cilantro". If we profess to be "Christian", then we should live up to that reputation. The very meaning of the word "Christian" is being "Christ like", so strive to be just that. Let no one question or mistake who you really are.

March 21

"Follow Me," Jesus said, "and I will make you a fisher of men" (Matthew 4:19)

Peter's journey began with Jesus giving him a vision of being something other than what he was. Christ saw him not simply as he was, but as he would be. And Jesus committed Himself to making Peter everything he had the potential of becoming. But Peter had to answer the call. Jesus sees in us what we can't, but in order to get there we too must answer the call.

Peter could have said no, and remained happy among his nets, boat and the fish. He could have followed in his father's footsteps. He could have remained in his home town, and lived out his days in anonymous mediocrity. And so can you.

But Peter said yes! And as a result, he not only walked on water, he walked into history! He became a cherished hero to millions of Christ-followers throughout history, who see in Peter so much of themselves.

Jesus gave him vision which produced passion that marked Peter throughout his life. His eagerness to impress Jesus, his crazy zeal in vowing to be faithful when others fell away stemmed from his deep, abiding passion for Christ.

Jesus fueled Peter's vision and passion with the right ingredient; discipline. Peter responded to being disciplined, and was willing and able to take remarkable risks as a faithful follower of Jesus. Vision, passion, discipline and risk, that's how Peter did it.

And now it's your turn. As Peter followed Jesus on the path of vision, passion, discipline and risk, and stepped into the pages of history, so can you. The only question I ask, "Will you follow?"

March 22

"Therefore we also pray always for you that our God would count you worthy of this calling, and fulfill all the good pleasure of His goodness and the work of faith with power" (2 Thessalonians 1:11).

Answering a call to follow Jesus is scary to say the least. The fear is of the unknown, things one must leave, fear of those who may turn their backs on you because of your newfound faith. I know because I have answered that call. One of my own sisters told me that I was "too religious", too changed for her liking. But I traveled into the unknown regardless.

Abraham traveling into the unknown, Joseph remaining faithful in Egypt, Moses crossing the Red Sea, Joshua conquering the Promised Land, Deborah lifting her sword in battle against the Midianites, Ruth returning with Naomi to the land of Canaan, David slaying a giant and becoming a King, Isaiah telling his visions, Zechariah telling his dreams, Daniel in the lion's den, Nehemiah rebuilding the walls, Zerubbabel rebuilding the temple, Peter left his nets, Paul preached the very gospel he set out to stop. Each one of these ordinary men and women heard and answered the call of God, and as a result lived extraordinary lives.

Following is allowing God to use you for a greater purpose. The bible tells of men and women called out of mediocrity into magnificence, who left their world better than they found it. Many men and women of modern day, who will never be read about, have done the same.

The Lord longs for you to answer the call on your life and be a part of His team. And in your heart you know it's what you want to do more than anything else in the world! So will you? I pray, in the words of Paul, that God would count you worthy of this calling, and fulfill all the good pleasure of His goodness in your life, and bring to pass with His power each and every work of faith you perform for His honor!

March 23

"He called ten of His servants." (Luke 19:13)

Have you ever been in a place where the phone kept ringing and nobody answered it? In moments like that it seems everybody is busy with something else, assuming that somebody else will answer the call. But no one does. It can get to be quite annoying. There is something irritating about an incessant, unanswered call.

Over the years I have noticed a similar thing in the lives of many people — a call that is not being answered. It is a call from God. Busy with so many other things, and sure that the call is for someone else, many men and women lose themselves in trivial stuff and miss the opportunity to answer the call of God on their lives. Have you answered the call?

Missing out on God's call for your life would be the worst thing that could happen. Research shows that one of the greatest fears people face is having lived a meaningless life; a life that didn't matter; a life that made no difference. This dreadful thought haunts even the most accomplished of individuals. Maybe it haunts you even now.

Os Guinness wrote, "Our passion is to know that we are fulfilling the purpose for which we are on earth. All other standards of success, wealth, power, position, knowledge, and friendships, all grow tiny and hollow if we do not satisfy this deeper longing."

Each of us long to know that our lives count; that we accomplish what we were put on this earth for. Yet, in an odd contradiction, nothing is more common than unrealized potential. Most of us settle for far less than we are capable of. On the one hand we want our lives to count; on the other hand, we seem far too willing to become marginalized into mediocrity.

Our only hope is to answer the call of God upon our lives. I know because for a long time I ignored that call. But once I answered the call and allowed God to use me, my life took on new meaning, purpose and direction. I am better for answering the call. So stop ignoring it, answer it.

March 24

"He delivered unto them his goods." (Matthew 25:14)

When I first answered my call to preach I knew nothing about it. Oh I had heard many, but had never really studied how to create a sermon, how to make points or to research adequately.

Few things are more frustrating to people than to be faced with a task and not be given the time, the training, or the tools to get the job done. And few situations are more likely to produce this frustration in a person than the general state of affairs in contemporary church life.

I believe one of the least understood and practiced Christian discipline is prayer. Very few actually know how, or feel adequately equipped to do so. Even the disciples, who must have heard Jesus pray often, didn't know how to pray. We can learn anything from Jesus, if we ask.

Jesus said to His disciples, *"Follow Me, and I will make you fishers of men."* I am sure at first they didn't understand, but they followed, and Jesus delivered on His promise. These two occasions show us that the desire to be taught the things of the Spirit is strong in the heart of godly men and women, and that Jesus is more than accommodating.

Furthermore, Jesus doesn't just train us, He also entrusts us with the resources to get the job done. As the scripture says, *"He delivered unto them his goods."*

How strange it must have been for a fisherman named Simon Peter to be called by an itinerant rabbi named Jesus, to follow Him so as to become a *"fisher of men."* In his later years Peter wrote, *"His divine power has given unto us all things that pertain to life and godliness"* (2 Peter 1:3). He was writing from personal experience. Jesus called him, trained him, trusted him, and entrusted him with the high privilege of presenting the Gospel to ordinary men and women with extraordinary results—thousands were saved!

Peter had no idea when he first met Jesus just how radically different his life would become. The same is true of you. Your life matters to God far more than you may realize. And by placing it fully in His hands, trusting Him to keep you in step with His Spirit, you can do whatever the Lord has called you to do—for He has also given you everything you need to get the job done.

March 25

"For out of the overflow of the heart the mouth speaks...The good man brings good things out of the good stored up in him, and the evil man brings evil things out of the evil stored up in him." (Matthew 12:34-35)

Dick and Jane walk into a church as first time guests. They are greeted by Sally who once attended Dick and Jane's current church. After the initial hello, Sally bombards them with negative words about Dick and Jane's pastor, ministry leader or other members of the church she left. It is very uncomfortable and awkward.

"If you can't say anything nice, don't say anything at all." Did your mom ever say this when you were growing up? Well I know mine did, plenty of times. Did I always listen? Not really. As I have grown older and more mature I have learned that this is sound advice.

When you were a kid did you ever say or hear: "Sticks and stones may break my bones, but words can never hurt me." To some it was a cute little saying, but untrue, because what we say really does hurt people.

Idle or negative talk, gossip, and rumors can cause more damage than one may think. It has the power to ruin someone's character, or tarnish an image. It has the power to turn people's opinions of someone without really knowing the truth. To be honest, someone who has a habit of spreading negative talk means to hurt, that is their sole intent in talking about someone behind their back.

I must say that this really disturbs me most when it comes from those who proclaim to be followers of Jesus Christ. We are called to be "love" and "imitators of Christ", someone who lifts others up, not try to break them down. What is in our heart comes out, and true followers of Jesus Christ have hearts filled with love, not bitterness, hatred and negativity.

Jesus wants our hearts to be filled with love. But if our hearts are filled with negativity, then that is usually what comes out. Matthew 12:36 tells us that those who spew venom will have to answer for it. *"But I tell you that men will have to give account on the day of judgment for every careless word they have spoken."*

So maybe mom was right, maybe some things are best left unsaid. Mom's advice should keep us from saying things we'll later regret, or that will hurt others. May our thoughts today be excellent and praiseworthy and our speech be gentle and kind!

March 26

"For all have sinned and fall short of the glory of God." (Romans 3:23 NKJV)

Remember the group Milli Vanilli? They enjoyed great success until it was revealed that they did not sing on their own records. Everyone found out the truth about them and they had to face the music, so to speak.

The phrase, "face the music," originated in Japan. A man was a part of the Imperial Orchestra, but he could not play a note. Because of his great influence and wealth, he demanded a place in the group. The conductor sat him in the second row and gave him a little flute. During each concert, he would raise his instrument, pucker his lips, and move his fingers as though he were playing. But he never made a sound.

This went on for two years until a new conductor took over and wanted to audition every player. One by one, the musicians performed in his presence. Then came his turn and he had to admit he was a fake. He couldn't "face the music."

None of us can live this life perfectly. All of us will fall short of God's glory from time to time. But there is a difference between a person who seeks to live a godly life, but has their human failures and weaknesses, and a person who tries to appear to be more spiritual than he or she really is.

It has been said that you can fool all of the people some of the time, you can fool some of the people all of the time, but you can't fool God any of the time.

March 27

"The Kingdom of Heaven is like a farmer who planted good seed in his field. But that night as the workers slept, his enemy came and planted weeds among the wheat." (Matthew 13:24-25 NLT)

Jesus told a parable of wheat and tares. He talked about a farmer planting a crop of wheat. And during the night his enemy, probably a competitor, came and sowed tares (weeds) among the wheat.

The tare Jesus described was also known as the darnel seed, which looks almost like wheat in the beginning stages of its growth. But after it grows a little, it becomes evident that it is a weed that uproots the wheat.

When one of the farmer's workers asked if he should pull the tares, he was told no. The plan was to let them grow together until the harvest, and then the weeds would be gathered and burnt, while the wheat was put in the barn.

Jesus' point was that there are people in the church who have infiltrated our ranks. While there is wheat, there are also tares. We don't know who is who, necessarily. You will find them sitting side by side in a pew, breathing the same air, and singing the same songs. One may be a believer, while the other may be a deceiver. One may be wheat, and one may be a weed.

We will have people who infiltrate our ranks, Ananias and Sapphira, were weeds. Judas Iscariots was a weed. But it is not our job to weed those people out, it's God's job.

Our concern should not be who the hypocrites are, but whether we are hypocrites ourselves. Our job is to take care of ourselves, to take heed and make sure that we are true believers, not weeds.

March 28

"Therefore go and make disciples of all nations, baptizing them in the name of the Father and of the Son and of the Holy Spirit, and teaching them to obey everything I have commanded you. And surely I am with you always, to the very end of the age." (Matthew 28:19-20)

How many of us love a lush, green yard? If you are like me, I am terrible at caring for my yard; I barely take time to keep it mowed. But I love the look of green grass so I pay someone to keep it that way. They fertilize it for me at all the right intervals, keeping it just the way I like it.

But yesterday I found a dandelion. You know the pesky weed with the bright yellow flower. Those things can take over a yard in a hurry. I couldn't believe it, all that money and I have a weed. But is it really a bad thing?

As I looked at that weed I couldn't help but remember a sermon I once heard, and yes it was about dandelions. So I did some fact checking and found out that the truth was preached, dandelions are considered beautiful flowers, not weeds.

Did you know what was once imported from Europe, is now the wildflowers we try to kill? Did you know that both common species in the U.S. are edible in their entirety? Did you know that the flower heads mature into spherical seed heads called "blow balls" containing many seeds? Did you know that each seed can be dispersed over long distances by the wind?

What I heard from that sermon, and I learned from that weed, is that those of us who call ourselves Christ followers should be more like dandelions. We may look out of place in the green yard, but we can be beautiful while being different. We can bring some color to the surroundings. We can produce something that can be consumed and we can spread into the other yards around us, and the yards miles away, by planting seeds. If we plant seeds and each one takes root, imagine what that would look like.

I can tell you, because I looked at my neighbor's yard and realized where the dandelion came from, his yard was full of them. So is there a lesson here, yes. We should spread our seeds (the gospel) and we should water that seed and watch as it takes root and grows. This world could use a few more weeds like us.

March 29

"...I am writing you that you must not associate with anyone who calls himself a brother but is sexually immoral or greedy, an idolater or a slanderer, a drunkard or a swindler. With such a man do not even eat." (1 Corinthians 5:11-12)

Have you ever heard the phrase, "Cut your nose off to spite your face?" My dad used to say that when people were to being stubborn. I have heard people say that the church is filled with hypocrites as an excuse for not attending. That to me is a good example of that saying. We all need it, but some let the actions of others keep them from it.

What is a hypocrite anyway? Well it is people that say one thing yet do another. For the church folk, I guess that would be people who pray, carry bibles and attend church, yet they live a worldly life. All the "religious" stuff has not changed them.

Our focus verse speaks of these people. Their life has no distinguishable change from non-believers. Paul tells us to expel them, have nothing to do with them. This may sound harsh but it's biblically sound.

Christians must be held accountable to live lives different from their counter parts. Their lives must take a turn from the "worldly" to the "holy" over time. Six times in Deuteronomy it is written *"You must purge the evil from among you."* This meaning that those that claim to be walking with Christ yet live lives contrary must be "purged" from the church.

Christians should hold each other accountable for how they live. Those not living according to the teachings should be warned, offered help and if they refuse to change, they must be expelled from among the church.

The expelling serves a purpose. First, so others are not corrupted. Second, so that the guilty person can see their ways and repent. Lastly, so that believers can understand that accountability is vital to Christian living.

How can Christianity offer hope to a lost and dying world if its members are no different than that of the lost and dying? Jesus lived a life on earth, one of Godly, Christ like, moral living, sinless, pure and holy. We are called to be Christ like, so we must also live that type of life. Are you up for the challenge?

March 30

"Yet the news about him spread all the more, so that crowds of people came to hear him and to be healed of their sicknesses. But Jesus often withdrew to lonely places and prayed." (Luke 5:15-16)

As a boy I loved to hang out with my dad. He wasn't much of a talker. We spent a lot of time in silence, but it was great. I watched him work, interact with people and how he carried himself. During those times with him I learned many valuable life lessons on how to be a man.

This is the Lent season, a time to reflect on the birth, life, death and resurrection of Jesus Christ. It is a time when most of us do something to get closer to Christ. Lent is often a period when people "fast" from something in order to withdraw to a lonely place to be with God. It is a time to be intentional, to escape the chaos and storms of life to be in solitude with God.

Our focus verse tells us that in the midst of Jesus speaking to large crowds, healing the sick and being in the middle of the chaos, He took time to slip away to a lonely place and pray. That verse almost seems out of place, but I think it is there to show the importance of time alone with God. If Jesus did it, it must be important.

More than once in the bible we read references of Jesus going off by Himself to be alone with God. On the night before Jesus was arrested and led to the cross, Jesus went to Gethsemane and prayed to His Father. Those times alone with God meant a lot to Jesus.

Prayer and time alone with God was very important to Jesus Christ. If we are followers of Jesus and we are called to "be like Him", then doesn't it stand to reason that time alone with God should be as important to us? In order to learn from God, to hear from God, we must carve out time to be alone with God. We must set aside things from our agenda, our busy schedule and slip away to a quiet place and sit with God.

We will find time to do what we want to do. So if we want to hear from God and be the person He created us to be, we must take the time to intentionally meet with God, one on one. So I ask, is getting to know God better important to you? I challenge you during this Lent season to find ways to be alone with God, and if you do, I promise you won't regret it. What about you? Have you felt the abundance Jesus offers? Have you ever received it? If not, what is keeping you from receiving the gift that is better than a truck load of candy, and lasts much longer?

March 31

"With a loud cry, Jesus breathed his last. The curtain of the temple was torn in two from top to bottom." (Mark 15:37-38)

I remember my very last "whipping" in public school. Oh yeah, they did that back in the day. I was walking past an easel, which had a crepe paper picture on it, on my way to sharpen my pencil. Not paying much attention, the point of the pencil touched the picture and ripped it slightly. The teacher thought I had done it on purpose and told me I ruined the piece. She sent me to the principle, where I "received justice", which was what they called the use of a wooden paddle with holes drilled in it.

Receiving what we deserve, or in my case what others thought I deserved, is a way of thinking in our world. Rightly so, we are all responsible for our actions and must pay the consequences of those wrongs. But for how long are they held against us?

With Good Friday and Easter upon us I thought about this. It struck me that the things I have done wrong and have asked for forgiveness for, someone else paid the price for those wrongs; Jesus on the cross. His death on that instrument of torture was for me and you, the one who should receive "justice for our wrongs".

I was drawn to the passage above, the part about the veil being torn. What does that mean? In the temple, that veil represented something of significance, something of honor. Only a select few could go behind that veil and get close to God.

But at that moment, the moment Jesus took His last breath, the veil of the temple was torn in two from top to bottom. This act of God indicates that by Jesus' death, all those who believe now have direct access to God Himself.

The tearing of that veil is something to celebrate and cherish. Because it was ruined, torn in two, we are given access to God and His Son Jesus Christ. The price for our forgiven sins is paid and we can share in the Kingdom of God. Isn't that the best news you have ever heard?

April 1

"A generous man will prosper; he who refreshes others will himself be refreshed." (Proverbs 11:25)

Have you ever had one of those weeks where things just seem to mount one on top of the other? I have had many, but one week in particular was even worse for me.

It started with an early phone call about a family I was ministering to. They had a house fire and lost everything. As I arrived at their house, I cried when I saw a family's life in ruins. To see someone's whole life in ashes was a little more than I was prepared for. But it sparked my determination and got me moving.

To this day I am still amazed at what happened in a short week in a community that has been hit hard by the economy. People came together for one of their own. It started with a few emails, a few phone calls and a couple of posts on social media, and then the out pouring of love that followed was overwhelming.

People from all over the area stepped up to support this family. People collecting money, cooking and delivering meals, donating clothing and household items, and praying for a family some have never met. A local business hosted a car wash and bake sale with all the proceeds going directly to the family. The local media joined in to promote the immediate need, running articles and news clips to let the area know their story.

I saw and heard all this and was immediately reminded of our focus verse. God loves a generous giver and I have seen some very generous giving through this ordeal.

I know God is pleased when His people step up with compassion to help the less fortunate. God wants His people to imitate Him and by giving, we are being exactly what he was. So, take a look around you. There is need, do you see it? Or better yet, what are you doing about it?

April 2

"Were not all ten cleansed? Where are the other nine? Was no one found to return and give praise to God except this foreigner?" (Luke 17:17-18)

I once went to a child's birthday party where plenty of people were in attendance and the gifts lay before the child like treasures at the feet of a king. The child was excited and waited until his mother told him he could begin. Then I sat in utter amazement.

Once the first piece of wrapping paper was torn, I was shocked. The child would open one gift, look at it for a mere second, cast it aside and begin to open another. He tore through them in record speed and then proclaimed "Is that all?" I sat in disbelief.

How often do we receive gifts from God only to immediately look for the next one? In our focus verse, ten people receive the gift of healing, yet only one takes time to give God the appropriate thanks. Why? Is it that they expected it, felt they deserved it or even were entitled to it?

What about us? Are we truly satisfied with each and every gift? Or are we constantly searching for the next? Do we take time to thank Him appropriately or do we expect Him to hand us another?

I went to another child's birthday party, still remembering the last. This time as the child opened each gift; he would look it over with excitement in his eyes and then thank the giver with a hug. He was truly thankful for each gift and took the time to let that gift sink in and to thank the one who gave it.

That is what God wants from us. I think if we all look closely we can see the gifts He gives. They may be simple things like the mere fact you woke up this morning, but the gift of life is something to thank God for. We can look and see family, friends and our homes, again worth a thank you to the giver of life and blessings.

True gratitude is born in the hearts of those who understand that the things we have are all gifts from God. He is the giver of everything and is worthy of our thanks. Take a minute today to thank Him for the things in your life that you hold dear.

April 3

"'Go,' he told him, 'wash in the Pool of Siloam'. So the man went and washed, and came home seeing." (John 9:7)

My one eyed dog is a good girl. She, for the most part, does what she is told. She is super funny at bathroom time. I take her out with the command of "go potty" and she wanders out into the yard. She usually makes sure I am watching her do her business and then she runs inside and does a trick in order to get her treat. I would give her treat without the trick, but I love watching her enthusiasm for her reward.

In John 9 we read about a blind man who meets Jesus. There is a big discussion as to why he is blind, but what I get out of this is that Jesus wants to do something for this guy. So he makes a mud pie out of spit, puts it in his eye and tells the blind guy to "go" wash it out. Now, if that alone isn't funny enough, the guy does just that and we read that he came back seeing.

As I read this today I couldn't help but see the correlation between the command (go), the obedience (he went) and the reward (sight). So I started to think, how often is this played out in scripture? Well, if we search we will see that every miracle Jesus did had the same sequence. John 5:8 tells of a lame man Jesus met. Jesus said to him, "Get up! Pick up your mat and walk." The man was given a command, he obeyed and he walked.

So what happens when we don't follow the sequence? My little dog goes outside every now and then and does nothing, yet she runs inside expecting a treat. No way, I don't care how cute she is, if you don't follow the instructions, no reward. It happens in scripture as well. Remember the rich guy who wanted to know how to get to heaven? Jesus answered, *"If you want to be perfect, go, sell your possessions and give to the poor, and you will have treasure in heaven. Then come, follow me. When the young man heard this, he went away sad, because he had great wealth."* Matthew 19:21-22. The rich man didn't obey and he was sad.

In a world that says all one must do is believe yet live any way they choose and still get to heaven, I say be careful with that. Scripture teaches otherwise. We have a role to play in the salvation offered; obedience. So the next time God gives a command, obey it and then see the reward He has waiting for you.

April 4

"The LORD is far from the wicked but he hears the prayer of the righteous."
(Proverbs 15:29)

One of my devotions this morning was entitled "I pray and read my bible too." It spoke of how we often give lip service to our being Christ followers. We say we believe, yet live like the world. We say we love God, but do nothing He says. Is that really what being a Christian is about?

We all have our checklist when it comes to God. We go to church, check. We throw some money in the plate, check. We read a verse or two a day and pray when we need something, check, check. But according to the above passage, God only hears the prayers of the "righteous." So is it more than a mere checklist?

"Righteous" means "a state of being perfect", "attribute of God" and "the goal of Christian life". Countless times in the bible we are told to "be holy because He (Jesus) is holy." We are told to be "like" or to "imitate" Christ. This is righteousness.

So in order for God to hear us we must be more than followers of a checklist, we must be willing to open ourselves up to God so that we can be righteous. Because the reality is, we can't be on our own. So, I challenge everyone to pray this prayer for a week. Try it by giving God permission to search you (Psalm 139:23-24), cleanse you (Psalm 51:1), fill you (Ephesians 5:15-18), lead you (Galatians 5:22-25), stretch you (Luke 17:5) and use you (2 Timothy 2:19-22)

April 5

"Make every effort to enter through the narrow door, because many, I tell you, will try to enter and will not be able to." (Luke 13:24)

I used to travel a lot for work. Once I flew to Boston and then drove to Taunton, MA. I walked up to the front desk of the hotel and said "I have a reservation." The clerk looked at her computer screen and said, "Sir you have no reservation here, but you do have a reservation in Baltimore, MD."

I use this funny story to help illustrate the false thinking that everyone is going to heaven. The reality is, not everyone has a reservation. In fact, a quick look through scripture tells us that there are two paths people travel, but only one reaches the gates of heaven.

Matthew 7 tells us that there is a wide and broad road that leads to destruction (hell) and that many will enter through it. And there is a narrow path, one that leads to eternal life (heaven) that few will find. Notice the wording here. The broad road allows many, a large number, to enter into the destination. While only a few, or a small number, will enter into the gates of heaven.

So, what must we do to have the proper reservation? We must first believe that we need Jesus as our Savior. We must accept His love, mercy and grace fully. We must start to live the life Jesus Christ modeled. And then, allow Him to transform our lives into the lives He desires for us. It is more than mere lip service; it is a way of life. It's all or nothing with Jesus.

Fortunately for me there were vacancies and I received a room. But on the final day, there either is or there isn't a reservation. Listen to what Luke 13:25-27 from the Message version of the bible says about that day: *"Well, one day you're going to be banging on the door, wanting to get in, but you'll find the door locked and the Master saying, 'Sorry, you're not on my guest list.' You'll protest, 'But we've known you all our lives!' only to be interrupted with his abrupt, 'Your kind of knowing can hardly be called knowing. You don't know the first thing about me.'"*

That sounds a little harsh, but it should wake people up. Heaven isn't a given, and hell is a reality. So, it's never too late to change paths. Make the decision to get on the right road before it's too late. I would hate for anyone to be left out and have to go to the one place that is on no one's "must visit list"; hell.

April 6

"But Jesus bent down and started to write on the ground with his finger."
(John 8:6)

Let me say up front, I write based on lessons God teaches me. I write because He is working in my life, gently nudging me, guiding me, correcting me and teaching me to be more like Him. So when I write, I write to myself, even though you may benefit.

After reading our focus verse, I thought, "What did Jesus write in the dirt?" What did Jesus write that convinced those accusing the woman to go away? Did Jesus write his name or his status in the dirt? Did Jesus write the sins of each man in the dirt, convicting them that they too have sinned?

Too often we look at others through eyes that don't see our own faults. I am guilty of that and for that, I am truly sorry. God used this passage to convict me that I need to look at myself before I look at others. Now I do not believe this is one of those passages that says "don't judge me", but a passage that says, clear the plank out of your eye before attempting to remove the dust from someone else's eye.

As Christ followers ,we are to hold each other accountable, but out of love and correction, not as an act of punishment. Just as Jesus reminds us of our sins and the need to turn from them, hence verse 11, we are to gently remind others of the way to live. But we are to do so with compassion, love and forgiveness.

April 7

"Enter through the narrow gate. For wide is the gate and broad is the road that leads to destruction, and many enter through it. But small is the gate and narrow the road that leads to life and only a few find it." (Matthew 7:13-14)

Have you ever been behind a "Wide Load"? They make passing difficult. As I followed one, I wondered how burdensome it would be to drive that thing. The driver must be constantly worried about his/her surroundings, whether they will fit through certain areas or get down some narrow streets. Kind of reminds me of a passage of scripture.

Jesus warns us about the path we travel. There are two types of paths and only one leads to heaven. I think our lives can look like that truck. We carry extra weigh like burdens, troubles, and cares. We live a lifestyle not pleasing to God.

Our focus verse is very clear. There are roads that lead to two different places, or outcomes. It also makes it clear that "many" will go through the wide gate, while only a "few" make it through the narrow gate. I'm no genius but "many" means "a large number, plenty, the majority", while "few" means "a small number, the minority of people". So it leads me to believe there may be a lot of people who won't make it to where they think they are going.

The drivers of those trucks make sure they know where they are going. They have the up to date maps; they know the current weather and road conditions. They follow very specific paths to get those rigs to their destination safely. We too must ensure we take every effort to make it to our desired destination.

Once Jesus was traveling through towns and villages and someone asked Him a very pointed question; *"Lord, are only a few people going to be saved?" His response is valid today. He told them, and us today to "Make every effort to enter through the narrow door, because many, I tell you, will try to enter and will not be able to."* Luke 13:23-24

Many say they believe, yet live according to this world, not Jesus' way. Jesus is very clear; they are on the wrong road. So how can we "make every effort" to enter that narrow door? By a close, personal relationship with Jesus and living according to His road map, the Bible. By staying connected to Jesus and following His example for our life, we can be sure to be among the few. And by doing so, when our journey is over, we will walk through that narrow gate with room to spare.

April 8

"So he immediately sent an executioner with orders to bring John's head. The man went, beheaded John in the prison, and brought back his head on a platter..." (Mark 6:27-28)

Ever had one of those "I wish I would have..." moments? That point in time where you think back and wish you would have done something? We all have once or twice in our lives. Sometimes we can recover from those moments, other times it may be too late.

Things happen fast in our world. One minute everything is going along okay, then POW, something happens. When that happens, that fast, it may be too late to do or say something that will affect our lives. Especially when we think about our eternal lives...

When it comes to our eternal lives, the things we do now can affect us. Waiting until it's too late is too late. Let me demonstrate how fast things can change. Take our focus verse, it comes from a story in which John the Baptist has been arrested, put in jail and suffered under the hands of Herod. Herod throws a party; and the daughter of Herodias danced and pleased Herod, so he allowed her to ask for anything and he would grant it. She conferred with her mother who had a grudge with John the Baptist and the mother wanted John's head on a platter.

Well, the girl told Herod what she wanted and immediately it was done. John the Baptist had no time to react, he was beheaded at once and his head was delivered to the girl. There was no time to tie up loose ends, make amends, and ask or plea for his life. It happened in an instant.

John the Baptist was a Christian and his eternity was heaven. He had at least made that choice some time before hand, but what about you? So, what if today is your last? What if this minute is your last? Are you ready to face eternal life? Do you know if you will face eternity in heaven or hell? Have you made that choice?

If you have made the choice for heaven, and my hope and prayer for you is you have, then you are ready. But if you haven't you need to stop what you are doing now and ask God into your heart. Accept Him as your Lord and Savior so you too can know your eternity will be spent in heaven. Don't wait until it's too late, do it now and fight the rush.

April 9

"Jesus replied, "What is impossible with men is possible with God." (Luke 18:27)

Often I have felt like my life is spiraling out of control. Things going way too fast, nothing working out the way I want, and no end to the madness in sight. I can often become so overwhelmed that I just can't think.

As humans we aren't capable of managing our lives without help. We must all depend on someone or something to help us get through this life. We can think we are able to, but the reality is we can't. Have you ever felt like you just couldn't do anything right? Ever felt insufficient?

God sometimes leads us to that place of insufficiency, a place where we are powerless. I am of the belief that God takes us there because that is the only place where He can step up and work in our lives. It is in that place of insufficiency where He can be acknowledged as the power to bring victory over the inability to meet our own needs.

Our focus verse reminds us that He can help us through the hardest of times and it is by His power that he demonstrates our inabilities in order to bring us face to face with His abilities.

So when life gets out of control, turn to Jesus. When things don't work out the way you want, look to Jesus to make sense of it all. He has the ability to make life calm again, if we will let Him.

April 10

"Very truly I tell you, whoever believes in me will do the works I have been doing, and they will do even greater things than these, because I am going to the Father." (John 14:12)

A young lady with three small children walked into church. Her husband walked out and she is being evicted because of her housekeeping habits. During prayer time some surround her and begin to ask God to help her. One elderly lady whispers in ear, "After church how about I go help you clean your house?"

Prayer is easy, but what if you are the answer to that prayer? Jesus wants us to help others, not just simply pray for them. Our focus verse tells us that those who believe in Jesus and walk in His ways will do greater things than He did while He was here on earth. How is this so? How can I do greater things than Jesus?

I think the "you" Jesus is talking to is the "church". Not the building, but the very people who profess to believe and follow Him. What if "you" (the church) did the "works" Jesus is referring to?

Suppose you knew someone that was struggling financially and you invited them to dinner one night. The money they saved on that meal could be used for some other need. If each of "you" did this (me included), we could very well feed more than the 4000 or 5000 the bible records that Jesus fed.

Suppose you knew someone that had a job interview but didn't have the proper clothes to wear. What if "you" took that person to Wal-Mart and bought them some appropriate clothing? They just may get the job and provide for their own needs.

The list could go on and on. In order to do greater things, we first must have the heart that Jesus had. The heart of Jesus was filled with compassion and willingness to do something for someone who was in need. To be Jesus' hands and feet, we must do more than pray, we must do the work.

So pray for others, but have an attentive ear because you just may be the answer to that very prayer. If we all listen to the prompting of God and did His work, how much nicer would this world be? What if every single believer of Jesus actually did one good deed? Can you imagine the impact it would have? So look for your opportunity and then get busy, God will be pleased.

April 11

"I give them eternal life, and they shall never perish; no one can snatch them out of my hand." (John 10:28)

When I taught my son to ride a two wheeler, I held onto the seat and ran along behind him. I reassured him I wouldn't let go until he was ready. As he peddled, He knew that I wouldn't let go, he had confidence in me. I didn't want anything to happen to him and he knew it.

In our focus verse that is the picture I get of God. He loves us so much that once He has us in His grips, He isn't letting go. His promise gives me confidence that nothing will force Him to let go of me.

With that being said, let me also say that this doesn't promise us that we will always be His. God won't let anyone snatch us, but there is a fear of us walking away. Intentional sin, denial and disobedience can result in us departing from Him. He doesn't let go, we walk away.

But, we don't need to live in fear of spiritually falling away. No one who has ever fallen away has done so against his or her will. Those who fall away make a series of choices that lead to spiritually destructive (and sometimes physically destructive) results.

Jesus' teachings seem like they are hard to understand, but really they are not. The reality is they are sometimes hard to keep. There is a pattern in the Bible: when people didn't understand Jesus, they hung around and asked questions. It was when they did understand him that they either joined his ministry or went elsewhere. They left because what they heard was so contrary to their own ideas. What about you? Are you willing to follow Jesus, to truly give your life to him? Or will you walk away?

April 12

"The LORD himself goes before you and will be with you; he will never leave you nor forsake you. Do not be afraid; do not be discouraged."
(Deuteronomy 31:8)

I have recently taken on the project of building an addition to my existing workshop. It's a "she-shed" for my wife. The two of us have been pounding nails, driving screws and digging out splinters for a week or more. Every muscle in our bodies ache, yet through all the hard work, we are having fun doing this together.

As I was putting the final nails in the shingles on the roof, I looked at the hammer in my hand and smiled. The old hammer in my hand was one my dad gave me when I was just a boy. It isn't much to look at, but I have driven a lot of nails with that thing. It's ugly and beat up. It isn't shiny and it doesn't have one of those new fancy handles. It doesn't drive nails as fast as a nail gun. Yet it still has value, to me at least.

I thought about what that hammer means to me. My dad gave it to me when I started working construction with him. I used that hammer on every job I ever worked on with my dad. I have carried that hammer around with me as I have moved countless times to countless places. Every time I work on a project, that hammer ends up in my hand. That hammer is a part of me.

Did you know that God looks at us like I look at my hammer? Well actually more so. He loves us no matter what we look like. He loves us and wants to keep us close. He doesn't throw us away simple because we get old, ugly or worn out. Instead He lifts us up, He makes us new, He encourages, He equips and He strengthens us.

So, as I take a few hours off from my project, and I let my old hammer rest, I thank God for loving me when others gave up on me. I thank God for not throwing me in the trash and getting something new. I thank God that He loves me unconditionally and forever. You too can know that love, simple ask Him for it and it's yours.

April 13

"If you remain in me and my words remain in you, ask whatever you wish, and it will be given you." (John 15:7)

I saw a cute commercial where a little girl dug all the money out of her mother's purse and threw it in a wishing well. She starts with change and then throws paper money as well. As I watched I wondered if this is how God sees our prayers, like throwing coins in a well.

The word of God tells us to pray, but do we treat prayer like throwing money into a wishing well? Do we just randomly throw out a prayer, in hopes that He hears and answers? Do we take the prayer so lightly that it's offered in a split second, and then forgotten until the thought reenters our mind? Do we think we can just throw out a prayer and God will answer, no matter how we live our life?

Praying is vital, but it isn't to be taken lightly. Do you know that the bible teaches that those that don't seek God, don't live by His ways, or fail to follow His commands, He ignores? Yet, those who believe and obey God catch His ear. Don't believe me, then read 2 Chronicles 7:14.

Our focus verse tells us that we must "remain" in Him, which means to continue to walk with Him, trust Him, and live according to His will on our life. When we do, then He will listen to the desires of our heart. But, we can't just go about and throw out prayers like coins thrown into a wishing well and think the sky is the limit. When we live by God's way, He hears, He answers and He gives us "whatever" we wish for.

April 14

"When I came to you, brothers, I did not come with eloquence or superior wisdom as I proclaimed to you the testimony about God. For I resolved to know nothing while I was with you except Jesus Christ and Him crucified. " (1 Corinthians 2:1-2)

My writings aren't for everyone. Some people really like what I write, while others pass it by. I don't really write for people, I write because God tells me to.

I write not to try to show how smart or knowledgeable I am, but merely because I have felt God tell me to use this media to spread His word to others. God gives me the power to be bold and speak when others may be quiet and speak when others may think it to be offensive.

I bet Paul felt the same. As our focus verse tells us, Paul wrote to proclaim and testify. Paul wrote because God was working in his life and he wanted people to know it. I write for the same reason.

Some must have thought Paul to be arrogant, overbearing and pushy. People can think what they want, but Paul was driven by God and obedient at all cost.

What about you? Do you speak truths even when you know they won't be popular? Do you speak out about Jesus in a world that is so far removed from Him? Do you accept that because of the Gospel people are going to dislike you as the bible teaches?

We must accept the truth that not all will understand or agree, but we must do as we are commissioned and spread the Gospel to all. So speak up and be bold to speak the truth no matter what. Take your role as a disciple of Christ serious and get busy. The kingdom is near, tell others about the greatest gift you have ever received, Salvation!

April 15

"...pray continually..." (1 Thessalonians 5:16)

When my son was small he was one of the most persistent people I had ever met. Especially if there was something he wanted. He would see something on TV and he would ask for it every day.

Have you ever had a prayer that you thought was too big to pray? What about a prayer that you asked once and "didn't want to bother God anymore" about? We all have prayers that seem to be inappropriate, too large, or the initial answer is no. True prayer means desperation outweighs protocol.

Jesus tells us to pray with boldness and persistence. He tells us that we must ask in order to receive, seek to find and knock for the door to be opened. Jesus is implying that we are to keep asking, keep seeking and keep knocking, and then we will receive. Prayer calls for relentlessness.

Most of us pray for a period of time, and then when we have not heard from God, we give up, assume it wasn't His will or He is too busy. Scripture never gives us permission to drop a request because we don't get an immediate response. Our focus verse tells us to "pray continually", never ceasing.

So I say to you, pray with confidence and persistence. Declare His will in a situation and expect His response to your request. While we should always be open for Him to redirect our prayers, or even say "no", we should never assume a slow answer, according to our standards, is a non-answer. Like the farmer who waits for the harvest, we are to wait for His answers. Jesus is very clear, keep on asking!

April 16

"All things are possible with God." (Mark 10:27)

Once while walking in the woods, I heard the sound of rushing water but could not see it. It grew louder and began to sound like a raging river. My vision was limited due to the trees and brush. My mind saw a mighty river, but when the trees cleared I saw a small brook. It was a run off from the mountain falling over several small waterfalls. It was beautiful, but much smaller than I imagined.

As I walked on, the road began to rise. I thought I would never reach the top. Why had I chosen this route? But I pushed on, drawing strength from within and soon I was at the top.

Often we can allow our current situations to overwhelm us. Feeling inadequate, or ill equipped and ill prepared to handle the tasks at hand can be great. But if we call upon the power within us, the Holy Spirit, we can gain inner peace, strength and the power to move beyond our capability. God will encourage us to rely on His power, His wisdom, His words and His hope.

Often our vision is limited to what we see, so we make the situation much larger than it is. I imagined the small brook to be a raging river. Often we limit our ability to what we think we can do. The hill is too steep to climb or the situation is beyond our capability. Often we limit our hope to the likely resolutions to our problems or situations. I am incapable, not ready, and can't handle it.

The bible is full of impossible situations. The Israelites stood before the Red Sea; David faced Goliath; three men was thrown into a furnace; Jesus dead on a cross. Each of these was an impossible situation, with no earthly way to overcome them.

Our focus verse tells us to take comfort in God and His promises to bring us through any situation. God said to Moses in Numbers 11:23 *"Is the LORD's arm too short?"* The answer is "no" and it still applies to us today. Do we not believe He can do what He said?

He promises to meet real needs and to minister to those with real faith. He has never failed: Moses led the Israelites through the Red Sea; David killed Goliath; Shadrach, Meshach and Abednego came out of the furnace unharmed; and Jesus rose from the tomb." Each believed in God, each relied on God's strength, God's power and God's ability, not their own. Proof, that with real faith, *"All things are possible with God."*

April 17

"No one knows about that day or hour, not even the angels in heaven, nor the Son, but only the Father. Be on guard! Be alert! You do not know when that time will come." (Mark 13:32-33)

I attended the funeral of a 49 year old woman recently. The family was in a natural state of grief. They were also in a state of shock, because she was so young and her death was so sudden. No one expects to die that young, or that sudden, but the bible tells us that we don't know the time of our demise.

We learn from scripture that the time of our death is not known by anyone but God. He and He alone holds that time secret and it isn't revealed until His purpose is to be accomplished. Scripture also tells us to be ready and to be alert. What does this mean? If we don't know when we are going to die, what do we prepare for, what are we on guard for?

We are to be prepared for the day our soul enters into eternity. The reality is we will all spend eternity in one of two places, heaven or hell. Both places are real and both places are forever. We must prepare ourselves now for that reality. We can't put it off until later, because later is not guaranteed.

What is the status of your eternal soul? Have you made the decision about where you will spend eternity? If you haven't, or you aren't sure, you need to know. Salvation is easy, ask God into your heart, believe He is your Lord and Savior and then start following His commands and His ways and teachings. If you want to talk, Jesus is listening....

April 18

"But if you do not worship it, you will be thrown immediately into a blazing furnace." (Daniel 3:15)

The news seems to be filled with the evidence of a declining and dying world. The media pushes decaying morals down our throats, trying to make the world accept this as the norm. Most people today dismiss bad behaviors as "only being human"! We must be reminded that "only being human" is what made us sinners to start with.

Thousands of years ago a man and woman were given everything they could ask for with only one rule and they failed miserably. They too could have been excused because they were "only being human" but God created us in His image; pure, righteous, and holy. God held them to a standard of conduct and because they failed, He expelled them from the Garden of Eden.

We too are faced with a standard of living and in order to live that way we have choices to make. We can either fall to the pressures of the surrounding environment or behaviors, or we can live a life of unwavering faith and unashamed devotion to the One True God.

In our focus verse Daniel and his friends were given an ultimatum; pretty much they were faced with "compromise your beliefs, or die" They could have found a variety of excuses for compromise, but they chose to place their faith in God, no matter what.

Very few will ever face such a "compromise or die!" ultimatum. We will be tempted to compromise our convictions and bow to things like financial gain, physical pleasure, personal recognition, or the fear of conflict. We are tempted with the entertainment we watch, the web sites we visit and the company we keep. Standing firm to our beliefs requires a determined effort to remain solidly on God's path.

God never asks us to compromise His standard in order to follow His path...NEVER! We can therefore be assured that ANY compromise represents a deviation from His plan.

We need to strengthen the convictions God has already placed on our heart and we don't need to be ashamed of, or fear, what we know is His true calling on our lives. We need to conduct ourselves daily, in public and private, so that what we believe in is reflected in the way we live our lives. Let's take a stand and live a God-honoring life...without compromise.

April 19

"I am Jesus whom you are persecuting" (Acts 9:5)

The Apostle Paul was once a persecutor of Christians. He went from house to house and dragged believers off to prison, and some he put to death. Paul set off for Damascus in order to rid the land of these "misguided" Christ followers, however, Jesus had other plans.

Jesus revealed Himself in such a magnificent manner that there was no doubt as to who it was. Paul encountered Christ and was blinded by the light - and his life was changed forever.

Most of us will never encounter Jesus in such a dramatic way as Paul did. One day, without any lights, voices, or great fanfare, Jesus simply meets us and forever changes the course of our life. And just as Paul was called to follow Jesus, we are called to follow and be obedient.

When we encounter Jesus, truly encounter Jesus, our lives can never be the same. We are new creatures, changed forever for God's purpose. Our attitudes, actions, way of living should change. There should be evidence of that change in our lives that others can see.

Just as a pregnant woman starts showing the signs of a baby in the womb around month 3 or 4, the new Christian should start showing signs of being born again soon after conversion. The change can come in drastic ways, but can also be subtle. The way we talk, the way we act, how we carry ourselves, the company we keep, we realize the old habits aren't becoming of the Godly life we are called to live.

What actions, behaviors, worldly ways do you still possess that you know would not be welcomed in Christ's body? As you grow in Christ, look at your life and ask God to change those things that aren't Christ-like. He will give you the power to change.

April 20

"But thanks be to God! He gives us the victory through our Lord Jesus Christ." (1 Corinthians 15:57)

The song "Through the Fire" is very powerful. It is a source of strength and reassurance for me. Read the lyrics:

> *So many times I've questioned certain circumstances*
> *Things I could not understand*
> *Many times in trials, weakness blurs my vision*
> *Then my frustration gets so out of hand*
> *It's then I am reminded I've never been forsaken*
> *I've never had to stand the test alone*
> *As I look at all the victories the spirit rises up in me*
> *And it's through the fire my weakness is made strong*
> *(Chorus)*
> *He never promised that the cross would not get heavy*
> *And the hill would not be hard to climb*
> *He never offered our victories without fighting*
> *But he said help would always come in time*
> *Just remember when you're standing in the valley of decision*
> *And the adversary says give in*
> *Just hold on, our Lord will show up*
> *And he will take you through the fire again*

We are called to be immovable, always standing firm in God's work. We are to be consistent in our faith and not allow the events of the day to sway us. Too often we are moved by anything that happens in the world. We get a flat tire and let it ruin our day. We get depressed and ask "Where is God?"

Our focus verse tells us God is going to give us victory always, even when things look bad. God always leads us to triumph, that's the promise. How do we have victory in God? If He is always going to give us triumph, then we can always be strong and unwavering. You can know that through every problem or obstacle, no matter how big or small, you are going to be led to victory. God wants us to become the person of dedication, always faithful. You have a God that is dedicated to you; so the least you can do is to stay dedicated to Him.

Just as the song states, "...it's through the fire my weakness is made strong." Let your strength come through weaknesses.

April 21

"A generous man will prosper; he who refreshes others will himself be refreshed." (Proverbs 11:25)

A man starts to mow his yard. As he makes the first pass in his front yard, he can't help but notice his neighbor's yard with knee high weeds. He is angered because of how it makes his own yard look, much less the neighborhood. As he mows his yard he gets angrier with each pass. He rehearses what he should say to his neighbor or what he should do, until he hears a small voice.

"What if they are sick? What if they aren't able to care for their yard? There may be a multitude of reasons of which you do not know." The voice starts to convict. The voice tells him if it bothers him so much, do something about it. The voice tells him to mow the yard himself.

So the man pushes his mower into his neighbor's yard. He is a little nervous, a little unbelieving that he is actually going to mow this yard. But as he makes the first pass, he feels a peace come upon him. As he makes the second pass, he feels a small smile come on his face. The longer he mows the more he feels that voice say, "Well done!"

As the man continues to mow he finds himself praying for the family that lives there. He asks God if anything is wrong, to protect them, care for them and provide for them. He prays that they are safe and well. He continues to pray, "Lord, let them get a blessing from this. Lord let no one see this, so that You get the credit." As he finishes, he finds that his heart is filled with a blessing of his own.

We have different ways of dealing with situations. We can complain and get angry, or we can reach out and bless. Jesus met many in their need. He reached out when people were down, in need or just couldn't do for themselves. Jesus teaches us to do the same; love others as ourselves, to do for the least, all for His glory, not ours.

One of my favorite passages is our focus verse. In this passage Jesus tells of times when people did for those in need and then tells us, it is as if we did for Him. Jesus is well pleased when people do for others, with no motives, other than to bless. Jesus knows the heart of those that do for others, and to me that is what counts, not the accolades of others.

So keep your eyes open for opportunities. They are out there, can you spot them?

April 22

"...just as Christ was raised from the dead through the glory of the Father, we too may live a new life. "(Romans 6:4)

Spring. I really like this time of year. Everything's coming alive. The flowers are blooming, trees are budding, and the grass is turning green. New life, or more accurately life regenerated, is evident all around us.

Even the pollen, as bad as it may be, is a welcomed sight. It is a clear indicator of a resurgence of life from the drabness of winter. It tells us that we are about to see change, newness and beauty.

One reason I like to share the good news of Jesus Christ is because I get to see new life, or regenerated lives of those who know, or come to know Jesus. Their eyes tend to sparkle when they come to know Him. They get excited when they speak of Him, or the things He is doing in their life. There is a spring in their step, new purpose in their walk.

This morning I can't help but thank God for His renewing power. I recall the day I knelt and asked Jesus into my heart. It was in December, but after that simple prayer, the sky seemed brighter, the world seemed to be less dark.

Coming to know, walking with, and having a relationship with Jesus Christ is like the onset of spring. The old is replaced with new. Your life begins to transform and change. You bloom, and the longer you walk with Jesus, the more you grow into the creation He wants you to be. So enjoy it if you know it. But if you don't, ask Jesus into your heart and see for yourself.

April 23

"Then Jesus came to them and said, "All authority in heaven and on earth has been given to me. Therefore go and make disciples of all nations, baptizing them in the name of the Father and of the Son and of the Holy Spirit, and teaching them to obey everything I have commanded you. And surely I am with you always, to the very end of the age." (Matthew 28:18-20)

Since my calling, my heart has been burdened for those that do not know the love of Christ and who do not have a relationship with God. I want to take serious the call God has on my life, to introduce people to God and make relationships with those who don't know Jesus.

Our focus verse is such a part of whom I am and who I try to portray. That verse has also given me a glimpse of the urgency of spreading the gospel. But it is a daunting task for one. There are so many people, so few hours in the day. How do you get others to see the same need?

Jesus told His disciples in Matthew 9 to ask for workers. You see, the same was true in those days. There were so many people, so few willing to spread the word.

But what would happen if we all did our part? You see, based on scripture, we are those workers, the ones that are responsible to work the harvest field. Our harvest field is all around us. In our schools, neighborhoods, workplaces, etc.

But in order to accomplish this task, we must grasp the greatness that the phrase *"All authority in heaven and on earth has been given to me."* implies. We need to step out of our comfort zone and believe that the greatness, the authority given us will equip us to reach people for Christ.

Dare to step out and be His faithful laborer.

April 24

"All Scripture is God-breathed and is useful for teaching, rebuking, correcting and training in righteousness, so that the man of God may be thoroughly equipped for every good work." (2 Timothy 3:16-17)

It never amazes me how people waste their time listening to people like some of TV talk show host. People will go to great lengths to get advice from someone they know nothing about, nor have their own lives in order.

In ancient days, people would travel across lands, oceans and seas to get counsel from the oracles of Delphi and Pythia. Oracles are a person or agency considered to be a source of wise counsel or prophetic opinion. They were thought to be portals for gods (notice the little "g") to speak to man. Kings and common man alike would go to great efforts to get counsel from the oracles. Today some talk show hosts are considered oracles' a "false" source of wise counsel and teaching.

Just as the oracle in ancient days couldn't provide accurate wise counsel, either can the self-help gurus in today's society. Most are self-serving, in it for fame and money and have no interest in you or your problems. It's all for show. People spend fortunes on self-help gurus and "psychics" to get "supernatural" counseling, but they get nothing that will help their lives.

So where do you go for answers? If you have a bible you have been entrusted with the very oracles of God. The Word of God isn't just a book, it's supernatural, and it's yours. You have the divine, supernatural counsel for your life, directly from heaven. You have the counsel of what to do in your life, of God's will for your life, and of how to be blessed, right in your very presence.

Are you going to let it sit on your shelf or your desk unopened? Why waste the treasure that has been written to you? Open the bible today and receive a word from the living God. Don't lose the treasure entrusted to you because it's for real. Make it a daily habit to spend time in the most divine word of all time; read it, receive it, and treasure it. God wrote it just for you!

April 25

"...you laid aside the old self with its evil practices, and have put on the new self who is being renewed to a true knowledge according to the image of the One who created him..." (Colossians 3:9-10)

When I was young I did things that were not right. I knew right from wrong, but sometimes chose to go down the wrong paths. There are parts of my life that are good, but some were downright bad and some that I would rather forget. There was a time in my life where I wore a mask, a façade that all was well and I was a good guy. But it was a lie.

But then later in life I realized that I couldn't hide behind a mask anymore, I couldn't continue to fool people and I especially couldn't hide from God. I found out through God that life can be better, the old can die and the new can come out. The old self isn't who I am anymore, the bad habits, the old things are dead and the new me is my true self now.

There are some from my past that will never believe that. They tend to think I am just hiding under a new mask, but through Christ I am a new creature. I took off the old mask of failure, deceit, bad habits and ways and that person died. I now choose to live in the beauty of the new, in the image of the one that created me. I live now as a beloved son of God. What about you?

"Do not go back to putting on what is no longer you. Being born again, you are a new creation. Put off the old; put on the new and live holy and pure." Jonathan Cahn

April 26

"Who do people say I am?" "But what about you...Who do you say I am?"
(Mark 8:27)

Have you ever heard "if they will talk to you about someone, chances are they will talk to someone about you." My wife has a good remedy for gossip. Before the tidbit is shared, she asks the person if she can use them as a source. That normally stops them dead in their tracks.

Jesus was teaching some tough lessons and doing some pretty amazing things. Some were amazed, while others may have been confused as to who He really was. Talk must have spread. Labels and names must have been given, but were they true?

Jesus hears and knows what others think. He heard the gossip, but what he really wanted to know is what those closest to Him thought.

So Jesus asked the question in our focus verse. The disciples had many different answers. They were relaying what others had said, but Jesus wanted to know a more personal answer, what did they think?

This begs the question, who do we say He is? Who do we deep down believe Him to be? Go beyond the pew, the church and the pulpit and go into your living room, your office, your social group for that answer.

Who we say He is must be the same on Sunday as it is on Friday and Saturday night. Our answer must be the same from the mountaintop as it is from the valley. The answer to who we say He is must be more than head knowledge, it must be heart knowledge.

When our situation is bad, a relationship is broken, finances are low, and a disease is pronounced incurable or tragedy strikes you or a loved one, who is He? Is He really your Savior, healer, friend? When temptation comes, immoral desires run wild, an ethical compromise would be easier than doing the right thing, or you are pressured to conform to the world's expectations, who is He?

If Jesus is the center of your life, He will help you when you are on the mountaintop as well as when you are in the valley. He will be the same in the good and the bad. He will be your strength, your righteousness and your refuge. Know Him in your innermost being. He doesn't help us much as the center of our theology, He helps us as the center of our lives.

April 27

"...what good things must I do to get eternal life?" (Matthew 19:16)

Ever been asked a very pointed question? You know one that took you by total surprise. In our focus verse Jesus was asked a pointed question, one He gave a very pointed answer to, *"obey the commandments."* Jesus tells the rich man to do the things taught in scripture, live a life as Christ modeled. The man quickly states he had done so, but asked further, *"what do I still lack?"*

I look at this statement and think, what about this guy's life made him think he needed more? Was his life still filled with hurt, pain, emptiness, and a void that he knew could only be filled with something he lacked? Jesus gives an answer, one that wasn't what he wanted to hear.

We read that the man *"went away sad..."* because he wasn't willing to do as Jesus said. In our small group I was asked, "Did Jesus really mean for him to give up everything?" The answer I gave was yes. Jesus said it, therefore He meant it.

Why do we make it so hard? Jesus is simply saying we can't serve two masters. And in "masters" Jesus means Him or the thing that controlled the rich guy the most. In the rich man's case, he loved his money more than eternal life.

To ask the question again, did Jesus really mean for the rich man to give away everything? I have to say yes. Jesus knew the man's heart and what he loved more than anything. In order for the man to fill what was lacking, the thing he asked about, he had to get the priorities of his heart right. He had to decide what he was going to serve, his love of money or his desire to have eternal life.

So, I ask you this, are you serving more than one master? Try this experiment, say to yourself:, "I cannot serve God and _____. Fill in the blank with the things you value in your life. It could be your job, career, motorcycle, friends, family, anything.

Then measure your defensiveness to your reaction to each. This may show you where God wants to work in your life and what is holding you back from the fullness He wants you to experience. A further test is to try living without whatever it is for a while. That will be the real test.

April 28

"But Daniel resolved not to defile himself..." (Daniel 1:8)

Remember the news of a county clerk who was arrested under Federal charges for not issuing marriage licenses to same sex couples? I don't really want to get into a debate about the whole issue, but I do want to make a point about her actions and the events that led to this.

A group of people, actually quite small in number compared to the population of the U.S., saw what they felt to be a wrong. They wanted change, so they took a stand, they organized, they wrote, pleaded, spoke, rallied, yelled, and even went to court, to get their way. Now I am not for what they stand for by any means, but I do admire the fact they did something.

Now a lot of people disliked the decision. A law was passed, one that went against God, the bible and biblical principles. One side celebrates while the other side fumed.

This clerk, all alone, saw something she felt to be wrong. She wanted a change, so she took a stand knowing the consequences. Now I am not condoning what she did, nor applauding her, I will keep that to myself. But I do admire the fact she did something.

Matthew West has a song out entitled *"Do Something."* She did something. Based on a 2014 survey, 70.6% of polled American adults identified themselves as Christian. Now I must ask, if that large a percentage of the population believes the word of God, and believes this "Same Sex Marriage" ruling goes against God's definition of marriage, then why did it gets passed in the first place?

My answer; "Christians" are so complacent that they sit and wait for God to do something. Instead of being His hands and feet, and His mouthpiece, they just watched. Or, that percent of people are only "Christian" when asked. Nothing about their lives is different from the world.

I think it's time for Christians to become "Christ followers" and stand up for what we profess we believe. Instead of merely mouthing the words, we need to live our lives set apart. We need to take a stand for Christ and make our views, opinions and ideas heard.

.

April 29

"Praise be to the Lord, to God our Savior, who daily bears our burdens."
(Psalm 68:19)

I'm not a huge Tim Tebow fan for his football ability, but I respect the guy for his approach on life. I respect the guy for what he stands for and for what he professes and lives. In a culture where everyone is looking for controversy, dirt, and something negative to say about someone, he gives them nothing.

Tebow once played in a pre-season game, not knowing if his performance was enough to keep him on the team. When the media asked him what his plans were, this is what he said. "Go to sleep when I get home, wake up, come work out, watch the film." "See what I did good, see what I did bad, try to learn from it and get better.'"

He isn't worried, he isn't complaining, he isn't even overly concerned. This is why I like this guy; he is what he professes to be. He is real; otherwise the media would have uncovered some dirt. If he weren't real, I believe his response would have been like many of the other "professional" players, whining, complaining and/or bragging.

If we profess to believe and follow Jesus Christ then how we live our daily life should reflect that. How we handle difficult situations, success, failure and stress should reflect that in which we believe. The bible teaches about worry, about how to handle situations beyond our control and how to rely on God to guide our lives.

I once heard Tebow say his future wasn't in football, it was in God. There is a lesson in there, one we all must learn. God is in control. God leads our steps and God handles our situations and He carries our burdens. As Christ followers we must lay our burdens at His feet and allow Him to work it out. All we have to do is sleep, wake up, "see what I did good, see what I did bad, try to learn from it and get better."

Here is the promise, *"And we know that in all things God works for the good of those who love him, who have been called according to his purpose."* (Romans 8:28) We do our part, let Him do His part, we do our best every day and leave the rest to God. He is ready, willing and able; all we have to do is allow Him. So, what are you facing today? Have you tried to do it yourself, or are you going to lay it at God's feet and ask Him to handle it for you? The decision and response is up to you, choose wisely....

April 30

"But the Lord is faithful, and he will strengthen and protect you from the evil one." (2 Thessalonians 3:3)

Andy and Buddy were playing in the yard one day. Andy's dad told them not to go over the wall at the end of the yard. Being typical boys, as soon as dad went inside, over they went. They immediately heard a grunting sound behind them. They turned to see a big, nasty bull charging them. Back over the wall they went. When they hit the ground in safety, they noticed Andy's dad was waiting for them. As he marched them to the house he said, "The reason I told you not to go over the wall is because I knew there was something on the other side that could hurt you. I knew the bull was there. I didn't want you to get hurt."

Well I must say that when I was a kid I did some things my dad told me not to do, and more often than not, I either got hurt or in some serious trouble. We were all guilty of this, when we were young.

Now that I am older and a little wiser, I know the meaning of "no" and "don't", but I can honestly say, as humans, we don't always obey. We adults tend to think we know what's best for us and we are our own bosses. We may have grown in stature, but we are still little defiant kids inside.

As I read my bible I see a lot of "no's" and "don't" and used to wonder why they were there. But, as I have grown in my faith I know they are there for a purpose, for our own good. But how often do we read something in the Bible where God says "don't", only to do it anyway? Some think God's only purpose is to spoil their fun. Some think the bible is filled with more "don't" than "do's".

I have come to realize that God has great wisdom and when He says "don't", it's because He knows there's something on the other side of that line we are about to cross that will hurt us. His "no" isn't to spoil our fun, but to save us from something that may hurt, cause us suffering or lead us down a path we don't need to go.

Out of His amazing love for us He puts boundaries in place, to protect, save, bless and provide for us as only He can. His "don't" is not just a restriction to kill our fun, but they are acts of His love for us to help us be the people He created us to be. So the next time we hear God say "don't", listen and obey, it's for our own good.

May 1

"Go home to your family and tell them how much the Lord has done for you, and how he has had mercy on you. " (Mark 5:19)

Have you ever asked "Who me"? I know I have. I recall the day I learned I would be a father. I think the first words I spoke were "who me?" I was young, inexperienced and knew nothing about raising a kid. Well, my son grew up okay and now has a son of his own. I guess I did alright, and so did he.

I recall getting promoted in the Army and put in a leadership role. I recall asking my Platoon Sergeant, "who me?" I didn't know how to lead, train or motivate people. I was a young soldier and felt unqualified and ill-equipped. He had faith in me. I learned and did okay.

But the biggest "Who me" moment was when God called me to be a witness to someone. Only a short time ago I was an atheist. I didn't have years of "Christian" experience or total knowledge of scripture. Who am I to share the gospel?

To be a witness for Jesus doesn't require all that, you just need to share your encounter with Jesus and be willing to tell about it. Jesus didn't need me to go to seminary, to study every word of scripture; He just wanted me to do what He told the demon possessed man to do, *"Tell them how much the Lord has done."* It's that simple.

So, the next time you feel Jesus calling you to do something, just remember that He equips. Jesus just wants people who have been changed by an encounter with Him and are willing to tell those who haven't. We over complicate it when we begin to ask or question "who me?" Jesus simple said "go and tell" and we simply have to take that first step. Trust me, it works.....

May 2

"So in Christ Jesus you are all children of God through faith..." (Galatians 3:26)

On a recent camping trip I noticed a flock of ducks swimming on the lake. A group of 20 – 25 bobbed in the water, dove for food, and mingled with one another. As I watched I noticed about 50 yards away was one lone duck. It floated all by itself and I couldn't help but think about my past, a time when I felt much like that lone duck, all alone.

At one time in my life I felt like I didn't quite fit in. Not being close to most of my family, I felt like an outcast. I considered myself to be a loner. I could blend into a crowd, unnoticed by most people. I imagine that lone duck felt pretty much the same.

Then one day that all changed for me. Someone invited me to join a family bigger than any I had ever imagined. The day I accepted the invitation to allow Jesus into my heart, I became a member of the family of God. I no longer stood on the outskirts alone. I was included in the gatherings, and I was a part of that flock.

As believers of Jesus Christ, we belong to a family. God is our Father and we are one big happy family. We don't have to go through life alone.

So with that in mind, I go back to the "family" of ducks and wonder, "which one will swim out and invite that lone duck into the flock?" I am thankful for those that swam out to me. If not, I would still be out there alone, floating aimlessly and hopelessly. But because someone cared enough for me to invite me in, I now experience the love of a heavenly Father and a family that surrounds and loves me.

If we look around, we will find someone who needs invited in. Do you remember what it felt like to be on the outside? And if you were invited in, do you still remember how it felt? If you do, will you be the one to extend the invitation to someone else? By extending the invitation to join the family, you just may help change a life. Don't be afraid to "swim" out to someone who is all alone, you just may gain a new brother or sister in the process.

May 3

"Is it lawful for a man to divorce his wife for any and every reason?"
(Matthew 19:3)

If you want a good relationship, never give up on it and never allow it to be pulled apart. I want to ask you to take the duct tape challenge. Take two pieces of duct tape and hold them with the glue sides facing one another. Stick them together and rub them until they are fully stuck together. Now, try to pull them apart; impossible, right?

Lesson one: marriage was meant to be two becoming one. One man plus one woman equals a permanent bond. Lesson two: if it's of God, no one can separate the two. If you took the duct tape challenge, that is what those two pieces of tape became, one. When a man and a woman love one another and get married, they should become stuck together like those two pieces of duct tape. They form a permanent bond, inseparable.

So, why has divorce run rampant in this country? Because we have made it too easy to undo what was done. Have you ever used painters tape? It is made to temporarily stick to another surface. It easily peels away from the other surface leaving no mark, no residue and no evidence it was even there. That is what some marriages today are like, temporary. Some go into a relationship with the mindset of if it gets too hard I will just unstick that which was stuck.

God wants man and woman to marry, to live as one, to be happy and to die together. Marriage is a covenant, not a contract. I learned this; a contract is based on mutual distrust. You sign a contract because the one wants to make sure they get what they plan on getting from the other. But a covenant is based on mutual commitment. You commit to something and then stick to it, like the duct tape. Remember in the old days when one's word was one's bond? That is commitment.

Last lesson: you get what you give. Give a little, get a little, give a lot, well you get the idea. The bible teaches that we "reap what we sow", so if you want your relationship to be good, sow into it and reap the benefits. Your relationship can be as good as you both decide it is going to be, so why not make it all it can be.

May 4

"...clean the outside of the cup and dish, but inside they are full of greed and self-indulgence." (Matthew 23:25)

My wife and I are doing some remodeling in our home. Who would have thought that cutting drywall would leave so much dust? After a day of destruction, what we were left with was a layer of dust that covered everything. No matter what we looked at, all we saw was dust. It covered everything and you couldn't tell what was underneath that layer until you wiped it away.

As I thought of that dust, I thought how people can hide what is really underneath. From first glance, one may see a good person, a loving person or someone that cares. But underneath the surface may hide a serial killer, an abuser or someone that uses others. We often hear in the news how no one knew the guy next door could be capable of some horrific crime.

So it goes with people who profess to be Christians or believe in Jesus Christ. On the outside they appear to be what they claim. They blend in, look like all those around them, but deep down they are really nothing like what they appear to be. It isn't until one wipes away the outer layer do they truly see what lies beneath. When that layer is wiped away, the true self is revealed.

So, what are you when the outer layer is wiped away? Who are you even when others aren't looking? Are you a true believer deep down, even under the surface? Be the person Jesus wants you to be, the same on the inside as you are on the outside. When someone wipes away the outer layer, they should see the true Christian you profess to be.

May 5

"Someone asked him, "Lord, are only a few people going to be saved?" He said to them, "Make every effort to enter through the narrow door, because many, I tell you, will try to enter and will not be able to." (Luke 13:23-24)

With so much loss, I can't help but write about eternity. I believe that we all will spend eternity in one place or the other. I believe that where we spend eternity is based on our decisions and how we live our lives. And I believe that only God knows for sure and has the final say.

We must face the consequences of our decisions, one way or the other. Our belief and our actions must be one in the same in order to pass from this life to the eternal life with God. Our commitment to Him, His ways and His teachings are crucial to our final resting place.

Suppose a man sleeps with a woman and gets her pregnant. He tells her he wants to "do the right thing" so they plan the wedding and exchange vows. But he doesn't really love her so he continues to chase other women. He may be a good man, he may provide for the child and its mother, but he isn't committed to her. Is he a good husband?

This is what happens when someone says they "believe" in God yet continue to live their lives with no change. They aren't bad people; they just aren't committed to God. Does being a good person or saying you believe in God guarantee anyone a place in heaven? I believe that the bible teaches us that many good people will end up in hell.

The reality is that God determines who gets into heaven. Being good, even going to church, doesn't guarantee a spot. The only way to enter through that narrow gate is to believe, follow, serve and live for God with all your *"mind, body and soul."* And the time to make that decision to live our life for and with God is now. We should never wait, life is short and death can come without notice.

I don't know the eternal state of anyone, only God does. But I do know that the decisions we make and how we live our life matters, now and eternally. I want to be reunited in heaven with everyone I know who has gone there before me. The only way to do so is to live my life fully committed to God. And I ask each and every person that reads this to make the same decision in their life. It is my desire that everyone I know experiences that reunion, so choose wisely, choose now and know without a shadow of doubt as to where you will spend eternity.

May 6

"It is for freedom that Christ has set us free. Stand firm, then, and do not let yourselves be burdened again by a yoke of slavery." (Galatians 5:1)

I have been reading about the persecution of Christ followers around the world. A group called ISIS captures Christians, tortures them and kills them. I have to ask myself, how does ISIS identify Christ followers? What about their lives cause these evil people to take them captive? How are they recognized?

Whether God's people like it or not, self-professed Christians live in "glass houses." People watch our behavior to see if we live consistent with our words and beliefs. They wait for us to mess up so they can use that to denounce Christ altogether.

True believers, those who not only proclaim, but live up to proclamation are subject to persecution. And one thing I know, those who are being held by ISIS, are the real deal. They not only are recognized as believers; they remain firm in their belief while being held. How do I know this? If one person being held denounced their belief, don't you think we would have heard of it by now?

I carry an article in my journal that constantly reminds me that no matter what we face, we aren't alone. Kayla Mueller was captured in 2014 and killed for being a Christ follower. The article is a portion of a letter she wrote to her family before she died. She writes these words: *"I have a lot of fight left inside me. I am not breaking down; I will not give in no matter how long it takes."* She goes on to say *"I have learned that even in prison, one can be free. I am grateful. I have come to see that there is good in every situation, sometimes we just have to look for it."* And lastly she tells her family *"Please be patient, give your pain to God. Do not fear for me, continue to pray as will I, by God's will we will be together soon."*

Our focus verse talks about the freedom Kayla references. That freedom helps us to be strong, even in the face of grave danger. True believers have that kind of freedom. So grab ahold of that freedom that only comes by walking with Jesus Christ.

Also remember that eyes are on you always. Ask yourself this, if someone came to arrest the true Christ followers in this part of the world, would there be enough evidence that you are one of them? Food for thought.....

May 7

"He who overcomes will inherit all this, and I will be His God and he will be My son. But the cowardly, the unbelieving, the vile, the murderers, the sexually immoral, those who practice magic arts, the idolaters and all liars— they will be consigned to the fiery lake of burning sulfur." (Revelation 21:7-8)

I was invited to join a club which had very exclusive membership. I noticed immediately that only those invited and knew the code could get in. The invited guests were given a onetime access pass. Some feel that heaven is a free access club. Anyone that "says" they believe in God is an automatic member and destined to gain total access into the most prestigious place known. Some feel that by being a "good" person they can gain access through the "pearly gates" of heaven for an eternity of life on the streets of gold. But as I read scripture I find this not to be true. There is a membership fee, one that is affordable, but must be paid before access is granted. Let me explain...

Our focus verse speaks of the "New Jerusalem" or the "Holy City" in which God resides, that will be the eternal home for His followers. This is the place of no more tears, no death, no mourning, and no pain. This is the place where the streets are paved in gold, God's glory shines upon us and we are given new bodies that never grow old. This is the place most of us here on earth look forward to going.

Most people will tell you, no matter how they live their lives; they are going to heaven one day. But as we read this passage, we find there is an entrance fee, and some won't be able to pay it.

Those that obey God's teachings and live according to His ways overcome this world and will gain access to heaven. They will have total access to the riches, blessings and promises of God. But, those that live life as the world lives will never gain access. The one word I keyed in on was "liar". These are the people who say they believe yet keep right on living as if nothing has changed. They will not be allowed in. They will stand at the door and never gain access.

Friends, we can all be overcomers by obeying God's word and live a life worthy to be called His children. By living a changed life we can gain access to the greatest place known to man. But we must do our part. If you believe in God, live as if you do.

May 8

"...if anyone is in Christ, the new creation has come: The old has gone, the new is here!" (2 Corinthians 5:17)

When my son was young we got him a new bike for Christmas every year for about 5 years, or at least that is what he thought. I couldn't afford a new one each year, so I took the old bike, stripped it down, cleaned it up, repainted it and added all new accessories. When I was finished with it, it looked like the new one he actually wanted. He would ride around the neighborhood showing it off, as proud of his "new" bike as where the other kids who did receive new ones.

Sometimes things can be made new instead of throwing them out and replacing them with new ones. Why throw them out when all they need is a little cleaning and a little fixing up. People are no exception. Before I gave my life to Jesus Christ, I felt old, tired, and beat down. I thought my life was ready for the trash heap. Then, my Heavenly Father took me and cleaned me up, made me new and then sent me out into the "neighborhood" to show off His handy work.

There is a story in Mark chapter 5 that speaks of a possessed man who had many demons in him. He had been cast aside and pushed into the tombs to live. He met Jesus one day and Jesus performed a miracle in his life. Jesus cast out those demons and made him a new man. Jesus saw something in him worthwhile and made him a new man. Verse 15 says that when the town people saw him, he was *"dressed and in his right mind."*

Jesus took an outcast, someone no one wanted, and made him new. Jesus did exactly what our focus verse says. Then Jesus did something He had never done before in scripture, He told the man to *"Go home to your own people and tell them how much the Lord has done for you, and how he has had mercy on you."* Jesus wanted him to go and tell others what had happened to him, how he had been changed. And we read he did exactly that.

You see, when Jesus changes a person, makes them new, they can't help but tell others. We should want to show off His handy work. We should want others to see and believe, so that their life can be changed as well. Just as my son showed off his "new" bike, this new believer showed off his new self. So, if you have been changed by Jesus, show it off, tell others and be the new person Christ wants you to be.

May 9

"If your hand or your foot causes you to sin cut it off and throw it away. It is better for you to enter life maimed or crippled than to have two hands or two feet and be thrown into eternal fire. And if your eye causes you to sin, gouge it out and throw it away. It is better for you to enter life with one eye than to have two eyes and be thrown into the fire of hell." (Matthew 18:8-9)

My dog Ziggy had glaucoma in one eye. Her eye ball began to swell and the vet said she lived with the constant pain equivalent to migraines. She slowed down and just wasn't acting like herself. Her way of life was affected and it showed.

The vet recommended we remove the eye but I really didn't want to disfigure her like that. I was afraid of what she would look like. I didn't take into consideration of how much better it would make her feel. But in time I was convinced it was the best thing.

Too often we have sin in our life that cause us pain and suffering. We go about life as if nothing is wrong; all the while we are miserable. We think we are having fun, or its normal behavior, or we learn to live with it, but it is causing us unbearable pain.

Our focus verse tells us to "pluck out" or get rid of that in which causes us pain if we want to live the life God intended for us. The bible talks about literally cutting off a hand, or gouging out an eye. What if not only is it literally, but figuratively as well? If we know things cause us to sin, stop looking, attending, partaking in those things in order to rid ourselves of the pain it causes. That is the advice of the bible.

We had her eye removed. Oh yeah, she looks like she is constantly winking at me, but she is back to her old self. She is more playful, energetic and loving than she has been in a long time. That thing that caused her so much pain is gone.

What in your life needs to go? Ask God to help you rid your life of the things that cause pain, discomfort and torment. He will and you will be so much better afterwards...just ask Ziggy.

May 10

"...cried out to the Lord" and *"God opened up the hollow place in Lehi, and water came out of it. When Samson drank, his strength returned and he revived."* (Judges 15:18-19)

To be honest, I have done some things that I am not proud of. But my past failures don't define me because I have moved on, I am made new. If I concentrate on the negatives of my life, I would consider myself unworthy of anything. If I focused on my past failures and nothing else, I would wallow in self-pity and regret. I am far from perfect, but I am working on being better.

Samson, a man anointed by God to bring God's people out of captivity, and was given supernatural strength, failed over and over. He was a strong man with a weak will and he messed his life up. He repeatedly fell for the wrong women, violated all three vows he was to follow and became self-absorbed in lust, entitlement, anger and pride. He messed up too, He lost his strength, had his eyes gouged out and was taken captive by his peoples captives.

It's a sad story, yet one that teaches a valuable lesson about God. A close look at the life of Samson reveals he knew exactly where to go when he needed strength. Samson escaped and killed 1000 men. Tired and thirsty, he cried to God as our focus verse tells us. He took his need to God and God fulfilled that need.

Later, when he was blind and a slave, Samson prayed to God and God restored his strength. He was able to reach the central pillars of the temple. He pushed with all his might, and down came the temple on the rulers and all the people in it.

You see, once my life was near ruin. I was lost, in need of something that I couldn't obtain myself, so I cried out to God. He strengthened me. He gave me a new life, one filled with hope, mercy, grace and love. He picked me up, put me on a new path, one that glorifies Him and serves His purpose.

My past failures are gone, forgotten by God. I never want to live that life again. I never want those things to define me, because now I am defined by the God that saved me, restored me, strengthened me and gave me greater purpose. So, if you have failed in life, so what? Call on God and know that He will make you new; never again to be a failure.

May 11

"The Lord GOD hath given me the tongue of the learned, that I should know how to speak a word in season..." (Isaiah 50:4)

I read a story about a guy who had hurt a lot of people with his words. He went to a pastor and asked him how he could control his words. He wanted to do better. The pastor told him to take a basket of feathers to the top of the highest building in town, wait until the wind started to blow, then pour the feathers into that wind.

The man did so and then asked what to do next. The pastor told him to take the basket and go collect all the feathers that he had released. The man said "There is no way I could ever collect them all." The pastor said "Exactly. Your words, once released, can never be gathered up again. You must remember that before you speak, because once released they are gone forever."

Words have the power to heal, encourage, strengthen and motivate. They also have the power to hurt. With today's many ways to communicate, words can easily be spread across the globe in seconds. Once released, they can never be reeled back in. So we must pick our words better as not to hurt those we love or care about.

A young lady told me she was off social media because of negativity. She said she chose to delete her account so she would not say anything that she may later regret. Good advice for all of us.

Choose your words wisely. Ask yourself if they encourage or lift up, will they make the situation better or worse, and if they are worth speaking at all. Chances are, when we take the time to think, we will change the words we were going to say.

May 12

"Feed my sheep." (John 21:17)

In a world where most think the only way to get food is go to the grocery store, we raised pigs, chickens and cows. The animal's purpose was to put food on the table. One of the things I remember my dad saying is, "It's feeding time!" Those words are engraved in my mind. I can hear him now, saying those words as he headed out to the barn. Those words were spoken twice a day, every day.

Growing up, needless to say, I had to help with chores. There were things to do and I was assigned certain things, no matter if I liked it or not. And some days, my attitude was as stinky as those animals. But, no matter what, it had to be done. The animals, my dad and our stomachs depended on it.

The more I walk with God, the more I cherish the time I spend studying His word. Each morning, I can hear "it's feeding time!" Feeding time does me good. It refreshes me, encourages me and lifts me up. It is what sets my day in motion.

A bible story comes to mind. The disciples had been fishing all night with no luck. Jesus shows up and tells them to throw their net in one more time; they catch a boatload of fish. Later, they arrive on the shore and see Jesus and a campfire. What does He do? He cooks them breakfast. It was feeding time. Early one morning, on a shore alone with Jesus, they were filled, not with just a meal, but instruction from Jesus.

You know the story. Jesus and Peter have a three part exchange that ends with Jesus telling Peter to *"Feed my sheep."* Peter was a fisherman; he knew nothing about stinky sheep. With Jesus' help Peter came to realize that Jesus wasn't talking about stinky sheep, He was talking about people. We are often asked to do things we don't like, or know nothing about, yet Peter took Jesus' words to heart and the church was founded, grew and became that which Jesus wanted.

I am thankful for my dad and my upbringing that molded me into who I am today. I am also thankful for my Heavenly Father and how He is molding me to be what He wants me to be. God has a purpose for us, but if we don't spent time with Him we may never know. So, is it feeding time for you? Take a few minutes a day and get fed, it just might change your life. It changed Peter's....

May 13

"I am not ashamed of the gospel, because it is the power of God for the salvation of everyone who believes..." (Romans 1:16)

I believe in spreading the Word of God and using every means available in order to reach as many people as possible. Often I think I am a little too bold, but when I talk about quitting, those closest to me tell me not to. The bible tells us to keep up the preaching no matter how many people are offended. Our focus verse tells us not to be ashamed of it, so why not share it?

If we aren't spreading God's Word, are we ashamed of it? Some people tell me they don't know what to say. They have no idea where to begin, what scripture to use, etc. Well, let's break it down in simple terms.

Let me use the popular social site Facebook as an example. When you open your page, what is one of the first things you do? You either look at the "status" of other people or you post your "status". You tell the world what you are up to, how your day is going, where you are, etc. Everyone who is a "friend" knows exactly what is up in your life.

The same thing should be true in your Christian walk. Your friends, or the world, depending on your security in your beliefs, should know your status when it comes to God. When it comes to spreading God's Word, all that is required is telling people what God is doing in your life at this very moment. It isn't rocket science.

When we talk to people about the God we serve, we just need to keep it simple. People don't expect you to be the next Billy Graham; they don't need a long dissertation, or a detailed presentation of the entire bible in five minutes. All they need is to know how God has changed your life. Tell them how you have been transformed and the role God has had in that transformation. Give them your status update.

So I ask you, fellow believers and followers of Christ, what's your status? How has God changed you? What has God brought you out of? How is God working in your life? Care to share it with the rest of the world or at least your friends? Update your status, the world needs to hear to good news!

May 14

"Come, follow me," Jesus said, "and I will make you fishers of men."
(Matthew 4:19)

If you have ever been fishing you know that you don't catch a fish every time you cast a line or net. Fishing is time consuming. If you want results, you must stay with it. Jesus used fishing as a way of illustrating the spread of the gospel. He called men to follow Him, promising that He would make them "fishers of men." Unless we understand fishing, we can't really understand that whole concept.

Spreading the gospel requires using the fishing method. You "cast" yourself out into the community that you feel the most comfortable in. For me, it's the biker community. I find the right spots and hand out bait in the form of my business card. I let people know who I am and how to get in touch with me. I don't push anything heavy on anyone, but I do offer the bait for their taking.

A few guys I knew admitted that for years they would take my card, walk away and throw it away. Every time I saw these guys, they got another card. I call that "recasting" my bait. One day came when I received a call from one who wanted to know more about what I had to offer. He eventually gave his heart to Jesus. He began to cast his bait (a business card). He gave his card to the other guy who had thrown my card away and it eventually led him to give his heart to Jesus.

Luke 5 gives us an example of this approach. The disciples were washing their nets when Jesus told them to push out away from shore and drop their nets once again. Simon told Jesus they had done that *"all night and haven't caught anything."* Their efforts resulted in no fish, but they did what Jesus asked them to do anyway. Scripture tells us that when they "recast" their nets, *"they caught such a large number of fish that their nets began to break."*

The disciples were so astonished at the catch; they followed Jesus and became fishers of people. They realized that the recasting of their nets, with Jesus as their source of power, resulted in a catch far greater than they could imagine. I have witnessed over the years that one cast may not net the kingdom anything, but recasting, under the power of the Holy Spirit, can lead to people eventually taking what is offered and their lives are changed. So, if you believe in the gospel, cast it everywhere you go, who knows what you may catch.

May 15

"I can do everything through him who gives me strength." (Philippians 4:13)

I took a maple tree out of the front yard and now my yard has a big bare spot in it. It is kind of hard to miss and I keep saying to myself, "I need to fix that." All I need is some top soil, some sod and a few hours and that spot will go away. I know it will look so much better once it is completed, but I keep avoiding the work.

This morning as I looked at that spot I thought, what in my life do I need to pay some attention to? Do I have spots in my life that are unsightly and in need of repair? I think we all have areas we need to pay close attention to, but getting to those spots takes time and effort.

God provides us the tools to "fix" the things in our life. Our focus verse says He gives us strength. His word guides us. His Spirit strengthens and encourages. His power in us gives us abilities. But like my yard tools, they are worthless if we avoid them.

So, today I am going to take time to first examine my life for those areas that need attention. Then I am going to make a plan to fix them and finally, I am going to ask God for His assistance. There is no better time than the present, so I begin now.

What in your life needs some attention? I bet if you take a moment to talk to God, He will help you see those areas and help you devise a plan to correct them. But it takes time, effort and determination.

So, what are you waiting for?

May 16

"'Come, follow me,' Jesus said..." (Matthew 4:19)

There was once a man who didn't believe in God, and he didn't hesitate to let others know what he felt about religion. His wife did believe and raised their children to have faith in God, despite his objections.

One snowy day, she took the children to church. They were to talk about Jesus' birth. She asked her husband to come, he refused. "That story is nonsense!" "Why would God lower Himself to come to earth as a man?" So she and the children left.

The wind blew and the night turned into a blinding snowstorm. He sat in front of the fire reading. He heard something hit the window. He looked, but couldn't see anything.

When the storm let up, he went outside to see what had hit his window. He saw a flock of wild geese. Apparently they had been caught in the snowstorm and couldn't go on. They were lost and stranded, with no food or shelter. They flew around the field aimlessly.

He wanted to help them get into the barn. It's warm and safe; they could wait out the storm there. So he walked over to the barn and opened the doors. They didn't seem to realize what this meant.

He tried to get their attention, they moved further away. He took some bread and made a trail to the barn, they still didn't catch on. He tried to shoo them, but that scared them away from the barn.

"Why don't they follow me?!" he asked. He then realized that they just wouldn't follow a human. "If only I were a goose" he said out loud. An idea hit, he went into barn and got one of his own geese. He circled the flock of wild geese. He then released his goose; it flew straight into the barn. One-by-one, the wild geese followed.

He stood for a moment as the words he had spoken a few minutes earlier replayed in his mind: "If only I were a goose, then I could save them!" He thought about his words to his wife earlier. "Why would God want to be like us? That's ridiculous!" Suddenly it all made sense. That is what God had done. God had His Son become like us so He could show us the way and save us.

He fell to his knees in the snow, and prayed his first prayer: "Thank You, God, for coming in human form to get me out of the storm!"
(Author Unknown)

May 17

"Your Father, who sees what is done in secret, will reward you. " (Matthew 6:18)

She was short, round and quiet, one of those who blended into a crowd. He was tall, broad shouldered and vocal, stood out in a crowd. As a non-believer it was odd that these two would be friends of mine, but I was drawn to them.

You would think that it would have been him who made me start thinking about Jesus. He was always telling me about Jesus and how Jesus impacted his life. But actually, it was her who intrigued me and made me want to understand more about the Jesus she worshipped. There was something about the way she lived her life that I wanted.

She reminded me of my mother-in-law. Both of these women quietly lived out their lives differently than others I had met. They loved everyone, had a sparkle in their eye and praised God no matter what the circumstance. They demonstrated a peace that I didn't understand, but wanted.

One of my biblical heroes is Peter. He was strong, a natural leader and stood out in the crowd. But we can pass right over the guy who led Peter to Jesus, his brother Andrew. Andrew was what we call a "bringer". He was introduced to Jesus and immediately wanted everyone to know Jesus as well.

So he brought Peter (John 1:41), he brought a little boy with a lunch pail (John 6:8-9), he brought some Greek men (John 12) all to meet Jesus. That was the Andrew we can overlook, a person who was so impacted by Jesus that he brought people to Him. He wasn't the one getting all the attention, but one who wanted to share the good news about the Savior.

During the Christmas season, we celebrate the *"good news of great joy that will be for all the people. Today in the town of David a Savior has been born to you; he is Christ the Lord.. "* (Luke 2:10-11). Jesus came on that day to save the world and we should all be Andrew's.

But shouldn't we remember that each and every day? We are Christ followers 365 days of the year, so we should never stop introducing people to the good news. Bring someone to know Jesus, not by mere words, but by the way you live your life.

138

May 18

"Whoever wants to be my disciple must deny themselves and take up their cross daily and follow me." (Luke 9:23)

Ever played "follow the leader"? The object of the game was to do what the leader did and if you failed, you were out. The last one following the leader was the winner. I remember playing that game and doing some crazy things just to stay in the game.

Living a life for Jesus is like playing "follow the leader". He is the leader and if we claim to be followers of His, we are in the game to follow his lead.

The challenge for every Christian is clear; to forget about our desires and to let Jesus lead us; put aside our will for His; forget our purpose and concentrate on His purpose for us. If we are what we claim to be, Christians, then we are to die to ourselves and follow Him.

Following Him at times isn't easy. Following Him may take us to places we don't want to go. Following Him may have us do what we don't want to do. Following Him may cause us to change things about ourselves that we may be reluctant to change. Following Him may seem crazy at times, but if we want to stay in the game we have to follow.

Following is hard. We must love Him enough to obey His ways, His teachings and follow Him. We must love Him enough to lose ourselves and follow Him daily. Then and only then will we reap the rewards He promises. So, are you ready to follow the leader?

May 19

"...whatever you did for one of the least of these brothers of mine, you did for me." (Matthew 25:40)

Jesus was speaking of giving to the hungry and the thirsty, inviting in the stranger, clothing others, visiting and looking after the sick and visiting the prisoners. What He was saying is that those that do for others out of love; it is like doing the same for Him!

I have witnessed a lot of people who did just this. They spent their time baking cookies for American heroes. Then they deliver hugs, handshakes and those fresh baked cookies to Veterans hospitalized in a Veterans Hospital in Columbia, SC. My heart is filled with joy just knowing that these people did this act out of love for people they had never met and will more than likely never see again. I have been touched.

Why do people do this? What makes people give of their time and energy to help others? I believe it is because they have a heart like Jesus and compassion for the less fortunate. Our focus verse tells us that when people do this, God is pleased.

So what act can you do to help those who need help? It doesn't take much, just a little of your time.

May 20

" You were taught, with regard to your former way of life, to put off your old self, which is being corrupted by its deceitful desires; to be made new in the attitude of your minds; and to put on the new self, created to be like God in true righteousness and holiness." (Ephesians 4:22-23)

One night while talking with a new Christian, he shared a story that just floored me. Seems he and two guys were out riding their bikes. These two guys are not currently believers and my friend has been witnessing to them.

The Christian was bragging that the other guys couldn't keep up with him. Seems my friend, the new Christian, the one doing the witnessing, was doing 125 mph in a 45 mph zone. I just sat there in disbelief. My first thought was, "why?" My next thought was "do you know what they will do to you when they catch you?"

But as I have thought on this, another thing came to mind. What type of witness was he being? All too often, we "well meaning" Christians try to witness to our un-churched friends and at times we do more damage than good. We are told that when we come to believe and follow Jesus, we are to no longer live as we once did.

Take a look at our focus verse. We are to put off the old for the new. To me that means the old ways must change to new ways. I must be different than those who don't profess to believe and follow.

When we talk to others about the advantages of living a life with Jesus, they should see the results of that statement in our lives. Doing 125 in a 45 zone doesn't look like this. Talking to a guy that is allowing alcohol to destroy his life while you are drinking with him; doesn't look like this. Witnessing to a person who struggles with lust and porn, as you invite him to Hooter's, the local strip club, or share a sexually explicit joke, doesn't look like this.

Sometimes we can be well meaning but destructive at the same time. If you are a follower of Jesus Christ, how does your life reflect that admission? Are you the same old guy or gal you used to be, or is your life different from that person you once were? If you doubt, reevaluate. Before you take the opportunity to witness, look at what you are doing and ask yourself "Am I going to be a witness for Jesus, or a stumbling block for the person I am talking to?" I pray you live out your life as a new creation, in Jesus' image. When you do, the kingdom will surely grow!

May 21

"Bear with each other and forgive whatever grievances you may have against one another. Forgive as the Lord forgave you." (Colossians 3:13)

Flipping through the channels I found a football game. I noticed a name from the past, Michael Vick. Again, I don't want to get in a big discussion about what he did, or your thoughts about his actions or punishment. What came to my mind was far different.

We all know what he did. We all know his punishment and the outcome of his actions. And we all have our own opinions of him. But, did you know he represents you and your life in a strange sort of way? Oh yes, you too have messed up in your life. Oh, you have done things that deserve punishment. You, and me for that matter, have done things in God's eyes that are just as bad.

I was in a conversation with a couple the other night and David, you know, the guy from the bible, came up. We talked about how he rose to fame, and then he fell. We talked about how his life was filled with ups and downs. One minute he was a hero, the next an adulterer. As we talked we couldn't help but realize that he was forgiven each time by God. He was restored and used by God, for God's purpose.

When we realize we messed up, and we ask for God's forgiveness, we are forgiven. We have a God of second chances, and sometimes third, fourth and fifth chances. He forgives us and restores us to our rightful spot in his eyes. The bible tells us that when He does that, He chooses to forget our past offenses. I want to repeat that, God chooses to forget our past mistakes; they are gone forever in His eyes and mind.

What about us? Do we understand we all mess up and need to be forgiven? Do we all realize that we fall short of the things of God and need second, third, and fourth chances? Do we hit our knees and ask for forgiveness? Do we forgive others for their past mistakes when they ask for forgiveness?

I thank God that he is a God of second chances, because I need that. I am human, I mess up. I also thank God for His lessons about forgiveness. I need to be forgiven, by Him and by those I may have wronged in my past. So, if you know you have done wrong, ask God to forgive you and know you are forgiven. If someone has wronged you and asked to be forgiven, forgive and then forget. If you have wronged someone else, ask for forgiveness and watch what happens.

May 22

"Lord, how many times shall I forgive my brother or sister..." (Matthew 18:21-35)

Grab a plate and throw it on the ground. Now tell the plate you are sorry. Did it go back to the way it was before? Well no. The world thinks that 'sorry' is all it takes.

Before I came to know God, I had thrown my life on the ground numerous times. I wasn't just broken but shattered. I had been told about God many times, but each time I threw that idea on the ground, shattering it as well.

Then one day I came to realize I was doomed without some intervention in my life. I hit my knees, I said I was sorry, asked God to forgive me and guess what, God forgave me. He picked me up, He put me back together and honestly, I am better now than I ever was. His forgiveness made me whole.

Our focus verse is about forgiveness. A man owes money to another man. He is taken to court, told to pay and when he couldn't his entire family was ordered to go to jail. He begged for forgiveness and he was forgiven of his debt and set free. Afterwards, he went out and saw a friend who owed him, he demanded repayment. That man also begged, but no forgiveness was given. The unforgiving man was taken into custody, since he was forgiven yet failed to forgive, and was thrown in jail.

Jesus says don't forgive and forgiveness is withheld from you. True forgiveness is a powerful thing. It can mend, heal and actually make things stronger. Paul wrote that Jesus forgave in such a way that He chose to forget.

What if Jesus forgave like the world today says to? What if He mouthed the words, but did nothing else? What if He mouthed the words yet still held a grudge?

As for me, I would be back where I was some 17 years ago, heading straight to hell. But I am thankful that I serve a God who truly forgives. When someone does something to me and I say I forgive you, I mean it.

143

May 23

"So if the Son sets you free, you will be free indeed." (John 8:36)

I met a rather interesting new friend named Ozzie. He isn't very good looking. His hair is a mess, he has big ears and his eyes are two different colors. As I talked with him, he started digging around in a wood pile. He picked a large log and carried it to me. He dropped it at my feet and then sat down and stared at me.

I thought that this was pretty odd and wondered what I was to do with it. Then he made his intentions clear, he looked at me, looked down at the piece of wood, looked out into the yard and barked. Yes, my new friend is a dog and he wanted to play catch with that large log.

So I did what he wanted and off he went. He retrieved it and carried it back to the porch where he began to chew on it. Once he got the bark off of it, he picked it up, carried it to my feet and dropped it again. Now we are in full-fledged fetch mode.

As I played with my new friend, I couldn't help but think how often we do the very same thing. We pick up more than we can handle, drop it at Jesus feet, He throws it away and we go pick it back up again. It is more than we can carry, yet we struggle with it and even try and whittle it down to a more manageable size, only to lay it at Jesus' feet again, repeating the process. We often continue to do the same thing over and over again, because we don't really want things to change.

But with Jesus, He offers us change if we truly want it. We can be free from the loop, as long as we let Him take it from us and we don't go chasing after it. We can be free of the heavy burden we lay at His feet, if we truly want.

I once heard that insanity was doing the same thing over and over again, expecting different results. That is a do loop and what most do that are caught up in sin. But here is some good news, when we get tired of it, we can lay it at Jesus feet and walk away. We can let Him handle it, throw it away, and as long as we leave it where we left it, we are free from it.

So, don't be like my new friend. If it is heavy and you want to be free of it, lay it down at Jesus' feet and walk away victorious. God's word says we can be free, so be free indeed!

May 24

"My God, my God, why have you forsaken me?" (Matthew 27:46)

My new friend Ozzie taught me another lesson. After a day of fetch he wore me out. By the end of the day I tired of the game and began to ignore him. He would bring me his log; drop it on my foot and bark. I stood firm and refused to even acknowledge him, his log and his bark.

As I walked out on the porch the next day, he just sat there. I scratched his head; he followed me around, but without the log. He was just content being in my presence.

I wonder how often God tires of our consistent dropping our burdens at His feet and then picking them back up again. I wonder if God tires of us praying that a certain sin leave us, only to do it again. Does He ever get to the point that He ignores us?

As Jesus hung on the cross, He bore the sins of the world and God turned His back. Our focus verse tells us that Jesus cried out because He felt God ignoring His pain. God wants us to live sin free, He even provided a way to escape that sin, but when we continue to sin, I think He may ignore us.

He doesn't stop loving us, but He wants us to realize that we need to leave that "thing" alone. My new friend figured that out and left the log out of our friendship. He was finally content to just go about life without the log and enjoy my company.

So what about you? Is there something that you keep carrying around? Is there something that you have taken to God only to pick it up again? Leave it behind and enjoy the company of God, knowing that when He takes it, you can be rid of it, for good.

May 25

"He who walks with the wise grows wise, but a companion of fools suffers harm." (Proverbs 13:20)

My wife and I just traveled 1850 miles on two motorcycles. I am so blessed that my best friend is also my wife. As we traveled, I realized how great we are together. Where do we eat? Anywhere there is food. Where do we stop? Anywhere we want. What do we see? Whatever is there. Neither of us are high maintenance, nor demanding. We enjoy what each other enjoys and both of us want what benefits the other. I can't help but believe that is how God intended married life.

Over the years I didn't always pick my friends wisely. I surrounded myself with some that got me in trouble. Some led me down wrong paths. I suffered at times because of my choice of friends, but I grew wiser, as our focus verse says, as I grew closer to God.

There comes a time in life that we must take inventory of our "friends". We must ask ourselves, are they the type of friends that lift us up, make us better? Are they the friends that encourage and build one another up? Do they have our best interests at heart? Do they want us to excel, overcome and be blessed?

Or are they the type that our parents and 1 Corinthians 15:33 warn us of; *"Bad company corrupts good character."* If they are the latter, we may have to walk away from them.

We should surround ourselves with people who lift us up, make our lives better and encourage us. We should have people in our lives that want what is best for us. This also goes for you; you should be a friend like that as well. When we all live with this mindset, then life becomes what God intended…full, rich and meaningful.

As this thought came to mind, I took inventory of my friends list and realized that I have many friends that want what is best for me. They care about me, they love me, and they bless my life. I have many friends that God has brought into my life that I can truly say; they lift me higher than I could ever be alone. I am thankful for those people and pray that each of you have a list of friends like that. If you find your inventory doesn't contain people like that, shed that list and look for new friends. God wants you to be happy and He wants you to have friends that make you a better person. Surround yourself with friends that want to lift you up.

May 26

"Your love has given me much joy and comfort, my brother, for your kindness has often refreshed the hearts of God's people." (Philemon 1:7)

We need people like the ones referred to in our focus verse. We need those friends who will offer us help when needed, encouragement when required, and grace when undeserved. We need people, who while living the faith authentically, will refresh our very hearts.

I can't know all the needs faced by each of you who will read this devotional thought. But I'm pretty sure that some of you have a heart that needs a little refreshment. You need a little joy... a little strength... a little hope... a little calmness... maybe a little sanity. I desperately pray that you have the people in your life that will provide you with such gifts. I hope that through prayers and conversations with others that you will feel renewed hope and will find in those friends the presence of Christ.

In the past week alone, I have had several friends speak to me of their prayerful support and encouraging thoughts as we approach another busy holiday season. It always means a lot.

Now let's play the flip side of this thought. Have you refreshed the heart of someone lately with your kindness? I know that you have some friends in your life that could use a little refreshment. Why not give them a call, text them, or send them an email? Why not look for a way to do something tangible to show them your support? Love is always a two-way street. We need to receive it and we need to offer it. I hope your day is encouraging as you both give and receive a little refreshment.

147

May 27

"Meanwhile a Jew named... was a learned man, with a thorough knowledge of the Scriptures. He had been instructed in the way of the Lord, and he spoke with great fervor and taught about Jesus accurately..." (Acts 18:24-25)

We had a pond on our farm where water run into it, but nothing ran out. It became stagnate and was a breeding ground for mosquitos. It was not a place we hung out at, in fact we avoided it.

Our focus verse tells us of Aquila and Priscilla, who heard Apollos speak and recognized that he needed further instruction. So they took it upon themselves to share the full gospel with him. As a result, he went to Corinth to preach about Jesus.

We are called to share the gospel and tell people about Jesus. If you don't believe me, I challenge you to read the New Testament. You either evangelize or fossilize. The truth God has given us is not to be hoarded, but to be shared. You have been blessed to be a blessing to others. And if you only take in and don't give out, you are running the risk of being like that pond on the farm, stagnate.

If you call yourself a Christ follower you have a commandment to follow and to share your faith. There are many believers who know God's word, yet pretty much think everything revolves around them. It is all about them being blessed, all about them growing and learning. And there is some truth to that, but it is also about taking these newfound truths and sharing them with others.

We, as Christ followers, have a part to play in the spreading of the gospel. You may think you don't know enough, but you know more than a brand new believer or one who doesn't know or believe at all. And when you let the gospel flow out of you, you grow, become vibrant and God can do a lot with a little.

On the farm my dad took his tractor and dug out a spot to allow the water to flow out of that tiny little pond. After a short time that stagnant pond became a source of water for the cows and a refreshing place for them to cool off. It didn't take much effort, but the end result was amazing. So get to work letting what flows into you flow out. In time, you will see that you have become a blessing to others and God will bless you.

May 28

"No one was strong enough to subdue him. Night and day among the tombs and in the hills he would cry out and cut himself with stones." (Mark 5:4-5)

Ever met someone that left a lasting impression on you? I have and some of them come from the bible. Their stories are so gripping that I use them to teach, to set goals for myself and to use as a litmus test on how I am doing in my walk. One such character is introduced in Mark 5.

He was a demon possessed man named Legion who confronts Jesus. He is so strong that even chains and irons can't bind him. Even though he was possessed by many demons, he recognized Jesus and went to him. Jesus calls out the demons and the man is set free.

The once demon possessed man is so pleased he wants to join Jesus and become one of his disciples. His heart was set, but Jesus did not let him. Jesus sent him home to be a witness to the miracle that had been performed. He was a living example of the power of Jesus and how Jesus can set even those that have demons free, to be a witness to His mercy.

All too often we think we need years of preparation, training, teachings and experience to be a witness for Jesus, or to be useful to God. This passage of scripture tells us otherwise. All that is required is an encounter with Jesus and the will to tell people about it. All we're asked to do is to "tell them how much the Lord has done" for us. It's very simple....

May 29

"Watch out for false prophets. They come to you in sheep's clothing, but inwardly they are ferocious wolves." (Matthew 7:15)

A "real biker" can tell a fake one when they see one. Fake bikers are known as RUBs (Rich Urban Bikers). They want to play the role of a biker because they think it is cool. A real biker knows by the way they look, act, how they dress and how they carry themselves.

Most people have a hard time picking out the real from the phony. Here's a quiz. What do you think when you hear the name Satan? Do you envision a guy with pointy horns and a tail? I remember as a kid watching old movies where Satan was portrayed and having bad dreams afterwards. I outgrew the nightmares, eventually. And as I study the bible, I am outgrowing the thought of Satan looking anything like the little creature we envision.

The bible teaches us a different way of thinking about Satan and his followers. He is sinister. He is evil. He is sneaky and always trying to lure people into thinking his way. But he doesn't necessary look as evil as we may think. He can often look like ordinary people.

Our focus verse tells us that people can give the appearance of being true believers, yet inwardly they are vicious unbelievers who prey on the immature, the unstable and the gullible. They blend in with those that believe. They may regularly attend church, sit beside you in the pews. But they are Satan's workers and do whatever it takes to deceive, corrupt, sway and cause people to stumble.

Want more proof that Satan and his helpers take on the appearance of ordinary people? Look at Acts 20:29-30, Romans 16:17, 2 Timothy 3:5, and 2 Peter 2:1. The warnings are numerous, but the lesson is the same, be careful.

We must guard ourselves against those that are actually workers for Satan. We must learn to discern God's will on our lives and be aware of anything that is contrary to that will. We must be ever mindful of the people we surround ourselves with and evaluate those that have motives that may not align with God's will. You can tell by the way people act if they are true believers or not, they take on the characteristics of the one they truly follow. Learn the difference and stay away from phonies.

May 30

"If you love me, you will obey what I command." (John 14:15)

I was given a gift card once and when I went to use it, imagine my surprise when I was informed there was no money on it. After some investigation I found the card had been issued over a year ago and the company took a percentage each month as a "service charge". So by the time I received it and used it, it was no good.

Ever received a gift that you didn't use? I asked Jesus into my heart in December of 2000, but for the first several years I simply didn't use that gift of salvation. Yeah I went to church. I occasionally read my bible. When times were tough I even prayed a quick 2 second prayer. But I never fully used the gift of God's love, grace, mercy and forgiveness. I never got to know Him on a personal level.

It took some time to completely surrender my life to God. I was tired of halfheartedly playing with religion. So one day I decided to go all in. It was time to live my life for God and allow Him to transform my life. Oh how my life has changed.

The bible tells us that the gift of salvation consists of belief and obeying. We must "use" the gift by applying His word to our lives. His will for our life must be our will. Our life should reflect His life. We must walk with Him, talk with Him, and spend time with Him daily in order that we know Him and His gift completely.

By not using the gift we risk hearing the dreaded words, far greater than *"sir, your card doesn't work"* but *"I never knew you. Away from me you evildoers."* (Matthew 7:23) These words we are told are reserved for those that know of Him, but don't truly know Him, or He us. There is a difference.

But by using the gift, the ability to get to know Him, obeying, following and being one with God, we can assure that the reward of that gift is valid when the time comes. By having a relationship with God we can hear *"Well done, good and faithful servant! Come and share your master's happiness!"* (Matthew 25:21)

The gift of God's love is priceless, but it must be exercised in order for it to benefit us. By getting to know God on a personal level and He us, we are assured the full price of salvation, eternity in Heaven with the Creator of the Earth. I am not sure about you, but that is one big gift card!

151

May 31

"Now if you obey me fully and keep my covenant, then out of all nations you will be my treasured possession. Although the whole earth is mine, you will be for me a kingdom of priests and a holy nation." (Exodus 19:5-6)

We live in a world where the word of God has been watered down. Pastor's preach love, acceptance and forgiveness, but fail to preach the "if" and "then" realities of scripture. The word of God says "IF" we do our part, "THEN" God will do His part. Failure on your part results in wrath from God.

In a world where people seem to think everyone goes to heaven, the reality is many go to hell. People that live lives contrary to the "if" and "then" don't magically end up in heaven. No, to live contrary to God's word results in a "Depart from me, I don't know you" statement from God upon arrival. There are eternal consequences for your behaviors and lifestyles.

We are told in scripture to "fear" God. For the longest time I didn't understand that. If God is love why should I fear Him? But then I realized it is no different from my earthly father. I knew he loved me, but I feared disappointing him or going against what I was told. I knew if I did what he told me not to do, I would suffer consequences. The same is true with God, my Heavenly Father. To live contrary to His word, there is "hell" to pay.

"Do not be afraid. God has come to test you, so that the fear of God will be with you to keep you from sinning." (Exodus 20:20) That fear kept me on my father's good side. It kept me in favor of him and resulted in more love from him. The same is true with God...obey and then reap the rewards.

June 1

"Now this is what the LORD Almighty says: 'Give careful thought to your ways. You have planted much, but have harvested little. You eat, but never have enough. You drink, but never have your fill. You put on clothes, but are not warm. You earn wages, only to put them in a purse with holes in it.'" (Haggai 1:5-6)

My 52 inch big screen TV is starting to show signs of wear. It appears that it is developing what looks like a wrinkle. One of them goes about a third of the way across the screen.

My wife and I were talking and I told her I thought we needed a new one. I have seen ones in the store that go up to 80 inches. So, naturally, as people often do, we want new, bigger and better. I told her I wanted a bigger TV. She tells me we are fine with buying a new one the same size. In reality, for our purposes, we are fine with the one we have and saving our money until this one gets to the point where it is of no use.

We all too often want more, bigger, and newer, when the reality is, what we have is suitable for our needs. We just don't seem to be happy with what we have and want more. Nothing seems to satisfy us these days. A look at the commercials or a walk through a store tells the story of today's society. Material things hold our priorities in life. We seem to work, or go in debt to buy the next great thing.

The people of Israel did just this. They were to rebuild the temple but when the going got tough, they stopped. Instead they began to build their own homes to the point that their homes were greater than the house of God. Boy, doesn't that sound much like our world today. But God has different plans for us and our priorities.

You see, we were created to fellowship with God, not the world. God wants our attention, not the TV, not the club, not the latest movie; He wants us to put Him first. And when we don't, well the things we focus on never seem to be good enough. Do you realize that the new Star Wars movie has made 1 billion dollars, while people in our country, in our neighborhoods starve? Where are our priorities?

God says *"Give careful thought to your ways."* Ever wonder why you always feel hungry? Ever wonder why that car, bike, TV never seems to be enough? Maybe it is because we are focused on the wrong thing.

June 2

"This is what the LORD Almighty says: 'Give careful thought to your ways.'"
(Haggai 1:7)

I recently made the decision to retire from my secular job. It was a tough decision until I thought of it this way, "When is enough, enough?" I have been blessed with a nice home, enough money to be debt free and enough savings to live comfortably the rest of my life. So why wait? I have my health, my wife, family and all the things God has blessed me with, and so enough is enough.

I know God wanted me to focus more on Him, so work had to go. I know God wants me to enjoy the things He provided, so I am satisfied to follow His lead. I don't need the newest phone or gadget to make me happy. No, I need the love of God, the love of my family and the peace that brings.

If you read the book of Haggai (it's only 2 chapters), the first thing you will see is God's warning to set the right priorities. Our focus verse makes it clear that God wants us to give careful thought as to what is important.

The people were living in riches while the temple laid in ruin. God suffered while man prospered. Is that right? No!

But then you will see that when the people put God first, He blessed them. When we put God first, that means tithing to Him instead of buying the new TV, worshipping Him instead of the game or the club, going to His house instead of wherever it is that you go on Sunday, He is pleased with you and your life will be blessed.

So be challenged to *"Give careful thought to your ways"*, and ask yourself, are they His ways? Try living like God wants you to live and I believe you will find a much better life.

June 3

"And you also are among those who are called to belong to Jesus Christ."
(Romans 1:6)

Jeremy Camp sings a song entitled "Give Me Jesus". The lyrics are simple, yet they deliver a lot of power. *"In the morning, when I rise give me Jesus. You can have all this world, just give me Jesus. When I am alone, give me Jesus. When I come to die, give me Jesus."*

This song speaks about the importance we must put on Jesus. When we wake up in the morning, before we face even that first cup of coffee, we must make a choice as to what we put our faith and trust in. Everyone will believe in something, but not everything is worth believing in. I choose to put mine in Jesus. I know He will help me face the day and the things thrown at me. Every decision, thought and choice I make, I make it with Jesus on my mind.

When faced with the things of this world, do we value them for their temporary pleasures, or do we focus on the promises of Jesus for our eternity? Our daily lives should reflect that in which is important to us, and for me, it is Jesus and His eternal promises. The eternal far outweighs the temporary, so I make decisions that lead me to that future.

Often, even in a world filled with so many distractions, we can feel like we are all alone. The world just seems to pass us by. But when we choose to focus on Jesus, we are never alone. He walks with us, talks with us and even carries us from time to time. But unless we choose to follow Him, we can be alone in a dark world.

So for me, if I were to die right now, I want to go to Heaven to spend eternity. And the only way to do that is through Jesus. So each day I choose to follow Him, with everything in me. So, no matter what, "give me Jesus" is on my breathe today, and every day.

155

June 4

"Taking the five loaves and the two fish and looking up to heaven, he gave thanks and broke the loaves. Then he gave them to his disciples..." (Mark 6:41)

When I was growing up there was always food on the table. We were dirt poor, but we always had enough to eat. In fact, whenever someone would visit the first thing offered was something to eat. It is what people did, and most still do.

Food is a focal point in nearly every household in America. It is not only a source of nourishment, but it is where people can gather and enjoy each other's company.

There are numerous places in the book of Mark where Jesus gave thanks for the food prior to distributing it to His disciples. One example is our focus verse. Jesus knew the importance not only of nourishment, but giving thanks to the one who provides, God.

We too must realize that the food we have is from the Father and we must give thanks for what He allows us to have. We must also realize that ALL we have is from the Father and give Him thanks, because without Him, we would have nothing.

Most of us thank God for the food that sustains us. But we should also give Him thanks for the "Bread of Life" that sustains our soul. I thank God for my life as it is now that He is in it. His "Bread" has made me grow to be the person I now am.

What about you? Are you growing in faith, belief and knowledge of God? I bet if the answer is yes, it's because you too are eating of that "bread". So share the "bread" with someone today, help them grow in Christ as you have.

June 5

"Jesus asked 'How many loaves do you have?'" (Mark 6:38)

In our focus verse, the Apostles were concerned about how to feed the crowd. It would require much more than they had. Jesus wanted to know how much they had, and then He did the impossible.

It is common for us to focus on what we lack. We usually zero in on the downside and try to figure out what to do about it. We ignore what we have and focus on what we lack. Our dissatisfaction and wants loom larger to us than what God has already provided.

Jesus did not look at His circumstances this way. He didn't teach His disciples to do so either. He knew what He had already been given and He knew the God who promised to supply all our needs. When faced with five thousand hungry men and their families, Jesus counted a small handful of fish and bread and gave thanks. He took what they had and looked to heaven and instead of focusing on the hungry people; He focused on God and gave thanks for what they had. It wasn't much, but it was what God had provided. And God never falls short in meeting a need.

Could we be missing out on God's supply because we focus so much on the need and so little on what God has already given us? Jesus teaches a lesson in praying for provision, and God provided enough. Resources are never insufficient when God is involved. So give thanks for what you have been given. Just as the five thousand ate and were satisfied, you too can be satisfied with what God provides.

"He who can give thanks for a little will always find he has enough." Anonymous

157

June 6

"If you love me, you will obey what I command. And I will ask the Father, and he will give you another Counselor to be with you forever... for he lives with you and will be in you." (John 14:15-17)

A Vivofit™ is a gadget that tracks movement, sleep, calories and activity. If you don't move enough you get an in indication that it's time to get moving. It is designed to encourage you to stay active.

What if there was a Godofit? It would track our movements towards God, our daily amount of rest with our Lord, our diet of spiritual matters and our activity for His kingdom? Can you imagine how useful that would be? Can you imagine what yours would reveal to you?

If it recorded the time spent reading His word, would it be enough? If it recorded your activity level towards being *"holy, because I am holy"* (Lev 11:44) what would it tell you? What about prayer, resting and listening to God, consumption of the scriptures? If there were such a thing, would God be pleased with your progress?

We don't think there is such a device, but is there? Do you at times feel distant from God? Do you feel like He is nowhere to be found? He hasn't moved, so maybe we need to move towards Him. Maybe your Godofit is indicating in the red, saying it is time to get moving. Feel empty inside? Maybe your Godofit is telling you that you need *"bread of life."* (John 6:35) Maybe your device is telling you that your diet is lacking the things of God, the things God uses to nourish us, replenish us and to make us stronger in Him.

Such a device doesn't exist as far as something to wear, but each of us who profess a belief in Christ has something to remind us of God. The Holy Spirit resides in us and as our focus verse tells us, the Holy Spirit *"will be in you."* The Holy Spirit will remind you of the need to be filled, to rest, to consume and to move closer to God, we just have to be willing. You see, I can wear this gadget all day long, but if I don't pay attention to it, what good is it?

We can have the Holy Spirit living within us, but if we pay no attention to it, will it stay? So I ask you today, what is your Godofit telling you? Do your daily habits, diet, etc. need to change to get healthy in Christ? Is it time to get moving? I recommend you stop what you are doing and consult your personal trainer who lives within, the Holy Spirit, and get started on a more fit, healthier, Godly you.

June 7

"Blessed rather are those who hear the word of God and obey it." (Luke 11:28)

As a little boy, I knew right from wrong, yet at times I did what I knew I shouldn't do. There were times when my dad would tell me not to do something and I would do it anyway. I can tell you I lived in the age of the belt and when I did what I wasn't supposed to do, I paid the price. There was no "time out" in my youth; I received punishment for doing what I knew not to do.

Our culture today seems to think that doing right or wrong is negotiable. A commercial shows a little boy sitting on Santa's lap and he is asked if he has been naughty or nice. The little boy asks Santa to explain "naughty".

Want another example? A college football "star" has been caught twice speeding excessively. Why? He knows speeding is wrong, he knows he is going to get caught, but he continues to do so. He even posed with the police officers who stopped him. The worst part is most people laugh it off, just as he did. Doing wrong or living contrary to the hard right over the easy wrong is common in our society and thought of as the new norm.

The human heart reveals who the master is by our obedience. Those of us who profess to believe in God should know that we are "blessed" when we do right. Jesus tells us in our passage that true blessedness is a matter of obeying the Word of God. We must choose to live by His standards, never compromising what we know to be right.

Living a life pleasing to God means we won't fit into this world. We are to live in this world, but not be "of this world". By professing Christ as our Lord and Savior, and living our life the right way, we will stand out, but we will be blessed.

I remember those times my dad took the belt to me for being disobedient. I know he loved me and didn't like to beat me, but he used those times to teach me a valuable lesson. I learned right from wrong and I learned there are consequences for our actions. The wrath of my dad was bad enough when I disobeyed; I can't even begin to imagine the wrath of God for disobedience. So I choose to live according to His ways, because I don't even want to envision God's belt....

June 8

"Enter through the narrow gate. For wide is the gate and broad is the road that leads to destruction, and many enter through it. But small is the gate and narrow the road that leads to life, and only a few find it." (Matthew 7:13-14)

I don't think I've ever been on a motorcycle trip that I haven't found myself on the wrong road and had to make either a U-turn or change my course. For me, this makes the trip more memorable and over the years I have many stories of these wrong directions and turn a rounds. To me they are a part of the journey and they make life on the road interesting.

There is a difference between being on the wrong road on a motorcycle trip and in real life. On the road trip it makes for interesting stories and memories, in real life it is the difference between winding up where you want to be verses where you do not want to be. In a Christian walk, it is the difference between heaven and hell, plain and simple.

Jesus warns us that the correct way to eternal life in heaven is narrow and difficult. Those who faithfully follow His teachings and stay on that path find the abundant and eternal life He promises. On the other hand, the wide gate, the life of self-indulgence, pleasure and total disregard to His teachings, leads to destruction.

How many people today assume they are saved and on the right path, when in fact they are going the wrong way and heading for that wide gate? How many profess to be Christians when in fact they treat Jesus' teachings lightly. How many think they will one day arrive in heaven when all along they were traveling in the wrong direction and failed to turn around? I have to admit, I was on the wrong road at one point in my life. I was traveling straight to hell, but thanks be to God, I turned around and am now on the right path.

The good news is if one finds themselves going the wrong way, they have the choice to turn around and get back on the right path. When one realizes they are on the wrong road and makes the necessary changes to their course, they too can enter that narrow gate, the one that leads straight to Jesus. The bible tells us how to live, tells us what road we need to be on, and gives us the course to follow. We merely have to follow that course and turn towards God.

June 9

"Do you want to get well?" (John 5:6)

I didn't put on 20 extra pounds overnight. It was a gradual thing. I enjoy food and often eat because it tasted good. I didn't think anything was wrong with a few extra pounds until the extra weight began to affect my health.

Not everyone who drinks too much wants to stop. Not everyone who does drugs or is living immorally wants to change. Some people are comfortable in their sinful lifestyles. Like me and my eating, they have grown accustomed to behaviors that are actually destructive, both physically and spiritually. So Jesus asks, "Do you want to change your life?"

I wanted to lose weight, so I said yes to change. I found an app for my phone that helps me track my calorie intake in order to reach my weight loss goal. But here is the catch, if I eat it, I must log it. Sounds simple, right?

In order to change, one must be honest. Take the things of God. If we want a better spiritual life, we must be honest about the time we spend in His word, prayer and worship. If we want to get rid of some sin, God can give us the strength to overcome those urges and desires. He, like the app, can be our accountability. In order to lose it, we must acknowledge it.

If we are honest with God and listen to His advice, He can make us a different person. But the key is to be truthful. Own up to the things you do and strive to make better choices. With God's help you can lose whatever it is that is causing you harm. It works...

June 10

"...love their wives as Christ loved the church and gave himself up for her."
(Ephesians 5:25)

Growing up in a dirt poor home had its challenges. It often looked as if there wasn't enough food to go around. My father always ate last. He put his kids first and, believe it or not, there was always enough to go around.

Putting others first is a novel thing these days. Everyone wants to be first. It is a selfish world we live in. My father's approach to being last taught me valuable lessons as I grew older. I have carried that lesson over into my marriage as well. Ask both my wife and I why we have a strong marriage, and we'll both tell you it's because we put the other first. My wife is the most important person alive and she will always be first. I live to make her happy, that is why I married her.

Marriage is about making your spouse happy and living your life to please them. It isn't about some false feelings or about making yourself happy, it's about them. In Ephesians 5: 21–33 the bible gives us some simple instructions to make a happy marriage. First, both husband and wife must *"submit to one another"*. When you put the other first, you both become first. No one in a marriage is more important than the other.

Then we read about the wife having to *"submit to her husband"*. This doesn't mean she is a door mat, but that she knows and expects him to be the leader of the household and the spiritual head. Believe me when I tell you, men, step up and be a man and your wife won't object to being the wife she is called to be.

Lastly, our focus verse tells us that men are to love their wives, and children, as Jesus loved the church (us). We are to place her/their needs above ours, live our daily life to provide for her/them, care for her/them and show her/them we love them.

Marriage is a partnership and both parties must work at it. It is not about you, it's about the other person. Jesus said to put others first. He meant that in marriage also. When a husband and wife practice these principles, their marriage, their home and their life will be what they expected on their wedding day. So, practice what my father taught (both my Heavenly Father and my earthly father); put your spouse first and see what happens. I promise you, you won't regret it.

June 11

"Now faith is confidence in what we hope for and assurance about what we do not see." (Hebrews 11:1)

When reading the Old Testament we read about mighty acts of faith. Some of these acts of faith seem unbelievable, if not impossible. But if we believe the bible to be true and the Word of God, we must have faith in the things we read. The writer of Hebrews gives us a clear picture of faith in action as told in the Old Testament.

By faith, we understand that God created everything. By faith we believe that Noah built an ark even though he didn't know about rain. By faith Abraham and Sarah became the parents of a nation even though they were near 100 years of age. By faith Abraham, when tested by God, offered Isaac as a sacrifice out of an act of worship. By faith Moses, though unqualified to lead, led the Israelites out of captivity. By faith, the people of Israel crossed the Red Sea on dry land.

The promises of Jesus in the New Testament teach us that because He came, died, was buried and rose from the grave, we too have power to overcome the impossible, live victorious lives and do extraordinary things. When stories are written or told of our lives, they could seem unbelievable or impossible, but true. By living a life of faith, we too can be the saints others will remember.

We also have resurrection power. Graves cannot contain those that have faith in the promises of Jesus. When we have faith in Jesus and live a life as fully devoted followers, *"we too will be caught up together with them in the clouds to meet the Lord in the air. And so we will be with the Lord forever."* (1 Thessalonians 4:17) One day, we will all enjoy the perfection of the resurrection glory. By living a life of faith, we can live in full glory of the cross. So, how is your faith?

June 12

"You must be on your guard" (Mark 13:9)

With 20 years of military service under my belt I can say that the one job soldiers don't like, but is one of the most important jobs, is guard duty. You have to sit or lay for hours, being still, quiet, alert, while watching and keeping an eye out for the enemy. It is a job that has to be taken seriously, one that needs 100% of your attention. The last thing you want is for the enemy to gain access and cause you harm.

In our lives today, we must take "guard duty" just as serious. The enemy is out there, ready to enter in and cause harm to you and your family. He lies in wait, looking for an opportunity, waiting for you to nod off, get distracted and allow him in.

You may ask yourself, what enemy, I'm not in a combat zone, I'm not at war. Oh, but we are at war every day, at war with Satan and he is waiting for just the right time to enter in and cause you great harm, eternal harm. He wants to catch you with your guard down, asleep at your post.

Jesus tells us in our focus verse to be on guard. He is warning us of the evils of this world that want to destroy us. The enemy is waiting and he will come in if we let him. If we aren't on guard, he will cause us great harm.

Jesus is also telling us in Mark 13 to be ready for His return. He isn't repeating Himself; He is telling us to be ready because it is very important to prepare ourselves for His coming. He wants our constant attention and for us to be ready for the day He comes and ends the battle.

We must be on guard against the enemy and on watch for Christ's return. We must live as those in a war zone, ready for anything and constantly on guard duty. If we are, the enemy can't strike and we will be ready for the day that Christ comes to take us to heaven. Take guard duty serious; be prepared for the battle, while standing ready for Christ's return.

June 13

"What can I do with you, Ephraim? What can I do with you, Judah? Your love is like the morning mist, like the early dew that disappears." (Hosea 6:4)

Commitment is defined as: *an absolute dedication and faithfulness to someone or something.* It's something we all claim to have, yet very few demonstrate. Many claim to have a strong commitment to the local church, but they rarely attend. Wedding vows, which include promises of commitment, are so easily broken. Nothing is as distressing to God as a half committed Christian.

The purpose of Hosea's prophecy was to provide Israel with a real-life example of her spiritual idolatry. The lack of commitment to him by his wife and her infidelity was but a minute calamity when compared with the spiritual infidelity of Israel and their lack of commitment to God. Hosea called Israel to national repentance much as he pleaded with his adulterous wife for personal repentance. Israel's commitment to God was shallow at best. God is never pleased with such a halfhearted commitment and a complacent attitude toward Him.

There is a tiny harbor town on the ocean shore where many ships hit the rocks during bad weather. This well-known town had a dedicated rescue team which aided mariners in distress. They rallied to the siren and rushed to the scene of the accident. They risked life and limb to save the sailors. The citizens raised money and built a rescue station close to the shore. Through the years the rescue station became a social club, where people gathered to have fun and relax. Ships would still crash upon the rocks; the alarm would still sound; but eventually no one responded. They didn't want to leave their comforts; their commitment to rescue was no match for their complacency.

There are many today who have a halfhearted attitude toward God. To some, Christianity has been reduced to a mere "country-club atmosphere," basking in the goodness of God yet unconcerned about commitment to the Father or the rescue of those who are perishing.

We can almost hear Hosea saying, *"Your goodness is as a morning cloud, and as the early dew it goeth away."* The fleeting goodness of uncommitted Christians is not goodness at all. It is just a temporary rest stop on the highway to complacency. Isn't it time to get off that road and back to God?

June 14

"Whoever sows sparingly will also reap sparingly, and whoever sows generously will also reap generously" (2 Corinthians 9:6)

My dad was a farmer. He would prepare his land well in advance of the growing season, watch weather patterns and study his seeds, all in anticipation for a good crop. He would plant the seeds, water the land, keep the weeds pulled and tend the soil to promote growth, all in anticipation of the harvest that would come. His attention to detail and dedication to his planting always resulted in a bumper crop come harvest time. He always got more out of his garden than he put into it. He would not only feed us daily off this crop, but would provide vegetables to his neighbors.

My dad knew that a good crop provided not only for our immediate physical needs in the form of a harvest of crops for his daily use but also for his future needs in the form of seed for next year's planting. The general principle was the more he planted and harvested, the more he was able to use and give away.

We can learn a lot from a farmer when it comes to sowing and harvesting. Preparation, determination, patience and study leads to a harvest that makes all the work worthwhile. We can also learn that the more we plant and the more we harvest, the more we have and the more we are able to give.

The bible gives us a clear lesson on reaping what we sow. This sowing and the harvest that comes from the planting are greater than vegetables and potatoes; it is souls for the kingdom. We harvest in proportion to our planting.

In order to sow we must trust in God for the seeds and in order to reap we must sow the seeds He gives us. As a Christian we have an obligation to sow the seeds, water them and wait for the harvest.

Are you a worker in the Lord's harvest field? Are you planting seeds in the form of the gospel? If not, take a lesson from a farmer's son, get God's seeds in fertile grown, tend the garden and then wait for the harvest.

June 15

"When Peter saw this, he said to them: "Men of Israel, why does this surprise you? Why do you stare at us as if by our own power or godliness we had made this man walk?" "By faith in the name of Jesus, this man whom you see and know was made strong. It is Jesus' name and the faith that comes through him that has given this complete healing to him, as you can all see." (Acts 3:12; 16)

We took the training wheels off, I grabbed the seat and off we went. As long as I held on, he was great. I kept telling him to pedal, don't look back, as I ran behind him. There came a time when I felt it was just right so I told him to pedal fast, look straight ahead, keep pedaling, as I let go of the seat. I kept repeating this as he got farther and farther away. It took him a while to realize he was doing it alone, and his sense of accomplishment was all over his face. He couldn't wait to tell all his friends that his daddy had taught him how to ride a big boy bike.

Jesus told His disciples over and over that they could do the things He had told them they could. He told them that by the power of God, they could drive out demons and heal the sick, but they didn't believe Him, or because He was with them, they didn't need to. Once a man brought his demon possessed boy to the disciples to cast it out but they were unable to do so. Jesus, frustrated at their inability, cast the demon out Himself. (Luke 9:37-42)

Then things changed. Jesus' talk about going away came true. The disciples were left alone. While they waited in the upper room, they were filled with the Holy Spirit. Suddenly they were empowered to do the things Jesus had told them all along. They preached and thousands came to believe. They spoke in foreign languages and people heard. They came upon a crippled beggar and healed Him.

I bet the disciples were excited. They had received the Holy Spirit and the things Jesus had told them they could do was happening. When confronted as to how, they couldn't wait to tell who taught them to do these things. Our focus verses above tell us that the disciples gave credit to Jesus for the healing. They took no credit, they were taught and empowered by Jesus and to Him all the glory goes.

What are we doing with the power of the Holy Spirit? Have we realized that Jesus expects us to keep going and do the things He wants us to do? Do you believe you have the power to cast out demons, heal the sick, and overcome evil?

June 16

"I have been crucified with Christ and I no longer live, but Christ lives in me." (Galatians 2:20)

As a pastor, I am often faced with things that I never thought I would ever have to face. I have been weighed down by the pain and suffering of others, not always sure how to handle it, what to say or what to do. I have felt inadequate, ill equipped and ill prepared for the role in which I have been placed. I have been focusing on these things to the point of carrying them as burdens.

As I rode my motorcycle, God spoke to me through song. God reminded me that He is in charge, He is in control and He strengthens and equips me for His service. The songs "Redeemed" by Big Daddy Weave and "Give Me Your Eyes" by Brandon Heath spoke words of truth to me and it was as if God was speaking instead.

I was reminded that I am not capable, but He is. God is in me and He works through me. Scripture reminds me that *"...in all things God works for the good of those who love Him, who have been called according to His purpose."* (Romans 8:28) I know I am called, so I am assured He will work it out.

As Christians, we are called to see people as God does. Once we are redeemed, we are called to love others and share their pain. We are called to a life of compassion and concern, even if it means sharing their burdens. That is when I started thanking God for allowing me to serve Him and others. I thank God for filling me with His Holy Spirit. I look forward to being what He wants me to be, in spite of my inadequacies. I am nothing, but He is everything.

June 17

"Some time later God tested Abraham. He said to him, 'Abraham!' 'Here I am,' he replied." (Genesis 22:1)

When my son was very little, he and I liked to play hide and seek. I would cover my eyes and tell him to go hide. I would count, then uncover and shout "Where is Bryan?" He would jump out from where he was and say "here I am." He hadn't fully grasped the concept of him hiding and me finding. He wanted me to know where he was. Over the years he has grown into a fine young man and to this day he always wants his father to know where he is.

While studying Genesis 22, I came across someone else that was quick to say *"here I am."* I read and find out that several times God spoke to Abraham and Abraham's response was *"here I am."* Not only was he quick to respond, I read how obedient he was to what God told him to do. God told him to take his son, the son God promised him, the son born to him at the age of 100 and sacrifice him to God. Abraham was willing and would have gone through with it if God wouldn't have stopped him in the nick of time.

Then I read the book of Jonah and see just the opposite. God called Jonah and told him what He wanted him to do. Instead of Jonah saying *"here I am",* Jonah went in the opposite direction. By failing to respond in a positive way, he was on a ship about to be shipwrecked, thrown overboard, swallowed by a giant fish and then thrown up after three days. Only then did Jonah do what God told him to do. Reluctantly, he spread the news of God throughout Nineveh. Jonah 4 tells us that he was angry with God for saving this town Jonah hated so much. The bad luck continued for Jonah. Go head, read the ending for yourself.

As I look at the contrast of these two stories I have to ask myself, which one am I? Do I respond immediately to God, obey what He tells me and then have Him provide a way out of a unpleasant situation? Or am I like Jonah, running from God and only obey in order to escape the pain, suffering and then once again turn my back to God and complain? I pray I am more like Abraham and try to live my in obedience to God. How about you? Could life be better? Could you use some relief? The next time you hear God calling, try saying *"here I am"* and see what happens.

June 18

"Repent, then, and turn to God, so that your sins may be wiped out, that times of refreshing may come from the Lord..." (Acts 3:19)

Is life hard? Are you having problems with your family, lost your job, not sure where you are going to get the money to pay your bills? We all have problems and we all think we are the only ones that are suffering. Some of us have no idea where to turn. We have no idea who to talk to or who we can take our problems to. Who will understand what we are going through? When life gets out of control there is someone that you can talk to. There is someone that can help and knows just what you are going through because He has been there.

Jesus can help. While Jesus walked this earth He suffered from the same things most of us suffer from and even suffered things that we will never face. Think about this: Jesus was from a questionable family line, He was poor, a blue collar worker, struggled to make ends meet. He got tired. He was tempted. He suffered from family tension. He was falsely accused. He was a very busy man; too busy of a schedule, too many demands on His time. He often needed to get away. He had leadership problems. He had employee and friend problems. His friends let Him down. He got hungry. He got angry. He wept. He was radical and misunderstood. He had responsibilities. He was afraid. He was hated. He was ridiculed. He was rejected. He was alone. He was penniless. He was thirsty. He was arrested. He was beaten. He was hung on a cross to die. He was sacrificed for many.

Any of these things sound familiar? Whatever you are facing, you are not alone. He knows how you feel. Jesus is able to understand, comfort your cries, and show you hope when things look bleak.

He is able to do this because He has been there! When we turn to Jesus for help, He runs to help us. Why does He do this? He knows how we feel, because He's been there.

So turn to someone that has been there and knows how you feel, who has walked in your shoes and overcame it all. Turn to Jesus for help because He's been there!

June 19

"What do you want me to do for you?" (Luke 18:41)

"I'll pray for you." How many times have we said this? These four words are good, biblically sound words, but I wonder how many people think in their mind "really? Will you?" How often do people hear those words and think it is just another way of saying, "I want this conversation to end." Are these four words enough?

What would happen if we used another four word phrase instead or along with the first? What would happen if we did as Jesus did and asked "How can I help?" When Jesus was confronted by a blind man in our focus verse, He asked "how can I help?" He wanted to do more than give lip service to this man's need. He wanted to help meet his need. And shouldn't that be our desire as well?

Isn't that what we are called to do? Aren't we, as Christ followers, called to do as Jesus did? We are to be His hands and feet, therefore we are to help others who are in need. I think prayer is great and a much needed discipline, but I also think we all need to do more. Jesus tells us we are to be like Him. I can't recall a single time in scripture in which Jesus merely used the words, "I'll pray for you", and leave it at that. No, Jesus listened, had compassion and acted. So, shouldn't we?

What would happen if we, as believers, actually asked "How can I help?" and did something to meet the needs of others? I think we could end up doing exactly what Jesus meant by *"greater things"* and not because of what we do, but *"because the one who is in you is greater..."* and works through you.

So the next time you talk to someone with a need, ask them how you can help. You may be surprised that it really isn't much more than an attentive ear, a little compassion, or a helping hand. A word of caution; be sincere and be prepared to actually do something. When we put Jesus' examples to work we will find out that not only do we bless others, but we receive a blessing as well.

171

June 20

"I tell you the truth, if you have faith as small as a mustard seed, you can say to this mountain, Move from here to there and it will move." (Matthew 17:20)

How much faith does it take to move a mountain? How much faith does it take to receive a healing? How much faith does it take to see a problem correct itself? It may be smaller than you think.

In Matthew 14 Jesus is preaching to a large crowd and as evening approached the disciples told Him that He should send the people away to get food because they didn't have enough to feed them. Jesus tells His disciples to provide for them. The disciples could only muster five loaves of bread and two fish, not enough for so many people. Surely Jesus was joking.

The disciples saw the problem as much bigger than they could provide for, Jesus telling them to use what they have, do something about the situation and feed the masses. The disciples forgot who they were with; they were with Jesus, the Christ, the provider. He is gently reminding them to have faith and see what happens.

Our focus verse tells us that we don't need large qualities of faith; He says we need just a little faith, but we must have faith. Jesus is waiting for us to do something, even offer meager loaves of bread and a few fish, even a small drop of faith no bigger than the head of a pin, anything to show we have faith that by us acting, He will provide.

Many places in scripture we read about small amounts of faith and the mighty miracles because of that faith. None of these people had great amounts of faith, they simply had faith. They believed Jesus was who He said He was and could do what He said He could do. They believed in His power to overcome.

Remember that every miracle began with an act of faith, a moment in time where they stepped out on a limb and trusted Christ to be who He said He was. So, what is in your way of being all God wants you to be? What problem is facing you? What mountain needs moved? Christ is there to provide for you, all you need is a little faith.

June 21

"And I pray that you, being rooted and established in love, may have power, together with all the saints, to grasp how wide and long and high and deep is the love of Christ, and to know this love that surpasses knowledge—that you may be filled to the measure of all the fullness of God." (Eph. 3:17-19)

Do you know how to remove air from a cup? You could get a vacuum and try to suck out all of the air, but you could end up destroying the cup. There is a much simpler way; you just fill the cup with any liquid. It's the same with getting sin out of your life.

Much of our walk is about trying to remove sins, habits, attitudes, and activities of sin from our lives. That's good, but it's not enough. We're trying to "remove the air from the cup." When we try to remove a sin, something else will come in. When we try to stop thinking angry and bitter thoughts or try not to worry, it comes back as a vacuum.

The key is in God! Whatever has to leave your life, don't focus on it. The focus isn't the sin. How did God remove sin from this world? Jesus did it by coming in, by bringing in His presence, He would push out sin; He would take it away. So, to take away sin from your life, fill it up with the presence of God. Like that cup, fill it up with His peace, His joy, His blessings, and His spirit. Get God into everything and sin will get out of everything. It is as simple as pouring water into a cup.

Today's mission: Fill up your day with the good things of God: His peace, His joy. His blessing, and His Spirit, until your cup overflows and there's no room for sin.

173

June 22

"Seek first His kingdom and His righteousness and all these things will be given to you as well." (Matthew 6:33)

God calls us to seek Him, to set our hearts on Him and deny ourselves of other loves. Self must die, possessions must be left and His kingdom must be chosen. It's all about the direction of our heart. Which way does yours point?

Many of our goals are easily recognized, like money, power and pleasure. Others may be more subtle like insincere worship and lukewarm living. Failure lies in making wrong choices. Wrong choices are the result of hearts pointed in the wrong direction.

Our heart points us to what is important in life. Our interests occupy our thoughts and our actions are what are really important to us. Do you believe that? Here is a test to see what is important to you. What is it you think about? Your schedule and your checkbook may indicate your priorities in life, but the better indicator is what do you think about. What fills your mind when you lie down at night, when you wake up in the morning, when you day dream in the middle of the day? If you detect a theme, know that this is where your heart lies.

If you want the forgiveness, the mercy and the blessings God offers, take this test and determine to make God the choice of your affection and your heart. Be careful of what you seek first.

June 23

"Brothers and sisters, I do not consider myself yet to have taken hold of it. But one thing I do: Forgetting what is behind and straining toward what is ahead, I press on toward the goal to win the prize for which God has called me heavenward in Christ Jesus." (Philippians 3:13-14)

A few years ago a friend and I took a motorcycle trip to Gaithersburg, MD. We were going on a business trip and decided to make it a pleasure trip as well. We left early one morning expecting a good ride. Little did we know what we would run into that day. As we rode, it started to rain and the further north we went, the harder it rained. We stopped and did a little checking, only to find out we were riding in the beginning stages of Hurricane Frances. We had two choices to make, stop and ride the storm out or keeping going and get out of its path. We decided to keep going and we rode out of the rain as we crossed into Virginia.

Sometimes we are faced with storms and we feel they are pounding down on us, flooding our life with turmoil and destruction. They can be overwhelming and make us feel like we are doomed. When we find ourselves in those situations, we have a choice to make, just as my friend and I did. We can ride the storm out where we are, or we can keep moving and get beyond that storm.

Paul gives us some good advice on how to face troubles and storms. Philippians 3 tells us to "press on" and get beyond them. The advice is not to stay in them, get out of them. The best defense is an offense.

We aren't to live trying to maintain our ground as the world, the storms of life and Satan attack. If you do, you will always be living on the defense and you will find yourself up against a wall. Instead, we are to live on the spiritual offensive. Always pressing forward, and taking new ground. When we stay on the offensive and move beyond the storms of life, we put the enemy on defense and he flees.

So, is there an area in your life where you feel the storm is too great and you are in the defensive posture, just trying to get by? Turn that around, press closer to Jesus, and take the offensive posture. With His help you can press on and defeat the enemy. You will always end up on dry ground and victorious.

June 24

"For I have not come to call the righteous, but sinners." (Matthew 9:13)

I've been around bikers most of my adult life. I've ridden since I was a teenager and have logged plenty of miles. I have ridden in all types of weather with all kinds of people. I've owned a variety of different makes and models of bikes. I prefer leather and denim over anything thing else. And as long as I can remember, there has always been the discussion among bikers, who is a "real" biker and who isn't.

I have been doing outreach ministry for 14 years and have heard the same discussion about the church. Just who are the "real" Christians and who aren't. If I have heard it once, I have heard it a hundred times, "I don't go to church because it's full of hypocrites." Well, I agree, the church is full of hypocrites, but I want to remind you, Jesus said that is who He came for. So with that said, isn't the church for the hypocrites?

Jesus tells us a parable in Matthew 13:24-30 about a man who sowed wheat seed in his field. Sometime during the night his enemy sowed tares among the good wheat seeds. Tares are small plants that look like wheat but don't produce grain. They are weeds disguised as wheat.

Jesus had a traitor disguised as a disciple among Him while He walked the face of the earth. Judas Iscariot was handpicked by Jesus yet turned out to be a hypocrite. He looked and acted like one of the disciples until the moment in time when he revealed his true colors. So hypocrites are nothing new. There always will be tares among the wheat.

It is true; hypocrites are among the Christians in the church. They may look and act like the real thing, but they will never bear fruit and sooner or later their true identity will be revealed.

It is Jesus' job to sort out the real from the fake. It is our job to grow to be the real thing. The fake will be burned and the real will get their reward in heaven. And, if you aren't in the field, then how can you grow? So by not going to church or being a part of the body of Christ because of the hypocrites is like my daddy used to say, "Like cutting your nose off to spite your face." And who knows, by you growing alongside one of those hypocrites, they just might sprout grain and produce a crop of their own.

June 25

"Not only that—count yourselves blessed every time people put you down or throw you out or speak lies about you to discredit me. What it means is that the truth is too close for comfort and they are uncomfortable" (Matthew 5:11 MSG)

Have you ever felt like saying, I am done with this! I am tired of being treated wrong and never being able to please people. So from this point on, I quit!

Life can be difficult. When things go wrong, when people hurt or disappoint us, often our first response is to just give up. Living a life as a Christ follower can be hard, some expect too much of you, others ridicule you. Because of how you live your life, people hold you to a higher standard than they even hold themselves. I, for one, have felt like quitting on numerous occasions. I get tired of the grind and sometimes just want to throw in the towel.

But then I read our focus verse and I am reminded to hang in there. It tells me that when I face these things to go on, and in fact, to expect it. The gospel makes some uncomfortable, yet Jesus is pleased.

The Lord knew that His true followers would be mistreated because of their association with and loyalty to Him. But Jesus said to suffer for His sake is a privilege that should give us joy. He tells us that a great reward awaits those who withstand the trials, the hardships and the persecution. But I, for one, find it hard at times to follow this teaching. I get beat down and want to quit.

When things get tough, people tend to fall away. The disciples did. In John 6, we read that when Jesus' teaching got hard, many turned away from Jesus. They couldn't stand the heat, so they quit.

But the words of Peter ring true, *"Lord, to whom shall we go?"* Peter tells us that he and the other twelve had faith in Him and His promise, that Jesus is the only way to eternal life, and to quit meant the alternative. When all else fails, where else is others to go other than Jesus?

So in order to withstand the trials of life, we too must have faith in Jesus and His promises. To do so means we win and we earn that eternal life in heaven. To give in is easy, to stand firm takes a strength we can only draw from Jesus. When we feel like quitting, we must rely on the promise that Jesus will give us strength.

June 26

"The Lord is with you mighty warrior." (Judges 6:12)

When it came time to take my son's training wheels off his bike, he was afraid and didn't think he could ride with only two wheels. He protested as I took those little wheels off the sides of the rear tire, asking me if it could wait another day. He didn't have confidence in himself, he didn't think he could handle the task at hand, but as his father I assured him I would not leave his side. I promised I would guide him along and be there if he needed me.

As he took that first try, I ran alongside him, reassuring him I was right there with him. He kept asking me not to let go and I assured him I would not until he was ready. As he pedaled, I sensed he was doing what was needed and I released my hand off the bike and off he went. Soon he realized that I was running along beside him, but I wasn't holding on. You could see the excitement in his eyes knowing he was doing it all on his own, but his eyes said he was grateful I was still by his side.

I have been feeling a little overwhelmed lately. My schedule has been crazy, some tasks before me have me feeling ill equipped to handle and I have felt like I am not giving the important things in life as much attention as necessary. This has left me feeling a little alone, afraid and feeling unable to do what I know I am called to do.

This morning, a friend led me to Judges 6. He reminded me that the angel of the Lord came to Gideon while he was feeling afraid. My friend told me to remember that the same Lord who guided Gideon, guides me today. The Lord reminded Gideon that He was the one sending him. The Lord told Gideon to go in the strength he had and that He would be with Him.

When we feel we can't continue, when we are unable to do the things we are being asked to do, we must remember that our Father in heaven is right there alongside us. We can only do what we have the strength to do and then rely on His strength to empower us to do the rest. He won't leave us any more than I would have left my son.

178

June 27

"Later the others also came. 'Sir! Sir!' they said. 'Open the door for us!'
"But he replied, 'I tell you the truth, I don't know you.' "Therefore keep
watch, because you do not know the day or the hour." (Matthew 25:11-13)

When I was young, a friend and I took a few of his dad's cigarettes, went behind the barn and lit up. Everyone smoked, it was the thing to do, so why not? As we smoked, coughed and choked, we thought we were cool. A voice from behind me brought me out of cooldom, (not really a word, but kind of describes me at the time). "Just what do you think you are doing?" It said. The voice of my dad was recognizable, and it brought fear at that moment. He wasn't happy, in fact, I remember it clearly, that voice sounded disappointed.

Well, you can imagine the end of that story. It didn't turn out too good for me and my bottom hurt for a while. But I knew from the moment he spoke the first words, I was in trouble.

Have you ever done anything you knew you weren't supposed to do? Have you ever done anything and in the back of your mind think, "I hope no one sees me"? Or have you ever done something and someone you least expected walked up? What was your reaction when you were caught? Were you embarrassed, or ashamed?

Let me pose it a different way, what if you were doing what you normally did on a Friday or Saturday night and Jesus walked in the room? What would you do if He strolled up to your table and sat down? Would you welcome Him, or would you want to hide under the table.

As Christ followers we are called to live in such a manner as to be ready for Jesus' return. If there are things in our lives that Jesus would not be pleased with, then we should work, with the Holy Spirit's help, to rid our lives of them. Our lives should be "worthy" of our calling.

Our focus verse tells the story of that day when Jesus comes. He will catch some off guard and they will be asking for the door to open up, but He will refuse. In fact He will tell them "I don't know you!" That breaks my heart.

The proof is in scripture, accept the free gift of salvation, turn from your ways, follow, obey and be ready. Then and only then will you enter in. Don't let the Father be disappointed in you and your behavior, turn from the evil ways, and be prepared....

June 28

"...the bread of life. Whoever comes to me will never go hungry" (Matthew 6:35)

I grew up poor. I was the middle child of seven. My father painted houses when there was work and my mother was a stay at home housewife. I remember nights eating a bowl of beans, with more broth than beans, and bread. We always had bread. My mother baked her own bread and there was always a supply to fill our stomachs.

When I grew up, we drank lots of water. Sodas weren't allowed or affordable and milk was a rare commodity. So I guess you can say at times I was raised on bread and water. I survived on my early diet and never once went hungry.

In my morning devotions I came across two passages of scripture where Jesus taught on the importance of bread and water. These teach us that bread and water are essential for life and Jesus provides both for us. They are our basic needs and without them we die.

In John 6 and 7, Jesus tells us that He provides the essentials for life, on earth as well as eternal life. He is the bread of life, necessary for life. And Jesus is the living water that quenches our thirst. He is the living water, necessary for life.

We have the constant need for food and drink. If you don't believe me, go a few hours without drinking or eating. Just as you become physically thirsty and hungry, our souls become spiritually thirsty and hungry as well. To overcome the thirst and hunger, one must eat and drink regularly.

To those who hunger and thirst for the needs He provides, he becomes our source for the essentials that never run out. He provides and fills, but we must receive. As a kid there was no such thing as telling mom I didn't like what was put before me. If I refused to eat, I went hungry. Jesus' conditions for the bread and water of life are basic, we must hunger and thirst, we must come and we must eat and drink. When we do, without reservation, we are filled in abundance.

June 29

"For my thoughts are not your thoughts, neither are your ways my ways," declares the LORD. "As the heavens are higher than the earth, so are my ways higher than your ways and my thoughts than your thoughts." (Isaac 55:8-9)

Years ago I installed a GPS on my bike to help me when I travel. One Friday morning as I loaded up for a trip to Marietta, GA, I keyed the address into my GPS. I noticed that it looked like it was going to take longer than I had thought. As I looked at the turn by turn directions, I didn't like the route it was taking me. So I changed a setting, reloaded the address and checked it again. Once again, I didn't like the results, or the arrival time, so back into the settings I went. I continued to do this until I got the route and arrival time I wanted.

As I rode, I couldn't help but think how common this is to humans. Don't like the direction, change it. Don't like how long it takes, take a short cut. We use GPS's to help us find our way, yet we manipulate them to get the results we want.

The same is true in our walk with God. We ask Him to guide our lives, we ask for direction, but try to change it when it goes against the way we want to go. We ask God for something, but when it takes too long we go on our own way in order to try and get it in our timing.

Our focus verse tells us our ways aren't God's ways and our thoughts aren't His either. God's way is perfect, His timing is perfect, yet may be different than ours. If we truly trust God, we need to let Him lead us no matter what. The quickest way to mess things up is to try to manipulate God in order to get what we want. God's ways are not ours....

Proverbs 8:32 tells us *"Now then my son, listen to me, blessed are those who keep my ways."* If you want to get somewhere in life, listen and follow God. His ways will get us there, in His perfect timing, and on His perfect path.

Lord, help me to trust your way....

181

June 30

"One of them, when he saw he was healed, came back, praising God in a loud voice... Were not all ten cleansed? Where are the other nine?" (Luke 17:15, 17)

I used to collect bottles and exchange them for candy. You used to pay a deposit on bottles and then return them to get your money back. I remember once I wanted a candy bar, but I didn't have enough bottles to pay for it. The man behind the counter let me have it anyway. Later that day I returned with some bottles to pay the man and to my surprise, he gave me a handful of penny candy for being a good boy.

Ten people, exiled from their homes because of a disease, call on Jesus to be healed and they are. No questions asked, no strings attached, they just receive their healing and are told to go to the priests to get a clean bill of health so they can return home.

So why did only one return to Jesus to thank Him? What happened to the other nine? Were they too busy? Didn't it mean as much to them as the one guy? Isn't that a true representation of the world today, to call on Jesus at a time of need, and then go about life as normal, as if nothing ever happened?

What I think is it's about gratitude and true faith. This speaks of changed hearts, not just clean outsides. True praise to God comes when one has been touched by Jesus in such a way that their lives are forever impacted and they can't control themselves from coming back and throwing themselves at Jesus' feet and thanking Him.

I often wonder about the meaning of Jesus' words *"Rise and go; your faith has made you well."* Did He revoke the healing from the other nine? I think not. What I do think is the one guy who came back, received even more from Jesus, much like I did from the guy behind the counter. He received not only the external cleansing, but he received an internal Spiritual cleansing as well. He was washed by Jesus' love, mercy, and grace.

What has Jesus healed you of? How has Jesus impacted your life? Have you thanked Him? Have you praised His name? It is never too late. Take time out today to thank Jesus for all His love, mercy and grace. Thank Him for your life, and thank Him ahead of time for all He will do in the days, weeks, months and years to come.

July 1

"The seed cast in the weeds is the person who hears the kingdom news, but weeds of worry and illusions about getting more and wanting everything under the sun strangle what was heard, and nothing comes of it." (Matthew 13:22)

Take a walk in my yard and you will find weeds among my flowers and hidden in the grass. There are some places where the weeds have totally choked out the grass, resulting in large patches of nothing but weeds. I wondered how long has that been there. I don't remember seeing that happen.

This choking out process happens over time. It's gradual and often goes unnoticed. Kind of like how this world gradually takes over our thoughts, feelings and desires. The things of this world infiltrate and, over time, choke out the things we know to be good.

Weeds hinder the growth of the good things that grow among them. In our spiritual walk we may say "I am a Christian" and perhaps we see some changes in our lives at first. But over the weeks and months slowly something happens. Our focus verse tells us that worry and illusions of more strangle the "good news" until it's nothing. It doesn't happen overnight.

Gradually the things of the world take over. Going to the movies or the lake becomes more important than church and parties more important than prayer or bible study. Things of this world become more important than treasures in heaven.

Are these people really converted or do they merely look as if they were? They were all in, until the weeds choked them out and they bailed, joining the weeds.

How do you know if you are truly saved? How can we tell if those we are close to really are? Time is the best answer, as well as visible results, like producing true fruit in our life. Spiritual fruit will be clear in those who are truly saved.

Ask yourself this, can people hear what you are saying over what you are doing? In other words, does my talk equal my walk? Don't let the weeds of this world choke out the grace and love offered or your eternal reward for living a fruitful life.

July 2

"Do not conform to the pattern of this world, but be transformed by the renewing of your mind." (Romans 12:2)

Ever felt as if you don't fit in? Ever walked into a place and thought you didn't belong? Believe it or not, I have. I've walked into places and immediately felt as if I was an alien in a foreign world. I remember watching old movies and seeing the good guy walk into a saloon and everyone stopped what they were doing, including the piano player. They all turned and looked at him. I have felt like that guy...

When I committed my life fully to Jesus Christ, I knew life would be different. I knew some would not like me, or at least what I represented. I knew that I would be an outcast in a world filled with darkness and evil. But I was determined to live my life as the bible teaches.

What God is doing in my life and in the life of other Christians is pure, beautiful and holy, but don't expect the world to recognize or understand it. It goes against the grain of this world and it can make one feel as if they don't fit in. The life of a Christian will always be different than the world. You will never fit in. But don't let that stop you.

As believers we are to live a life as if we don't belong in this world. We are to be set apart and we are called to be different. Being totally sold out to Jesus and living the Christian life is scandalous in today's world, but we are called to do it anyway.

As Christians we are also commanded to *"Go into all the world and preach the gospel to all creation." (Mark 16:15)* Spreading the gospel is scandalous, but do it anyway. Loving your enemies or those that don't look like, act like or believe as you do is scandalous, but do it anyway. Stepping up and out in faith is scandalous, but do it anyway. The life of a Christian will always be viewed as scandalous, let it be so. Don't fear scandal, embrace the Christian life and live different than the world. Live your life as if you don't fit in.

July 3

"God said, "Let there be light," (Genesis 1:3)

I have a confession. When I was a kid I was afraid of the dark. I remember before going into a room I would reach around the corner as far as I could and find the switch and flip it on before ever looking into that room. We used to have an outhouse and if I had to go late at night, I would turn on my flash light, point it down the hill towards that little building and then run as fast as I could. When I got there I would open up the door and shine my light in before entering. I even looked down that disgusting hole before taking a seat.

Darkness is not a friendly place and God knew this. His very first act of creation was to create light. God brings light out of darkness. This is important and profound because most of us fear the dark. This is true in the since of day and night, but also in good (light) and evil (dark).

The reality of life is that most of us may encounter some darkness in our lives that we may fear or look upon as a negative thing. But according to scripture, if we believe and follow God, we are told to walk in light.

Darkness is the raw material from which miracles come from. If we follow God, He will lead us out of darkness into light. When we walk with God we can say "Let there be light" and He will bring us peace and comfort.

By walking *"in the light of the Lord"* we can never be afraid of the dark again. We have a permanent flashlight that floods the darkness and pushes it away. So no matter what you face, no matter how dark it may seem, God created light to guide your path. Bask in it....

July 4

"Deborah, a prophetess, the wife of Lappidoth, was leading Israel at that time." (Judges 4:4)

I like summer. The grass begins to turn green, the trees bud out and the flowers start to bloom. As all that happens, we start to see bees. They aren't anyone's favorite insect, but they are important to nature. I believe they may even be a little biblical. Bees can teach us a lesson. This may sound crazy so give me a minute to explain.

Research shows that when a certain number of bees are removed from a hive, immediately other bees fill in for them. The remaining bees do the job for the missing ones.

Each bee has a purpose, to work in the hive. They don't have to be commanded to do so, they simply go where they are needed and work. No one has to make a public announcement, or recruit, or even beg to fill the vacancy; it's just their nature to fill in the gaps.

So you ask yourself, what does this have to do with Christians? Why are bees biblical? In Judges 4 we learn of Deborah, a Prophetess. She was one of five women in the bible called a prophet. A look at her life reveals that she was one busy woman. She saw needs and did what she could to meet those needs. Deborah was not one to sit around and let others do the work; she didn't have to be told. Deborah was like a bee in a hive, filling in when work needed to be done, making things happen for the sake of the kingdom.

What would the kingdom of God look like if we all made ourselves more like a bee? When we become active in our churches, the end result is a hive full of sweet honey. When we start being active Christians our church is filled and overflowing with the fullest of God's purpose and the sweetness of His love.

We, the body of Christ, can learn a lot from the actions of bees. There is work to be done, and the church, your church, my church, the body of Christ needs workers. Let us be like bees and fill in the gaps, pitch in and get it done, in order for God to get the glory. When we become so active that if someone steps away the work continues, we have become like bees and become the people God calls us to be. So let's get active and be like bees in a hive.

July 5

"If you hold to my teaching, you are really my disciples. Then you will know the truth and the truth will set you free." (John 8:31-32)

One morning on my ride to work, I passed a guy driving down the interstate with his head stuck out the window. My first thought was how weird he looked. But as I thought on this I came up with a possible explanation for his weirdness. Maybe he works the night shift and he thinks if he hangs his head out in the morning air, then he will stay awake and make it home safely. His thinking is "if" I do this, "then" the result will be....

I remember my mother telling me "if" you eat your vegetables "then" you will get dessert. There was a condition and only "if" I complied with the condition did I receive what I wanted. I learned early in life to appreciate vegetables, because they equated to dessert and I love dessert. I came to realize that the words "if" and "then" are connected to one another.

This concept applies to our spiritual life as well. Our focus verse tells us "if" we hold on to the teachings of Jesus and the bible, "then" we will know the truth and be free.

Only "if" we obey, "then" we receive the blessings and rewards He offers. There is a condition, it's more than merely believing or saying we believe. The "if" condition says we are to be devoted to following the things He teaches and go beyond the "profession" of faith. We must remember, Satan believes in God but he does nothing God teaches. So, "if" he believes yet does nothing God teaches, "then" how is that working out for him? So "if" you want the eternal reward of heaven "then" you must follow His teachings and then, and only then, will you be free indeed!

July 6

"It is not the healthy who need a doctor, but the sick. But go and learn what this means: 'I desire mercy, not sacrifice. 'For I have not come to call the righteous, but sinners. " (Matthew 9:9-13)

An accident happens; an ambulance arrives, loads up the uninjured people, and transports them to the hospital. The uninjured people are then taken ahead of all those already waiting. They are checked out and found to be okay. They are then released while the broken, sick and lame sit in disbelief. It's a pretty farfetched story, right?

Scripture tells us Jesus was in the Emergency Responder business. Jesus told Matthew, a tax collector and one worse than a sinner in those days, to follow Him. He then went to Matthew's house and had dinner with a bunch of sinners. When the Pharisees saw this they wanted to know why. Jesus' response in our focus verse tells us He was on earth not for those who claim to be well, but for those who needed help.

Jesus came for the hurting, the sick, the lonely, the broken hearted and those that feel like they don't fit in. He prefers the company of those who know their brokenness, their need, their sinfulness. And here's a good point we "Christians" should not miss, so should we. If He dined with the unlovable, he put it in us to do the same, if we are "like" Him.

With whom do you fellowship? If we are honest with ourselves, would we react to Jesus' dinner party like the Pharisees or Jesus Himself? Why would Jesus, the Savior of the world, tarnish His reputation this way? Why? Because the gospel was meant for people such as these. The gospel was meant for the likes of people like me prior to the year 2000. I had been an atheist, a druggie, a drinker, smoker, cussed, and one of the worst sinners you could imagine.

The gospel changed me and I thank God for it. But it doesn't give me the right to forget where I came from. In fact, I should be more intentional in welcoming others to the same gospel that saved me. Those of us who have been affected by the gospel should see others with their need in mind. Know the gospel of mercy…savor it, and never forget it. Most of all don't keep it to yourself, but share it!

July 7

"As you know, the Passover is two days away—and the Son of Man will be handed over to be crucified." (Matthew 26:2)

Matthew 26 reveals that Jesus faced many difficult things in a very short time. There was a plot against His life. A close friend plots to betray Him. He predicts that another friend will deny ever knowing Him. He is about to take on the sin of the world. Then He is arrested, tried, and sentenced to death. A bad set of circumstances; one most of us will never face even on our worse day.

At the height of this crisis, Jesus said this has to happen to fulfill scripture. He put aside Himself; God's word was to be lived out. He knew all this was true, because He had prayed and heard from God. There was no other way.

How do we reach a point in our life where we are calm in the face of a crisis? How do we reach a point in our life where we know the events of our life fulfill God's will on our lives?

We must be in a relationship with God as Jesus was. Constant contact with God is required. We must seek God's will regardless of the cost. We must have a God saturated life, one in obedience to Him and His will.

How we respond in the face of a crisis determines our true belief. Is our response "why me" or "what next"? Or is it "this must be to fulfill God's will?" Do we cling to God's promises; allowing His will be lived out? Or do we react in a worldly manner, allowing the events to steal our joy?

Paul preached the gospel and people came to know Jesus. Some were angry and persecuted him. Paul's reaction shows us he understood God's will on his life, even in the face of persecution. In Acts 13:51-52 we read how they responded. *"So they shook the dust from their feet in protest against them and went to Iconium. And the disciples were filled with joy and with the Holy Spirit."* Paul knew it wasn't easy, but it was God's will to preach His word. So in the face of it, he was *"filled with joy and the Holy Spirit."*

So the next time you are hit with a crisis, how will you respond? If you have a relationship with God, look at it as fulfilling God's will and be *"filled with joy and the Holy Spirit"* and that crisis won't look quite the same.

July 8

"My son, if you accept my words and store up my commands within you...
then you will understand the fear of the LORD and find the knowledge of
God." (Proverb 2:1, 5)

As a young child my mother was a stickler for eating our
vegetables. We couldn't leave the table until they were gone. She
never cooked anything she knew we didn't like (like Brussels sprouts)
so we should have been eager to eat. But kids will be kids. So I often
heard "if you don't eat your vegetables, then you get no dessert."

Most people would tell you that the promise of the gift of salvation,
like all other promises in the Bible, is free. They will quote John 3:16,
which to them says all one must do is believe and they are good to go.
They are saved and Heaven bound. But, I will tell you, I don't believe
that. There is so much more to salvation and that is why the bible also
tells us that "many" will go to hell, while only a "few" will go to
heaven.

We live in a world where people think everyone who dies goes to
heaven, or is in a better place when they die. They go through life
foolishly kidding themselves that they can go on sinning, yet just
believe, and end up in heaven. I contend they are heading in the
opposite direction.

If you spend any time reading your bible you will see that there are
expectations of us as believers. God is conditional. God says, "IF you
will, THEN I will; and IF you won't, THEN I won't."

God's promises are conditional; they are only "free" if you obey
certain conditions. If you are sincere, if you are authentic, if you are
humble and if you are taking action to rid sin from your life, then yes,
God promises to hear your prayers, God promises to save, God
promises a place in heaven.

The word "if" sets the prerequisite. The word "then" activates the
promise. The "if" is the action in which "then" you get the result. They
go hand in hand with God.

So just like my mother used to say, if you don't do one, you won't
get the other. "If" you want the free gift of salvation, "then" there are
things you must do. You play a part in your salvation. You do your
part and God will fulfill His part. It's pretty simple. Are you ready to
make that choice? I can tell you, my mom cooked some great desserts,
so a few beans or some corn was a small price to pay for the treat I
knew I would receive. The same goes for that reward in heaven for
those who obey.

July 9

"This is war, and there is no neutral ground. If you're not on my side, you're the enemy; if you're not helping, you're making things worse." (Matthew 12:30 MSG)

The quickest way to win a battle is cut off the enemy's lines of communication. In the Army, I learned to provide a means of communication to our troops. We knew how important it was for the soldiers to coordinate their movements or get information to and from the front lines. Take away the communications and our soldiers suffered loss.

This also applies to the enemy of your soul, Satan. If he can keep you from communicating with God, there is no way you can fight the good fight or win in life. The enemy will do anything to distract you and interrupt your communications with God.

The enemy uses people, events, sports, and even family to distract you from God. The busyness of life is his number 1 weapon. How many times have we claimed we don't have time for Church, bible study, or to pray? That is a tactic Satan uses to make us too busy for those things. Remember this; there is always time for what we truly want to do.

Some may wonder what harm missing a few church services or a few days of reading your bible could hurt. Not communicating with God for even one day can allow the enemy a foot hold, one that starts to tear down walls and enables the advancement of the enemy. A constant line of communications halts that advancement and allows us to know how to handle the things we are faced with. And it is more than a mere few words said before you scarf down your food.

Anything that goes against God or hampers God's work is of the enemy. Sounds like winner take all, so whose side are you on?

The enemy wants to stop you from communicating with the God who supplies power, who helps us overcome and who leads us to victory. We must recognize the ways the enemy can subtly break down that line of communication. It may only take a little break, just enough to lead you down the wrong path.

So the moral is: be aware of the enemy and fight against those temptations to "take a break" from talking with God. When you have no communication with God, you have no power and you lose. It's pretty much that simple. So, arm yourself and be on the lookout. The enemy lurks…will you stop him?

191

July 10

"Jesus said, 'It is finished.' With that, he bowed his head and gave up his spirit." (John 19:30)

I like to work with my hands. I seem to always have a project or two going. Often when I complete a project, I look at my work with pride and in my mind think, it is finished. Completing a task to me is fulfilling and enjoyable. But today I think about the project Jesus took on, to come to this world and save the likes of me.

The last supper was complete. The disciples feet had been washed, Jesus' final lesson had been taught. The betrayer had done the unthinkable and the arrest had been made. Jesus stood a mock trial and received the sentence. His best friends fled, even denied Him. He heard the people call for His death. The people had spoken. He took the beating. He carried the cross. He took the nails and He took our pain. Then, Jesus spoke His last words, "It is finished."

I wonder what went through Jesus' mind at that very moment. Was it pride? Was He happy with His work? I can't speak for Him, but as I read my bible I know that God was. And if we follow the story days after, we will read of Jesus' return and of His final instructions.

Even though Good Friday leaves me sad, I think Jesus' final words were words of hope and a future for those who believe, follow and obey. Jesus completed the biggest project known to mankind and it was for all to enjoy. "It is finished" means that our price has been paid, we are cleansed and we have hope for an eternity with Jesus.

So celebrate what Jesus did, for you and me.....

July 11

"You must not simply look the other way and hope it goes away on its own. Bring it out in the open and deal with it in the authority of Jesus our Master. Assemble the community—I'll be present in spirit with you and our Master Jesus will be present in power. Hold this man's conduct up to public scrutiny. Let him defend it if he can! But if he can't, then out with him!" (1 Corinthians 5:3-5)

I was a wild child growing up. I got into trouble more often that I should have. I, like many, used the excuse, "everyone else is doing it." My father would ask the age old question "if your friends jumped off of a bridge, would you?" We can get caught up in doing the things others are doing to fit in, to be like them and to look like everyone else.

Our Heavenly Father tells us not to conform to the world, to live lives contrary to the way non-believers live. He also tells us to be real, set apart, holy, because He, the very image we are created in, is holy. So what happens when people within the church live lives contrary to the ways of God? Do we say something or do we turn a blind eye?

Paul wrote a lot about misconduct within the church. Paul wasn't concerned with that old adage, "don't judge me." Paul's teachings were that those who profess Christ are to be more like Christ. He tells us to live unlike the world. Our focus verse gives us some pretty stern ways in dealing with those who aren't living up to what they profess.

Christians are not responsible for the judgment of the unsaved. Wicked people in the world will be judged by the Lord Himself in a coming day. Yet we DO have a responsibility as far as judging those who are inside the confines of the church, in other words, the professing Christians. It is the duty of the body of Christ to exercise godly discipline.

Some will say, *"Judge not that you be not judged."* We are not to judge motives because we are not competent for that type of judgment. But the word of God is equally clear that we are to judge known sin within the body of Christ, so as to maintain its reputation for holiness and to restore the offending brother or sister to fellowship with the Lord, and the very body of Christ.

So before you do something that you know is not right or against God's ways, ask yourself that age old question, "If your friends jumped off of a bridge would you?" Decisions we make have eternal consequences and it is my prayer that no one is willing to forgo their eternal life for the things of this world or just to fit in.

July 12

"...clothe yourselves with the Lord Jesus Christ, and do not think about how to gratify the desires of the sinful nature." (Romans 13:14)

There is a children's book named *"A Snowman Named Just Bob."* It's a story with a powerful message about friendship that is meant to warm the hearts of children and adults alike. I know it warmed mine.

The name Bob has a special meaning for me. You see, I know two men named Bob and both of them have impacted my life in one way or another. I love each of these men and would not be who I am today if not for them in my life. They have each taught me to be a better man, even though they may never know it.

Bob Tanner was standing in the foyer of the church I was visiting. He had a warm smile, a short joke or story, a friendly embrace and an infectious love for Jesus. He was a fun loving guy who took interest in me and over the last 14 years, he has poured Godly qualities into my life. He was instrumental in my spiritual growth and was so proud the day I was accepted on staff at our church.

Bob Deckert, a retired Army vet, I met through a friend. He was a strong man, independent and fun to be around. Warm hearted, loving and positive, even when his health started to fail him. He treats me like one of his own and was always ready with a word of encouragement. Bob inspired me one morning when he gave his family one of the best gifts a man can give his children. Bob prayed that God the Father would accept Him home when his time was up. He asked for forgiveness and told God how much he loved Him, all while his daughter sat by his side.

Both of these Bobs have impacted my life. Both have been examples of what Godly men are supposed to look like. Both Bobs loved freely, gave openly and are children of God. Both men are now with Jesus, and I hope they are putting in a good word for me.

My life is better because of these two men who just happen to share the same name. They are not "just Bob" to me. They are men that I will cherish and love because they took the time to share life with me. They made me better and they modeled how to live and love God openly. I just pray I can be a "Bob" to someone along the way.

July 13

"His mother said to the servants, 'Whatever He says to you, do it.'" (John 2:5)

When I was young, I didn't always do what I was told. I know, I am not the only one who is guilty of this, or am I? Maybe I am the only one willing to go on record and say it. But we all are guilty of not following orders or commands.

Mary, Jesus' mother asks Jesus to do something and then turned to the servants and gave them these instructions. *"Whatever He says to you, do it."* Christian faith thrives on obedience. The more we are willing to do the things of Christ, the greater the impact of our faith.

Many people say they believe, many claim to be Christ followers, yet as we see the world through the lenses of TV, social media and daily life, how can that be? Why is the world in such bad shape if so many profess to be followers of Christ? The answer lays in obedience.

We, as Christ followers, are called to love our enemies, pray for those who persecute us, forgive, love, share sacrificially, pray fervently, heal, preach, teach, feed, clothe, and rescue. So why do we see so much fighting, so many without, and so many lives in ruin? Is it only a matter of obedience or can we add to the problem our definition of Lordship. If we profess to follow Christ and he is truly our Lord, then we should live to obediently act as His ambassadors each day. But maybe for many, they have only given Him temporary authority over just a portion of their lives. They live with their own agendas, only obeying what they are willing to do or give.

I must ask, what would happen if we all would live our lives saying, "I will do whatever You (God) tell me to do"? Can you imagine what He would do to our lives if we offered ourselves so freely to His will and His purpose?

The rest of the story our passage comes from tells us that Jesus turned some plain, ordinary pots of water into the best wine ever. If He can do that to ordinary water, then he can turn our ordinary, plain lives into something extraordinary. By allowing ourselves to be obedient to His will, and doing as He says, His glory will shine and we will be transformed and blessed. So, as for me, I will do as He says and I ask God to transform me into His likeness by doing so.

July 14

"Ask and it will be given to you; seek and you will find; knock and the door will be opened to you. For everyone who asks receives; he who seeks finds; and to him who knocks, the door will be opened." (Matthew 7:7-8)

A woman shared a story with me about a brother she never knew she had. Seems way back in the Vietnam War, her dad met a young Vietnamese woman and out of that meeting came a child he knew nothing about. This boy grew up knowing that his father was an American and he was determined to find him. He searched and searched until, just prior to Thanksgiving this year, if I remember correctly, the young man showed up at the door step of his American family. His search was over. He had found the family that he, or they, never knew of.

I get chills every time I recall that story. I can't imagine what it took for that young man to find a family so far away. I can't imagine the hours of research, digging, asking and searching it takes to find someone he knew nothing about.

Our focus verse talks about persistence. We are to ask and keep on asking; to seek and keep on seeking; to knock and keep on knocking. Wisdom and power for the Christian life will be given to all who earnestly and persistently pray for it.

Taken out of context, this might seem like a blank check for believers, i.e., we can get anything we ask for. But this is simply not true. The verses must be understood in light of the whole Bible's teaching. For example, from Psalm 66:18 we learn that when we ask, there must not be any unconfessed sin in our life.   We must ask in faith (James 1:6-8) and we must conform to the will of God (1John 5:14). Asking, seeking and knocking must be offered persistently (Luke 18:1-8) and with sincerely (Hebrews 10:22).

When we ask, seek and knock with the right heart, we will find what we are searching for. So keep searching. Good things come to those who are persistent.

July 15

"Watch and pray so that you will not fall into temptation. The spirit is willing, but the body is weak." (Matthew 14:38)

We recently took a trip to the mountains of North Carolina. While we were there we went to an apple orchard to pick apples right from the trees. It was a cool, rainy, dreary day, yet we enjoyed ourselves none the less. While there, a friend posed for a picture. As I looked at it, I couldn't help but think of old children's stories where someone offered little boys and girls an apple, poisoned and ready to put them in a deep sleep. It was quite comical.

We have heard that story before. It's *"good for food and pleasing to the eye"* (Gen 3:6) who can say no to such a treat. Surely it poses no harm. But we know what happened don't we? If not for that temptation, or should I say the giving into that temptation, we all would still be living in the Garden of Eden.

Temptation lurks all around us. We are hit in the face with it at every corner, every minute of every day. It's an age old problem, one that will never cease. Even those who walked with Jesus knew of it. When Jesus took a few of His closest friends into a garden so He could pray, they too fell into the temptation to please the flesh.

Jesus found them sleeping. It's a sad commentary on fallen human nature. Jesus warned Peter against sleeping in that crucial hour. Only recently, Peter had boasted of his willingness to do anything, even die for Jesus, yet he couldn't even stay awake. If a man cannot pray for one hour, it is unlikely that he will be able to resist temptation in the moment of extreme pressure.

Things of this world look good. They tempt us to go against that in which the Lord would have us do. We must find a way to say no to temptation. A few ways is by staying grounded in God's word, surrounding ourselves with likeminded people and having people in our lives that hold us accountable to live according to God's ways, not man's ways.

Temptation will come, how we handle it is up to us. Give in and lose, or stand firm and win, the choice is yours. So, what will you do when temptation comes?

July 16

"The elders who direct the affairs of the church well are worthy of double honor, especially those whose work is preaching and teaching." (2 Timothy 5:17)

I write this in support of all my pastor friends, not solely out of things that have happened to me. A pastor's job week in and week out is a calling, and they do it willingly with little money, lots of demands and often little to no off time. They are God's messengers, yet they have a role in the church just like you and I. So read this and think about your pastor.

How the church can kill a pastor: In most churches, this one person, the pastor, carries the burden of being the one to hear from God, establish a vision, equip the people, raise the money, execute a strategic plan, visit the sick, proclaim Good News, launch new ministries, and exhibit all of the spiritual gifts that are supposed to be present throughout the church.

We pastors soon learn we can't actually be who the people in the pews think we should be. We aren't good enough to meet their every need. We get tired, we juggle too many things. We forget and we run out of time to do everything that is demanded of us. That is when the complaining starts....

Do you have any idea what kind of complaints pastors get? *I didn't like that song. The music was too loud. The lyrics on the screen were too small. The parking lot was too full. We ran out of coffee. There wasn't enough food at the potluck. The kids are too loud. A visitor sat in my seat.*

The complaints take their toll and cut a pastor deep. Paper cut after paper cut, our strength is sapped and the life flows out of us. Why in the world do we expect any one person to fulfill all of our spiritual needs?

So here is my thought. It is time for all of us, pastor, layperson, and pew sitter, to be "the church" and pitch in. Let's all ask ourselves, "What am I willing to do about...?"

I encourage you to spend a day with your pastor and see just how hard they work. Then ask yourself, what can I do to help them, not kill them? When "the church" does that, everyone gets a blessing. So be a blessing today to your pastor.

(Adapted from an article from "Holiness Reeducation")

July 17

"But there's far more to life for us. We're citizens of high heaven! We're waiting the arrival of the Savior, the Master, Jesus Christ, who will transform our earthy bodies into glorious bodies like his own. He'll make us beautiful and whole with the same powerful skill by which he is putting everything as it should be, under and around him." (Philippians 3:20-21 MSG)

I have always liked to work with my hands. At a young age I tagged along with my father from one job site to the next. I learned carpentry from him and really enjoyed it. But my career path took me in a different direction, but building things was always in me.

So I use the things my father taught me to make things for others. I like to take a pile of lumber and turn it into something useful. Like yesterday, I took a pile of pine boards and made a headboard for a friend. I like to see a pile of raw material be transformed into something beautiful.

God does that in our lives. He can take what we currently are and transform us into what He sees within us. He shapes, molds, and changes us into what He sees as beautiful. Oh, sometimes it hurts, sometimes it's uncomfortable, but it is always worth it in the end. He is a master at it and has been doing it for centuries.

My friend merely asked if I would be willing and I said yes. God is waiting for you to ask, and trust me; He is willing, able and ready to get to work. So are you ready for change? Would you like to see yourself as something different? God is open for business, all you have to do is call out. He will start today.

July 18

"Jesus answered, "I am the way and the truth and the life. No one comes to the Father except through me." (John 14:6)

Several of us took a weekend motorcycle trip to the mountains. There was a leader and then the rest of the motorcycles lined up behind him. As we rode through the curves, I noticed from my vantage point in the rear how people followed the bike in front of them. Each rider rode their line and their pace, while following single file behind one another. We went where the leader took us, through the curves and straightaways. At the end of the ride, we all arrived safely at our destination, each having a story of their journey.

As I watched, I was reminded of how in our Christian walk, we each have to follow the one leading the way, Jesus Christ. In our focus verse, Jesus tells us He is the only way to God. He tells us that by following Him, we can get there. Jesus is our road captain and by following Him, we too can arrive safely at the place we want to be, Heaven.

A close look at John 10 tells us that Jesus leads those that follow like a shepherd leads his flock. By following Him we are safe, protected and end up where we need to be. Oh, we may take a few turns, ride a couple of curves, even stay on a straightaway for some time, but if we stay behind and in step with the leader, we get to where He leads.

Following Jesus takes us through the gates of heaven, safely arriving at the end of our journey, in a place we will spend eternity. With this in mind, I say lead on Jesus, I am right behind you!

July 19

"A student is not above his teacher, but everyone who is fully trained will be like his teacher." (Luke 6:40)

As a boy I loved to spend time with my father. We went everywhere together. What he did, I did, or at least I tried to. He taught me at a young age to drive, to build things and how to fix things. He taught me manners, morals and ethics, and most of all, how to be a man. His teachings shaped me to be the man I am today.

At the age of 11, he took me to the job site with him during summer vacation. He put me to work, taught me skills and taught me his trade. My first job in the construction trade was puttying nail holes. I had to learn how to use just enough putty as to fill the hole, yet leave a smooth surface to be painted over. I later moved on to other tasks, but only after I successfully completed the one at hand. I soon became a pretty good painter, but only because my father took the time to teach me, and I was willing to listen and learn.

I believe the same principle applies to a Christian's walk. It is more than just believing or calling yourself a Christian. It's having a relationship with God. It comes with spending time with Him, listening, learning and doing what the Father teaches. In Luke 6:40, Jesus shares with us what He expects of a disciple. He teaches that a disciple is a student, being taught by the Master, learning the skills and becoming like the Master.

We are to take the lessons of the teacher (God) and let them transform us from what we were to what He wants us to be, more like Him. He teaches, we learn, we apply, and we become like Him in action, word, and deed. Our life reflects Him in everything we do.

Just as I learned from a master painter to become a painter, we are called to learn from the Master of the universe, to become like Him. I was never the painter my father was, but I was close. That is what we are called to do with God, to be as much like Him as we can. So, let God the Father teach you how to be like Him and then let the world see you for what you really are, Christlike!

July 20

"They chose Stephen, a man full of faith and of the Holy Spirit..." (Acts 6:5)
"Now Stephen, a man full of God's grace and power, did great wonders and miraculous signs among the people." (Acts 6:8)

A lot can be learned from just a little. I spent about 13 hours yesterday alone, quiet, reading, writing and meditating on God's word. I learned that some of the biggest lessons can come from the smallest of things. We can learn how to overcome the troubles in our lives with the right attitude and mind set.

Life is hard. We are all faced with troubles and problems that can weigh us down. They can get to us and bring us down. When we are faced with life's troubles, how we respond says a lot about us.

The bible spends a lot of time talking about people like Noah, David, Abraham, Moses, Peter, Saul/Paul and John. We can take away from the bible that the ones that get the most mention are the ones that are the most important, right? Remember I said I learned a lot from a little? Sometimes the least mentioned are the best ones to learn from.

Stephen was picked to fill a need; to lead a food bank. Stephen was an unknown, yet he gets busy working for the kingdom and that is when things get crazy. Falsely accused, blamed for things he didn't do, people are jealous of him for what he can do and what he is empowered to do. They become envious and soon he finds himself facing his opposition. Sound familiar?

Stephen had a choice to make, fight back and make matters worse, or he can face the problem knowing he is doing God's work. As he sat there being falsely accused, they notice something different about him. His face was like an angel, very odd at a time like this.

What a lesson. Stephen knew what was important, he knew that he was doing God's work and no matter what others said, he was doing it because he was filled with the Holy Spirit. He allowed the Holy Spirit and God's grace within him to bring him through this trouble. He faced it with God on his side, he was not alone.

What are you facing today? Is it an angry mob, false accusations, lies, hurt? How you respond to that situation will define you. Be a Stephen; a man empowered by God not only to do wonders and miracles, but a man empowered to face the enemy and come out victorious.

July 21

"Praise be to the Lord, the God of Israel, because he has come and has redeemed his people." "...because of the tender mercy of our God, by which the rising sun will come to us from heaven to shine on those living in darkness and in the shadow of death, to guide our feet into the path of peace." (Luke 1:68, 78-79)

While walking my dog Ziggy, I noticed that every so often she would squat and do her business. She does that when she walks. She will squat and "leave her mark" from start to finish. As I watched her my mind went to a few years ago...

A few years ago Ziggy got out of the back yard during a storm. We weren't home so we have no idea how long she was out. When we got home she was gone. We frantically looked for her. We searched until there were no places to search. We called her name, we hung flyers, and we even prayed that God would protect her and bring her home.

Just before I went to bed, I went to the front door to turn off the porch light and I heard a noise. I opened the door to find my little girl, soaked, dirty and cold. She had found her way back home. To this day I believe she followed her "marked trail" back home. Oh, what rejoicing....

I can't help but wonder what mark am I leaving in case I get lost? Is there some way for me to get back to where I belong? As I think on it I can say yes. I have stored up scripture in my heart, I have friends that love me enough to help me find my way, and I have accountability partners who help guide my steps and keep me on track.

But I want to take it a step further. What mark am I leaving to help others who may be lost? Am I helping people find their way? Am I leaving a clearly marked path that others can follow? Do I speak words of encouragement? Do I speak truths in others' lives? Do I leave calling cards to help others who stumble and are lost? Everyone needs a hand once in a while. We are our brother's keeper, and the bible clearly tells us to help others find their way to God.

So, do you have a clearly marked path? Are you leaving a mark for others? Think on this and if not, get busy. There are lost people who need to find their way to God.

July 22

"Forgetting what is behind and straining towards what is ahead, I press on toward the goal to win the prize for which God has called me heavenward in Christ Jesus." (Philippians 3:13-14)

Most of us today live for the now and not the future. We normally don't think about future generations and how they will view us. We seldom think about our legacy.

But all of us will leave a legacy, what we will be remembered for, so why not leave a good one? Take a moment to think about this, if you died this very moment, what would your legacy be?

This is a true story: "The merchant of death is dead!" That is how the obituary read for Ludvig Nobel in 1888. It was a mistake, because Ludvig's brother Alfred was known by that nickname. Alfred had become rich for inventing dynamite and contributed to every war.

Alfred decided to change his legacy. So seven years before his death, he set aside money to fund annual prizes, the most notable being the Nobel Peace Prize. Now Alfred is known as a man of peace, not of war and death.

Alfred changed his actions, which changed his reputation, which, in turn, changed his legacy. He couldn't change his past, but he could, and did change his future. This is a good lesson to us all. It is never too late to change the legacy we are leaving behind.

We need to leave the past behind and look towards the future as Paul writes in our focus verse. Paul, before his conversion was a killer of Christians, yet once saved he understood that God doesn't restrict our futures by our pasts. Imagine what kind of legacy we could leave if we shared Paul's passion for the things of God? Imagine what our legacy would be if we lived everyday serving a God who forgets pasts and sets us up with a bright future.

An old song said "My future is so bright I think I need shades..." Well when we walk in the light of Jesus Christ, our futures are that bright. So put on your shades and leave a legacy worthy of calling ourselves Christ followers. It is never too late to change.....

July 23

"Which of the two did what his father wanted?" (Matthew 21:31)

I like to spoil my wife Joy. It brings me as much pleasure as it brings her. Often she will ask me to do something and I'll tell her "no", only to do it anyway. I may say one thing, but my actions tell a different story.

So often I see people who say one thing, yet do another. Case in point, once a guy told me he would help me put some vent cap on a new roof. I waited all day for him to show, and just before it got dark, I climbed the roof and did it myself. I found out later he took a motorcycle ride instead. His actions that day said more than any words he had spoken.

Our focus verse speaks of two boys who said one thing, yet did another. Jesus asked a simple question, which one did what their father wanted? What they did mattered to Him. It is positive evidence of their true beliefs.

True children of God act as if they really are His children and He really is their Father. True children of God know their service in the vineyard really does matter. True children of God know that their actions are an accurate indication of where their hearts lie. True children of God obey the Father.

So, think about that the next time you hear the Father tell you something, convict you of something, or try to steer you away or towards something. What you do, not what you say you will do, matters to Him.

"A man's real belief is that which he lives by." George MacDonald

July 24

"...there is a friend who sticks closer than a brother." (Proverbs 18:24)

Just this morning I cannot help but reflect on my life and how over the years God has enriched my life with good friends. To be honest, my family (blood brothers and sisters) aren't very close and I only have one close relationship out of six siblings. The rest, well, let's just say they tend to leave me alone.

The bible puts great emphasis on close relationships and surprisingly Proverbs rates friends higher than family. The bible tells us that when we come to walk with Jesus, family members may separate themselves from us. But in our focus verse we are told that a friend is closer than a brother.

The secret is to pick your friends wisely. There are good, close friends and there are fair weather friends. The wrong kind of friends can bring trouble, but a true friend loves at all times, even when you are facing hard times.

There are friends in the valley of life and friends that are on the mountaintop. You know, they need you when they are struggling, but as soon as they get on top, they desert you. These are seasonal friends and as sad as they make us, they are good for that season. They enrich our lives, even if just for a season.

I am thankful for all my friends, and I hope they are thankful for me. I have many who love me and I know without doubt they are there for me, no matter what. I am blessed to have friends that I can say live according to Proverbs 17:17 *"A friend loves at all times..."* even when I mess up, they still love me.

I had a guy tell me once that as his "brother" he would take a bullet for me. Then we had a small disagreement and off he went. From that moment, his words cut deep and try to ruin me. The rest of proverbs 17:17 says *"...and a brother is born for adversity."*

In the biker world we use the word "brother" and "sister" freely. In my eyes it doesn't mean what it once meant. So for me, if you are close to me and our relationship is a blessing, I call you "friend". Thank you for being a friend and a part of my extended family.

I hope you have friends like I do. Friends that are closer than blood and are there for you when you need them and even when you don't.

July 25

"Love the Lord your God with all your heart and with all your soul and with all your mind and with all your strength." (Mark 12:30)

I have learned a few life lessons from my dog Ziggy. After being left outside all day, no matter the weather, when I come home, she is waiting for me. Her excitement is so great her whole body shakes. When I let her in she has to perform for me. She literally runs around in circles and then jumps up and gives me a high five. No matter the day I have had, she puts a smile on my face.

Ziggy craves my attention. She follows me around, sits in my lap, licks my nose (I call them kisses) and will do anything for some petting. I can ignore her, get mad at her, leave her out on a 100 degree day and she loves me anyway. Her love is unconditional.

Wouldn't it be nice if humans could love like this? Think about it. Most of the time we are too busy trying to get ahead, meet a schedule or fulfill our own agenda that we hardly love anymore. For some, love only comes conditionally, you do for me, then I will love you.... This is often true in our love towards Jesus. We love Him when we want something, but ignore Him when His presence isn't needed.

Jesus tells us in our focus verse that we are to love Him with everything. Our first obligation is to love the Lord totally. We are to love with the heart, our emotional nature; our soul, the conscience choice; our mind, with intellect; and our strength, physical love. Nothing should rival our love for the Lord and we should love Him no matter the situation or time.

We should all strive to demonstrate love like Ziggy. When we love our Lord and Savior with that type of love, it puts a smile on His face. Jesus loves us unconditional and He asks us to love Him and others the same way.

July 26

"The eye is the lamp of the body. If your eyes are healthy, your whole body will be full of light. But if your eyes are unhealthy, your whole body will be full of darkness"(Matthew 6:22-23)

There are things in my past that I am not proud of. I wasn't always the way I am now, and I thank God for that. I have seen all sides of the biker world, good and bad. I used to run in different circles and my life was far from where it is now. I look back and I am amazed at how far I have come and how things have changed.

After I gave my heart to Christ I thought I could go on living that same lifestyle, while maintaining my Christian walk. One night I came to the stark realization that it is impossible to live a double life. I found myself in a place where I should never have been, doing things I know God never wanted me to do, and I sensed evil all around me. It was as if I was suddenly shaken awake and I heard God tell me to get out, leave that life and live as He intended me to live. I left that lifestyle and never turned back.

Jesus uses the eye to teach us about spiritual sight. If the eye is good, we are flooded with light (good). But if the eye is bad our vision is impaired, we see darkness (evil). The good eye belongs to the person who desires to live as God wants them to and to accept His teachings. Their life is flooded with the things of God. On the other hand, the bad eye belongs to the person who tries to live in both worlds. They don't want to let go of the earthly things, while trying to claim the treasures of heaven. Jesus teaches that this is impossible. One must make a choice, light or darkness, you can't live in both.

After I left that old lifestyle, the one filled with darkness, new sight came to me. My eyes were opened to the things of God and He began to bless me beyond my wildest dreams. Is life perfect? No, but is it better than my old life? YES! When you see light verses darkness you get a clearer picture of what life is really all about. Where are you today? Are you living in the light or are you finding yourself in the dark? It's not too late to change, light is available to you. Ask God to open your eyes and let the light shine in!

July 27

"The eye is the lamp of the body. If your eyes are healthy, your whole body will be full of light. But if your eyes are unhealthy, your whole body will be full of darkness" (Matthew 6:22-23)

Fishing brings to mind an image of a solitary figure equipped with a rod and reel, standing on a bank. But it can also bring to mind a commercial boat with nets that are spread wide, ready to catch many fish at one time. Both images depict the art of fishing, but with different results.

I wonder what kind of fishing Jesus had in mind when He called His first ministry team. Did He picture them as a solitary fisherman or net-fishers? An interesting thought to consider.

Jesus' fishing metaphor describes evangelism and disciple-making. Often this is an individualized task and a lot of us came to faith through an individual who went fishing. But I submit to you that when Jesus called the first disciples, He wasn't talking about pole fishing. Jesus called commercial fishermen of the day, wanting them to cast nets to catch many for the kingdom.

So what does "net fishing" look like today? It is spreading the gospel so that souls are reached for Christ. It is about going where the fish are or hang out. It's about the body of Christ living in such a way, everyone they come in contact with sees a difference and wants what they have.

"Net fishing" is the body of Christ going out into the neighborhoods and being the hands and feet of Jesus. It requires being bold witnesses and sharing our faith. There are certainly times when our witness will be one on one. But, we must not forget that Jesus said *"they will know you are my disciples by the love you have one for another."* That's not something anyone can do alone. The gospel is primarily a net of grace and truth that we boldly and broadly cast ... together.

So, if you are a Christian and you believe in Jesus' command to be a "fisher of men", are you ready to help cast the net? Or are you standing on the bank with a pole waiting for a bite? They won't come to you!

July 28

"...exchange the truth of God for a lie, and worshiped and served created things rather than the Creator..." (Romans 1:25)

During a camping trip I was startled out of my sleep by a dragging sound. I grabbed a flashlight, the broom and out the door I went. To my surprise I found a raccoon dragging my 100 quart cooler out from under my camper. I tried several ways in an attempt to get him to turn loose, but the little guy was determined to hang onto what wasn't his. It took me tapping him on his nose with a broom handle to convince him to let go.

How often do people hang onto the earthly things that really aren't theirs? We are told in scripture to "put off the old ways" and think like "new creations". Yet many tend to hang onto the things that they should let go of, just like my little friend the raccoon. They need a new focus.

Our focus verse teaches us that the ungodly live for the things of this world. We, Christ followers, live under a different set of standards and look towards the heavens, not our government, or the things of this world. The bible tells us to *"Set our minds on the things above, not earthly things."* (Col 3:2)

My little friend climbed a tree and hissed at me as we put the cooler in a safe place. Are you hissing because of the things you really want, yet know that you shouldn't have? It is hard to let go, nothing worthwhile is easy. Lean on the strength of God to help you overcome the power of "things" and the evil one. Jesus said in Luke 10:19 *"I have given you authority to trample on snakes and scorpions and to overcome all the power of the enemy; nothing will harm you."* The Lord gives us protection over the forces of evil and nothing can snatch that away from you!

July 29

"Why, you do not even know what will happen tomorrow. What is your life? You are a mist that appears for a little while and then vanishes." (James 4:14)

I minister to the biker community and my heart gets heavy every time I read of another biker passing away. I am often the one who gets called to visit the family and to be honest, there is not much any of us can say that will take the family's pain away.

I can't help but reflect on how fast a life can be taken. Our focus verse reminds us just how short life is. If our eyes are open, we see the truth in this. Life is short and the future unknown.

I am very persistent about asking people, "What if today was your last day? Do you know where you will spend eternity?" During these times as I talk to other bikers, I am compelled to ask what if it would have been you. Would you be ready to meet Jesus face to face? Would you go to heaven or hell? Better yet, would your family know one way or the other?

I remind people that life is too short to put off the biggest decision of your life. There are a lot of people who think because they know of this man named Jesus they are okay. Because they say they are going to heaven and they are a good person, they are okay.

But the reality is it takes more than knowing "of" Jesus and believing you are going to heaven to actually get there. Matthew 7:13-14 gives us a clear picture about the gates of heaven and hell. Jesus tells us than many go through the gate leading to hell and only a few will enter heaven. Not sure about you, but there is a big difference between "many" and "few".

So I ask even those reading this today. Have you made a decision to follow Jesus completely? Do you know without a shadow of doubt, that when your time comes (and it will) that you are going to be one of the "few"?

It takes more than just knowing, it takes a relationship with Jesus, a life of following Him, His teachings, His ways. I am talking about a relationship in which not only you know Him, but He knows you. The decision is yours to make and I urge you to make it before it is too late.

July 30

"Rejoice always, pray continually, give thanks in all circumstances; for this is God's will for you in Christ Jesus." (1 Thessalonians 5:16-18)

Our focus verse is my life verse. Not sure why, but God put this passage in my heart and I try to live it out daily. Sometimes we are challenged and it takes everything in us, and the total reliance of the Holy Spirit, to get through the day rejoicing and giving praise.

Daily we are faced with loss, hardship, trials and struggles. Often we can get bogged down with the woes of the world; we don't much feel like rejoicing and giving thanks. We just want to get through the day with our sanity, much less anything extra.

But we must know that as Christ followers, there is a brighter future. We have hope for a better day and someone in heaven that has our back. Knowing who we belong to helps get us through a bad day.

Life is short, so how we respond to the day to day life here on earth matters. We need to live a life of loving God and others. Live life as if today was your last day.

Do we want to waste our days being frustrated and frazzled, or rejoicing and thankful because we do have a better future to look forward to? I want the latter. I want to live my life as if today is my last and that Jesus is going to call me home. And when I get there, I want a smile on my face, not a look of scorn.

Rejoice and desire heaven. Look forward to an eternity there. If we believe in God, Heaven is the prize we should strive for. But until you get there live, laugh and love. Live the life God intends you to live here on earth.

How is your day going? Take a minute to look real hard at the events; maybe God is speaking life lessons to you. Are you listening?

July 31

"Still other seed fell on good soil, where it produced a crop, a hundred, sixty or thirty times what was sown."(Matthew 13:8)

I was raised in a day when everyone had a garden. We raised our own vegetables and ate what we raised. My dad taught me how to prepare the soil and what soil produced the best crops. He also taught me that the best gardens came out of soil that has lain dormant for some time. He called it fallow ground; ground untouched.

In the Book of Acts we read of the new church and how it grew, multiplied and produced. Throughout the book, we read story after story of people coming to believe in Jesus and giving their lives to His ways. The church plants sprang up everywhere, even though they were persecuted. What makes the Book of Acts church so exciting, so powerful? The Gospel was falling on fallow ground.

In the Book of Acts the people hearing the Gospel were new believers, hearing the good news for the first time and in places where it had never been preached before. The message was 100% evangelistic and discipleship was taking place. There were conflicts, fighting, beatings, persecutions and slander because the light was coming into the darkness for the very first time.

The Book of Acts has never ended, but it can only be visible when the Gospel falls on fallow ground out into the world. When we start spreading the Gospel and God's love to the lost and unsaved, start getting outside the walls of our church buildings, out of our comfort zone and take the Gospel to those that don't know God, we will see the same things found in the Book of Acts, rejection, struggles, and battles. But we will also see something else, miracles, salvation, lost souls finding Christ and a Book of Acts type church of our time.

Our mission is to take the message of Christ out into fallow ground. No matter where we are, we should spread the Gospel to those that need to hear it, even if they reject us, make fun of us or even battle us. We are to be warriors for Christ, taking His message to all we come in contact with. Take the "Light" into the darkness, live a Book of Acts life and watch the seeds grow!

August 1

"Light has come into the world, but men loved darkness instead of light because their deeds were evil. [20] Everyone who does evil hates the light, and will not come into the light for fear that his deeds will be exposed. [21] But whoever lives by the truth comes into the light, so that it may be seen plainly that what he has done has been done through God." (John 3:19-21)

Who remembers the days before the digital camera? Film came packaged in canisters and was loaded into a camera. You took pictures, rolled the film back into the canister and had it developed.

How many of you ever opened your camera before you rewound the film ruining the entire roll? I, for one, have done that on more than one occasion. Film, in that state, was sensitive to light. A roll of film had to stay in darkness until it was loaded into a camera. Then frame by frame it would be exposed to light through the camera lenses in order to create the image in which you were trying to capture.

Our focus verse reminds me of that process. It is interesting in the use of the words "light" and "darkness". This passage reveals that the natural human instinct is to live in darkness, afraid of the light, in fear of exposure. That exposure causes pain and reveals the evil in one's life. But, those who make a choice to live in the light welcome the transforming work and the exposure of a Godly image.

The light creates an image and as believers we are called to reflect the image of Christ in all we do. Isn't that what is supposed to happen when we are exposed to the truths of Jesus and His light? We leave the darkness behind and live in light. If that is so, then why do so many who profess to believe in John 3:16 still live as the world lives?

If we truly believe in Jesus, we should ask ourselves "am I still living in darkness, or am I allowing Jesus' light to expose me to be more like Him?" We need to ask ourselves this question before doing anything "Is what I am about to do, say or think something that Jesus would do, say or think?" If the answer is no, yet you still do it, you are living in darkness. If the answer is no, Jesus wouldn't do that, and you don't do it, you have been exposed and reflect His image.

Let the light expose you making you look more like Jesus. By doing so, you are not only believing in John 3:16, you are living it. Your actions and your image will be pleasing to Jesus and be a beautiful picture for others to see.

August 2

"Here is a boy with five small barley loaves and two small fish, but how far will they go among so many?" (John 6:9)

We support a school back pack program in which back packs are filled with snack foods for children to take home. It seems that some children leave school on Friday and may not eat again until they arrive back at school on Monday. Sad but true. I recently read where a teacher found a student taking food out of his backpack and dropping it into a collection bin. When confronted, the student stated that he was being helped, so he wanted to help others.

He shared what he had, even though to some it may have seemed insignificant. Our focus verse tells of a similar story. Thousands had assembled to hear Jesus and dinner time came. Jesus asked the disciples to come up with a plan. Based on their calculations, there were too many people and not enough food or money. Then along came a little boy who was willing to share.

With what equated to sardines and crackers, he gave it to Jesus. The boy was insignificant, his lunch insufficient, yet in the hands of Jesus, it became both sufficient and significant.

So what problem do you have? Do you often feel insignificant or insufficient? Put your life in the hands of Jesus and watch what happens. Trust Him and have faith that what He says He can do, He will do it.

215

August 3

"… let your light shine before men, that they may see your good deeds and praise your Father in heaven." (Matthew 5:16)

The world is into the "status update." People seem obsessed with telling the world where they are. It would make one think that the world really cares about our minute to minute status.

I have an idea. If we are so determined to give a "status update", why not give the status of what God is doing in our lives? Our focus verse says we are to place the light of God on a stand and let others see it. We are to be a beacon, and shine that light for the world to see. So our status should be that God is in us and we want everyone to know it.

But for those who don't, Jesus explains that we are about as worthless as tasteless salt or invisible light. Not my words, HIS! This may sound harsh, but Christians are called to be set apart from the world, live drastically changed lives.

Jesus teaches that we should be like salt. Salt causes other to thirst for God. He teaches we are to also be light, which illuminates truth and shines compassion into dark places. He teaches that just as tasteless salt lacks value, so does a professed disciple (Christian) without genuine commitment. A Christian whose life doesn't reveal God's works is like salt that has lost its taste; it is worthless and needs to be thrown out.

Jesus also teaches that His people are to be a light to this dark world. We cannot be content to remain the world's light in a mere academic sense; we must BE what we profess, letting our light shine for God's honor. A Christian whose life doesn't reveal God's works is like invisible light: useless.

People are watching us. What they observe can either turn them away from or draw them into a relationship with God. People aren't looking for perfect Christians; they are just looking for authentic ones. They want to see people that demonstrate consistency between their beliefs and their behaviors.

We must live a different life from the one the world lives. Wouldn't it be a tragedy to "deter someone from experiencing Christ because of cosmetic Christians, whose skin deep spirituality look pretty on the outside but doesn't penetrate deep enough to change their behavior and attitudes"? (Lee Strobel) We must live a life that is so different from the world that it is noticeable.

August 4

"But just as he who called you is holy, so be holy in all you do; for it is written: "Be holy, because I am holy." (1 Peter 1:15-16)

Often people think of *Holiness* as something pertaining to preachers, priests, or people who are not like the normal person. They are set apart, held to higher standards and live lives that others can't live. Some people have negative images of holy people, but when we research the scriptures, we find that we (each and every Christ follower) are called to be holy.

Take a look at our focus verse. God's word tells followers of Jesus Christ to be holy just like He is holy. We are to emulate Him, be like Him, our lives should be mirror images of His. Can a mere Christian live like that?

When we confess the name of Jesus we are to separate ourselves from the secular and live a life towards the sacred. That is what being Holy is about. We must die to everything God doesn't want or like in our lives and dedicate our life fully to Him. It is an individual's responsibility to God to live holy lives.

If we read the book of Romans we find that the first 11 chapters tell us in depth about Jesus and then chapter 12 and beyond we get instruction on how we are to live because of Him. Listen to the transition found in Romans 12:1 *"Therefore, I urge you, brothers, in view of God's mercy, to offer your bodies as living sacrifices, holy and pleasing to God—this is your spiritual act of worship."* That is the turning point. We must understand who Jesus is, what He came to this world for and what He did for you and I, then live a life worthy of that.

When we start living our lives because of who Jesus was and what He did for us, we can start living up to the reputation of the family name, God's family. We should do nothing to tarnish that name or that heritage. We can live holy lives and we can be set apart from the world, but only when we put our minds, hearts, body and soul into it.

August 5

"Now faith is being sure of what we hope for and certain of what we do not see." (Hebrews 11:1)

Ever heard the phrase "live by faith"? What do you think of when you flip a light switch? You have faith that the light will come on. What do you expect when you turn on a faucet, water, right? We go through life having faith in the things of this world, but do we have the same faith in the things of God?

Our focus verse describes what faith does for us. It makes things hoped for as real as if we already had them. It provides unshakable evidence that the unseen, spiritual blessings are certain and real. How does that play out in our lives?

In Hebrews 11 we read about faith. Enoch showed faith in God and lived to please Him. Enoch was taken before death so he didn't have to experience a physical death. By faith Noah built an ark because God told him to prepare for something he hadn't seen, rain. Noah never hesitated. By faith Abraham, he believed the promise of God. He became the father of a nation.

We see many examples of living by faith in the bible and they make for great stories, but have you ever seen anyone today live by faith? I can submit to you that yes, I have. I have seen men who were laid off continue to pay their tithes, and never miss a bill or go hungry. I have seen people by faith ask for healing and the doctors can't explain the change in their health.

When we live by faith that God is who He says he is and can do what He says He can do, we receive power to overcome anything this world offers. It takes courage to live by faith, and it takes understanding that the things you need are far greater than the things you want. Living by faith is easy once you know that God is in control and no matter what, He always comes through according to His plan.

If you want to understand more about *"living by faith"* I suggest you read Hebrews 11. The examples in the bible are clear proof that living by faith in God is worth writing about. Once you read it, look around and see for yourself. I would imagine you won't have to look far to see that there are people living by faith all around you.

August 6

"I have set you an example that you should do as I have done for you." (John 13:15)

As we grew up our parents had an idea what they wanted us to be; a doctor, lawyer, maybe the president of the United States. I am going out on a limb to say not all of us lived up to those expectations. Many of us let our parents down, or failed to live up to their expectations for us.

Throughout the bible Jesus teaches us to live as He expects us to live, do as He does and be more like Him. His expectation for us is high; He wants us to grow up to be like Him. He goes through His life on earth being an example on how we should live. He came to earth to live, love and serve and He expects us to do the same.

Many believers make little effort to live up to their beliefs and the expectations of God. There is often a gap between what a Christian says he or she believes and what he or she actually practices. Jesus was very aware of the human tendency of failing to meet expectations. So He set out to give us examples to follow.

Jesus said He *"...came to serve, not be served..."* (Matthew 20:28) He came to serve, we are to be like Him, and so we are to serve as He served. In John chapter 13 Jesus teaches how we are to serve. It is a touching story of Jesus washing the disciple's feet. This was a task meant for a slave, not someone of the character and importance of Jesus. He takes off His outer garment, wraps a towel around His waist and one by one He washes and dries the feet of those that had been following Him for the past three years. This was a humbling and lowly task, yet one with so much meaning, power and purpose.

In our focus verse we see that Jesus sets the example and expects us to follow His lead. He calls us to do as He did, serve as He served, pray as He prayed, sacrifice as He sacrificed, live radical lifestyles different from the world, and live radically different from our culture. We are not living up to His expectations for us if we fail to live up to the way of life He called us to live. Live, love and serve as Jesus did, and then we can live up to the expectations of our Lord and Savior.

August 7

"...the water I (Jesus) give them will become in them a spring of water welling up to eternal life." (John 4:14)

I have visited many strange and interesting places in my life, one of them being *Healing Springs* in South Carolina. A group of us took a motorcycle ride there one beautiful summer day. We enjoyed the ride and the fellowship, and even enjoyed a refreshing drink from the springs. But for me, one sip just made me want another on that hot summer day. It was good, but it didn't satisfy. I also have to say that I don't believe it has any healing powers at all. What I do believe is it is a gift from God, a spring that provides a source of drinking water for our enjoyment.

Jesus knew of thirst. He knew there were different kinds of thirst and He mentions the differences in John 4. As He sat beside a well, He told a Samaritan woman that he provided a kind of water that quenched a spiritual thirst. His promise was that the water He provides would heal and by drinking it, we would live forever with Him. His water not only quenches the thirst, it heals the soul.

When was the last time you took a drink from the "living water" Jesus offers? Have you even tried it? The woman at the well asked Jesus to give her this water. Once she realized who He was and what He offered she went to tell her family and friends. The result is that many came to believe in Jesus that day.

Take it from someone that has had that "living water". It's refreshing, it quenches the spiritual thirst and it heals the wounds of the heart. The promise of the eternal life after drinking this water is a ray of hope in a dark world. The woman's testimony led others to drink of and receive the "living water". So let my testimony lead you to that same source. Drink of the promises of Jesus and live an eternal life in God's kingdom.

August 8

"But you walked away from your first love—why? What's going on with you, anyway? Do you have any idea how far you've fallen? A Lucifer fall! "Turn back! Recover your dear early love." (Revelation 2:4-5 MSG)

My first love was a girl named Linda. We planned on spending a lifetime together. We would ride all over town in her daddy's Corvair. Then one day she moved away. I lost her and that car.

A sad tale, but I think we can apply this to our spiritual lives. Often people come to know Jesus and begin a relationship with Him. They go everywhere together and have such a promising future. They one day something changes. They feel like Jesus has moved away.

She sat in the front seat on the far right side; he sat in his usual place behind the wheel. She asks, Honey, do you remember when we first met, how close we used to sit? You used to put your arm around me. What happened?" With one hand firmly attached to the steering wheel, and the other resting on the empty seat between them, he said, "I haven't moved." The separation was because she had moved away.

In our bible reference, the Ephesians had distanced themselves from their first love. They no longer loved the Lord Jesus as they did when they first came to know Him. They not only took their eyes off the Lord but they lost fellowship with Him. They had moved away like Linda did. They left Jesus standing there watching them go away, and He was probably as heartbroken as I was.

If we are feeling distant, detached, or lost, then we must take a look at our relationship with Jesus to see if we have moved away. He doesn't move. He is there for us; that is His promise. He tells us He will never leave us nor forsake us. So if we aren't feeling close to Him, then we are the ones that packed up and moved away.

The best thing about Jesus, He is still standing there waiting for you to return to Him. He loves you so much that He never gives up on you. But, time is running out; don't wait too long, because no one is guaranteed another breath. Get moving and return to your first love.

By the way, I guess I should tell you I was 6 when I lost Linda and that car was sitting on cinder blocks in the back yard. She never came back and I have moved on. I have found my true love, Jesus! And, He gave me the woman of my dreams, a woman named Joy and the car was replaced with a Harley.

August 9

"But the fruit of the Spirit is love, joy, peace, patience, kindness, goodness, faithfulness, gentleness and self-control." (Galatians 5:22-23)

My dog Ziggy loves my son. When my son was living with us, she couldn't wait for him to come home. She sensed about the time he was due and she sat patiently and watched the door. I tried to distract her, but she just watched and waited.

Waiting isn't something most of us do well. We live in a culture where everything is about "now". I call it a time of instant gratification. Microwaves, instant loans, fast food, etc.

David teaches a lot about patience. He was anointed king at a very young age. God chose him, yet two years later, he was still tending sheep. In fact, he was called into service to play music for the current King, who was unfit to rule.

Did David rush in and take over? No, he waited, he learned and he watched. He knew God had a plan and he stayed in step with God. He waited patiently for God to call him to rule. And if we read the story of David, we learn that the wait was worth it.

We all pray for the "fruit of the spirit", but most tend to leave out the "patience". Sometimes waiting is hard. We just rush into things that don't always turn out well. Things like marriages, careers, financial decisions, etc. Waiting isn't built into our DNA, but is so vital; especially if we want what God has for us. But in the lesson from David, waiting is what is best if we truly want to be blessed and to serve God.

When my son walked through the door, Ziggy got so excited. The wait was worth it. She got his full attention, petted and maybe a treat, but most importantly, she got the love she so desperately wanted from him.

Waiting is hard, but if you want the fullness of God, it is worth it. God has a plan for your life. Are you willing to sit back, listen for His voice, learn the lesson He wants to teach and watch what He shows you? If you do, the reward is great and well worth the wait.

August 10

"On hearing it, many of his disciples said, "This is a hard teaching. Who can accept it?" "...many of his disciples turned back and no longer followed him." (John 6:60, 66)

For me, rainy days define a love/hate relationship. I love them, especially if I can sit on the back porch and enjoy it. But I hate the feeling I get deep in the knee that still carries two screws from a past surgery.

The primary reason my knee aches and throbs on rainy days is because I didn't do what I was supposed to do. Being hard headed and wanting to do my own thing, I didn't do my physical therapy and I now suffer the consequences. Make bad choices and you get bad results.

Well, we can often have the same thing in our life. We say we follow Jesus, but when the teachings get hard or we decide we want to live by our own rules, we too can suffer the consequences. It's easy to follow when we are receiving blessings; God is answering all our prayers just as we want them. But then we are tested, a prayer is answered but not like we wanted, or we hit a rough path. That is when we often decide to do our own thing, in spite of what we know to be right and the consequences come. We love God, but often we hate the hard lessons He wants us to go through.

In our focus verses we learn that some of those following Jesus were having a hard time with His teachings. They loved Jesus when He was feeding the multitudes, performing miracles and blessing them, but the truths were more than they could handle, so they went back to living their lives as they once did.

Jesus wants followers who will obey and be changed because of hard teachings. He wants doers, not consumers. He wants followers like Peter who when asked *"You do not want to leave too, do you?"* he answered *"...to whom shall we go? You have the words of eternal life."* Peter stuck it out, it was hard but he made it.

I wish I would have applied this to my therapy, but I was hard headed and stubborn. If only I would have persevered. I pray that the Lord helps me, and you to stick it out with His teachings, no matter how hard it gets. I pray none fall away, that everyone stands strong and true to the end.

August 11

"Husbands, love your wives, just as Christ loved the church and gave himself up for her..." (Ephesians 5:25)

A few years back someone asked how long I had been doing ministry. He asked if my wife and I had been together the whole time. The answer is we were married long before ministry.

I asked why he asked, he said we acted as if we were newlyweds. We had to laugh because people often tell us that we act as it we just got married. If you know us, it is no secret that we are very much in love and we take every opportunity to tell and show each other how much the other means to us.

Love is an emotion that takes effort to keep alive. You don't wake up in the morning with this "feeling" of love. You don't walk around with a love "feeling" bubbling within you. You must make a choice to love someone and it takes a conscience effort.

I choose to love my wife and I choose to show her that I love her every chance I get. I wake up every morning and choose to keep my love for her alive and exciting. I think that is how everyone who is in love should live and I strongly believe it is biblical.

We live by Ephesians 4:21 – 5:33. This passages of scripture is a must read for every married couple. It teaches married couples how to treat one another if they want a strong marriage and a happy life together. It gives good biblical principles for mutual respect, the treatment of each other, and the responsibilities of each partner of the marriage.

For me, our focus verse tells me to love my wife as much as Jesus Christ loves the church, not the building but the people. He loves us so much; He left the throne of Heaven to lie in a manger. He loves us so much He took on sin, something He never experienced, and He hung on a cross and gave His life so that we can know salvation. Wow, can I love my wife that much?

You bet I can. I believe the bible to be true and it teaches me how to live. The bible is my handbook on life and if it teaches a principle, I choose to put that principle in action. So, if the bible tells me I must love my wife *"as Christ loved the church"*, then I choose to do so. I know some don't care for our public display of affection, but God openly loves and so do I.

August 12

"Here is my command. Love each other, just as I have loved you. No one has greater love than the one who gives his life for his friends. You are my friends if you do what I command." (John 15:12-14)

Growing up I was a small kid. I entered the Army at age 25 and only weighed 135 pounds. That should give you an idea as to my size. Being a small kid has its difficulties. Let's just say there were kids at school I didn't like very much. Once I got in a fight and my mother told me that I had to apologize to the kid no matter what he did to provoke my behavior. Are you serious?

We are told in scripture that we are to *"love one another..."* That is hard at times, and with certain people, but that is the command. At first glance this may seem easy, but if we look hard at this command it gets tough. Jesus says to love *"as I have loved you."* Are you kidding me? Not only do I have to love everyone, but love as Jesus loves me, no way.

So how does Jesus define love? Take a look at John 13, Jesus shows us the full *"extend of His love"* by washing the feet of His disciples. We are commanded to love by serving others and putting them before our own needs. Can we actually do this? No. If we attempt to love like this under our own power we will fail. But, if we remain in Him as John 15:5-17 teaches and allow Him to be our source; His love will flow from you to others.

So, are there people in your life that you really just don't like? Are there people in your life that have made you mad and you don't want to like them? Are there people in your life that seem to grate on your nerves, but they won't go away? If so, try this, love them. Better yet, do something nice for them. Soon you will find that you actually like that person. Love because Jesus loves....

That kid I was forced to apologize to became my best friend. We hung out together and because of our friendship, he kept the others from picking on me. So it was a good thing I listened to my mom. It is even better if we listen to God.

225

August 13

"Set your minds on things above, not on earthly things." (Colossians 3:2)

I have a friend who loves rocks. No matter where she goes she could spend hours staring at the rocks on the ground. She collects them, saves them in zip lock baggies, from all over the country. She likes different sizes, shapes, and colors. She can spot a rock and, to her, it becomes something she has to have. The more unique it is the more she likes it.

During a trip to *Hopewell Rocks* in New Brunswick, Canada, we walked among some pretty spectacular rock formations. Actually the water recedes so far that you can walk on the ocean floor at low tide. As I walked along, snapping pictures of the rocks and cliffs looming above me, I couldn't help but notice my friend with her head down, staring at the ground. My first thought was does she not see the things above? Why is she so focused on the ground?

I know what she was doing, but still couldn't help but wonder how often do we go through life so focused on the little things, that we miss out on the things that are far greater? The bible tells us to focus on the bigger picture, the things of God. He provides us with so much, but if we are always looking down, or focused on the wrong thing, we may just miss what God wants us to see.

Now I know my friend saw all the things I did, but doesn't the illustration give us good food for thought? When we say we trust in God, yet go through life only seeing the small things, do we miss out on the blessing that may be right in front of us? God wants us to live in abundance, but we must look beyond our current situation to see the riches that are there for us.

So keep your head up and focus on the things that really matters...the things of God. You may not see them just yet, but God has some pretty spectacular things in store for you, don't miss them....

August 14

"I know your deeds, that you are neither cold nor hot. I wish you were either one or the other! So, because you are lukewarm—neither hot nor cold—I am about to spit you out of my mouth." (Revelation 3:15-16 NIV)

Have you ever ordered a meal only to have it brought to you lukewarm? If you are like me, I struggle with this. Do I send it back, or do I just eat it? It makes the dining out experience less enjoyable. Often it even angers me. Lukewarm food, or food improperly prepared, can even make me sick.

This is exactly how Jesus was feeling about lukewarm people of Laodicea. Our focus verse tells us of Jesus' dislike for lukewarm believers. Some things make Jesus weep, others make Him angry, and then there are lukewarm people that make Him sick.

What does this mean to us? Keep in mind that these words were spoken to a group of people in a church, to believers. Jesus is talking about their spirituality. He says He would rather have followers that are hot, on fire for the things of God. He said He would rather they be cold, outsiders of the church and at least open to the gospel. But what we should take note in is His feelings towards the lukewarm Christian, those in the church, yet neither hot nor cold. They claim their devotion, but deeds, actions and words say otherwise. These people make Jesus want to throw up! Not a pretty picture.

So the question is, if we claim to be a Christ followers, are we spiritually hot, cold or lukewarm? Don't answer too quickly, because the lukewarm person is often the last to know. Take note of what Jesus said, *"I know your deeds..."* Or as the Message puts it *"I know you inside and out..."* He knows us, deep down, in our heart and there is no fooling Him. So we must think hard and take note of our spirituality, because He already knows.

So unless we just don't care if we make Jesus sick, I propose we all take a long hard look at our spirituality. If I have said it once, I have said it a hundred times, life is short and we all die. Judgment is inevitable and we must face Jesus. So let's rekindle that fire, let's turn up the heat on our spirituality. Let's recommit our hearts, minds, bodies and souls to follow Jesus with all the passion and devotion we can muster. By doing so, when we are presented before Jesus we will be sizzling like the fajitas in a Mexican joint.

August 15

"Make a joyful noise unto the LORD, all the earth: make a loud noise, and rejoice, and sing praise." (Psalm 98:4) *"Rejoice in the Lord always. I will say it again: Rejoice!"* (Philippians 4:4)

There she was, lying out on the sofa; coming out of what could have been a deadly diabetic coma. A smile came across her face and praises to God came from her mouth. My response "How in the world can someone nearly die and praise God?" She replied, "I am alive, and God brought me through yet again, so I rejoice."

It was another example Leeann Thrasher lived out before me that helped lead me to accepting God and starting my walk. She lived out our focus verse, over and over again, no matter what life threw at her.

In Acts 16, Paul and Silas were arrested, beaten, and thrown in jail. While they sat in a cell, their feet in stocks, they did the only thing they knew to do, pray and sing. "How in the world can someone praise God in that situation?"

How we respond to our situations, trials and circumstances says a lot about us. If we truly know the Lord, and trust *"that in all things God works for the good of those who love him"* (Romans 8:28), then we can weather any storm. We can get through any difficulty and overcome whatever life throws our way.

The rest of that story tells us that God threw open the cells and unlocked the stocks that bound them. Yet no one escaped because they were too busy singing and praising God. The end result of that situation was a family coming to know Jesus and I bet a lot of other prisoners came to know Him as well.

Leeann lived with diabetes her whole life, yet she never once let it get to her. Nothing could steal her joy; nothing could separate her from the God she loved so much. Leeann got her reward for being faithful and she is in heaven now. I often think of her when I am going through things. I ask myself, "What would Leeann do?" I can't carry a tune, but I will make a "joyful noise" singing the praises of my God. How about you?

August 16

"When I heard these things, I sat down and wept. For some days I mourned and fasted and prayed before the God of heaven." (Nehemiah 1:4)

I heard about a little girl who discovered her friend was sick. She was so saddened by the news, and I bet much like Nehemiah in our focus verse, she cried. Her heart hurt for her friend, but then something happened, she acted.

As believers we are called to be people of compassion and action. What would happen if we all kept our eyes open to the things around us and we wept and mourned when we saw need? What would happen if we all prayed and asked God to show us what we can do to help? Then, what would happen if we all acted and actually did something for others, something that impacted lives for the Kingdom of God?

Well, this little girl did just that. She began to collect toys for the children at the Children's Hospital where her friend was undergoing treatment. She loaded those toys in little red wagons and then she delivered them to the girls and boys in that hospital. She didn't do this just once; she has been doing this for three years.

Not sure what to do? Ask God. Nehemiah had a tendency to shoot "Arrow Prayers" at God when he wanted clarity. In Nehemiah 2:4, Nehemiah met the king who asked *"What is it you want?"* Nehemiah, not sure how to answer the king's question *"...prayed to the God of heaven and I answered the king, If it pleases the king and if your servant has found favor in his sight, let him send me to the city in Judah where my fathers are buried so that I can rebuild it."*

We should be like Nehemiah and this little girl. We should have a broken heart for the things in this world that need our attention. We should weep and mourn, and then we need to get on bended knees. We should pray and fast for direction and strength to do something. Then we should have bold feet and act. Nehemiah did just this and the wall he mourned over was rebuilt.

So, what breaks your heart? Have you wept, prayed and are you doing anything about it? If so, God is pleased, if not, what are you waiting for? Get busy....

August 17

"He humbled you, causing you to hunger and then feeding you with manna, which neither you nor your fathers had known, to teach you that man does not live on bread alone but on every word that comes from the mouth of the LORD." (Deuteronomy 8:3)

Wednesday's are typically long days for me. I go all day, have bible study late in the evening and don't normally eat dinner until close to 8pm. By the time I get to the restaurant I am starved. Hunger is not a good thing. I get hunger pains, my stomach grumbles and sometimes I even get lightheaded. I get so hungry that I crave food.

Hunger is a natural feeling created in us. Have you ever had that same feeling deep in your soul? Have you ever felt like you were spiritually hungry? Have you felt like something was missing in your life but not knowing what it was or how to fix it?

Sometimes we just need to be fed by God. While the Israelites were wandering through the desert, they got hungry, so God provided manna for them. All they had to do was pick up enough to last them the day, then the next day more came. They were instructed to not store it up, or it would rot. Why?

God wants us to come to Him hungry each day. He has things for us daily; instructions, lessons, tests and blessings, but we must be willing to gather it, kind of like the Israelites did in the desert. He wants that interaction, and honestly, that is what we need. We need to be fed, we need fellowship and we need to know God provides, each and every day of our lives.

Our focus verse tells us that God causes us to hunger, He feeds us what we need, and we can't live on bread alone, we need "daily bread" in the form of His word. But we must come humbly, ready to accept that in which He offers. Are you willing to come and receive?

August 18

"For we are God's masterpiece. He has created us anew in Christ Jesus, so we can do the good things he planned for us long ago." (Ephesians 2:10)

I am a woodworker and I like to make things. Since I retired I have found the time to go back into my workshop and create. I like to take an idea, a stack of raw materials and make something that can be enjoyed. With my hands and tools I shape, mold and join the pieces of wood to become something new.

The other day I was in my shop turning old pallets into Christmas trees. When I was finished I stepped back and looked at them with pleasure. I had taken a thought and a picture, some old pallets and turned them into something that I hope will glorify our Lord and Savior.

Now I know that the Christmas tree isn't a symbol of the birth of Jesus, but it is the most common reminder of that day. People's decorations are different, not everyone puts up a nativity scene, but almost everyone has a tree. Christmas isn't Christmas without one. So it is a symbol most use to mark the day of the birth of Jesus Christ, the Savior of the world.

God created us from dust, breathed His breath into us and did so, so that we could glorify Him. We were created to worship the God who created everything and to worship the one who was sent to earth to pay the price for our sins. We must never lose sight of that.

From nothing, we were created to be God's masterpiece. We must live up to that as we live out our life here on earth. We must become the people He expected us to be so that one day we will meet Him face to face. We are His masterpieces, from a pile of raw materials, to something He considers beautiful and pleasing. Remember, when He was done creating, God stepped back and admired what He created and said *"it was very good."*

Live as God's masterpiece, glorify Him daily and in everything you do, be pleasing to His eyes. The end result will be eternity in heaven with the one who created you in the first place.

August 19

"...if anyone competes as an athlete, he does not receive the victor's crown unless he competes according to the rules." (2 Timothy 2:5)

Johnny was a little upset. The team had counted on him and he lost the match. If he had won they would have gone to the state championship, but now they just go home. It came down to match point, the serve from the opponent hit very close to the line and Johnny missed the ball. He could have said the ball was out and got another chance, but instinctively he called it in and handed the victory to his opponent.

How often are we faced with a decision to do right or wrong? Have you ever been faced with the choice between the easy wrong over the hard right? Life can deal us those decisions often, especially in the world we live in. But how we live our life, even when others aren't watching, or can't see us, determines the type of person we truly are.

Johnny was upset. He thought his team and coach would hate him. He couldn't get out of there fast enough. The coach caught up with him just before he got in his car and put an arm around his neck. The coach said he was busy and didn't get a chance to see the match point, but he heard about it. He told Johnny how proud he was of him. He told him a lesser player would have called the ball out. He told him the other coach was standing behind Johnny and saw how close it was and was impressed with the call Johnny made. He told him it could have gone either way.

When we are faced with a decision between right and wrong, we must think of the greater picture. We must look at ourselves in the mirror every day and those tiny decisions start us on major pathways. Honesty, integrity and a willingness to do right is what truly matters.

I also want to remind us that even though we may fool others some of the time, we can never fool God. You see, every decision we are faced with, every situation in life, God is standing right there watching. He is like that coach, standing behind us waiting to see what call we make. He knows the choices we make and He knows if they are the right ones or not. And when we make the right ones, He is proud of us.

How many fall out of the game before they reach the finish line, disqualified because they did not maintain an unquestioning obedience to the word of God? In order to receive the reward, we must obey the rules of the game. The choices we make in life dictate our true character and who we serve, so pick wisely!

August 20

"His (God) eyes are on the ways of men; He sees their every step." (Job 34:21)

I have many projects started around the house and some I want finished more than others. One project I am in somewhat of a hurry to complete is my stairs. I stripped the carpet off the stairs and started replacing the risers and treads. As I began cutting the treads, I was focused on getting each step as perfect as possible. I remembered my dad telling me "measure twice, cut once." His instructions spurred me on to take my time, pay attention to what I was doing and do it right the first time.

We only have one life to live and how we live it matters. How we do things, what we say, our actions and deeds will determine where we end up once we die. Our eternal resting place, paradise (heaven) or gnashing of teeth (hell) is determined by the steps we take here in this life time.

God is the judge of our fate and where we will spend eternity, and it's based on how we live. Each step we take in this lifetime does matter and it is very important to please the God who is watching. So knowing that it only makes sense to do everything possible to get it right, doesn't it?

The steps on my staircase turned out really good, if I say so myself. I looked at them with a little pride; I had done a good job. I can only pray and strive to do the same with my life. In the end, I hope it is pleasing to God and that I hear Him say *"Well done, good and faithful servant!"* (Matt 25:21)

So what about you? Do your steps please the God who wants everyone to join Him in heaven and have eternal fellowship with Him? We know from scripture that not everyone will. What you do now matters, so I give you this friendly advice, measure each step twice....

August 21

"That man will bear the consequences of his sin." (Numbers 9:13)

As I said yesterday, I am in the process of remodeling my stairway. I took the carpet off, removed all the old wood and am replacing the treads and risers. The treads are 2" x 12" pine and I had to buy 12 foot long boards. As I took the time and effort to cut each one (remember, measure twice cut once) I made a slight err of judgment.

I learned all my woodworking skills from my father and he taught me to operate all sorts of power tools. One thing he stressed was safety. Well yesterday I was in and out, back and forth from the house to my workshop, and since I normally don't wear shoes in the house, I was slipping on and off a pair of flip flops.

A 12 foot long 2 x 12 is hard to handle alone and after one cut, I was wrestling with the long end of the board while the piece I cut fell off the saw and landed square on my toe. And since I didn't have on work boots, my toe is all swollen, black and blue. I can't blame anyone but myself and I can hear my dad now saying, "Son, what have I told you about..."

We all make bad choices and decisions once in a while. Not everything we do passes the common sense test or turns out good. A slight err is one thing, but a willful disobedience or doing what we know to be wrong will most likely result in something far greater than a black and blue toe.

The point I want to make is we are responsible for those choices and we must suffer the consequences for those decisions. If we know right from wrong, yet choose to go down the wrong path, the penalty could be great. It's on us, not anyone else.

So, I can tell you the next time I cut a 2 x 12, 12 foot long board, I will have boots on. And the next time I go into something knowing that it is wrong and I could suffer consequences, I will think twice. We have a choice; we also have a way out. Jesus will guide us, help us to make better decisions and when we do make a slight mistake, He will forgive us if we ask.

August 22

"If anyone is ashamed of me and my words in this adulterous and sinful generation, the Son of Man will be ashamed of him when he comes in his Father's glory with the holy angels." (Mark 8:38)

A group of us were minding our own business, sitting on Folly Beach soaking up the sun, when up walked four young people. They were in their teens and just strolled up on us. Not really sure what my first thought was, but what came out of their mouth floored me.

"We are from a youth ministry and we wondered if there is anything we can pray with you for?" Right here, on the beach in front of everyone? That wasn't my thought, but I imagined that would have been some responses they must have received. In fact, we were pretty quick to rattle off a few that we had been talking about and praying for ourselves.

Now, at this moment, I was wondering what would happen next. The one young man who was obviously the spokesperson asked "Can we pray for these needs right now?" His hands were spread out, inviting us to stand and take them, so we did just that. Right there on the beach, in front of everyone, we joined hands, formed a circle and the young man led us in prayer. Wow, what a remarkable moment. I bet God was beaming!

Our focus verse tells us to be open about our faith or God will be ashamed of us. The Message Bible puts it this way, *"If any of you are embarrassed over me and the way I'm leading you when you get around your fickle and unfocused friends, know that you'll be an even greater embarrassment to the Son of Man when he arrives in all the splendor of God, his Father, with an army of the holy angels."* (Mark 8:38 MSG)

Honestly, I see a lot of "superficial "Christians. They speak a good game at church or among their "church friends", but their true self comes out when they are around everyone else. Our passage tells us that is a slippery slope and very dangerous when the times comes to determine our eternal fate. We can't say one thing and live another. So what about you? Are you ashamed to be a Christ follower 24/7? Are you saved and living that life, or are you "saved" in word only? It's not too late to take a stand and be all in for Jesus. Don't be ashamed, be bold. Be the type of person God wants you to be and then feel His embrace, power and love.

August 23

"Saving is all His idea, and all his work. All we do is trust Him enough to let Him do it. It's God's gift from start to finish!" (Ephesians 2:7 MSG)

A few years ago I looked at myself in a mirror and decided it was time to do something about my weight. I started exercising regularly, drinking plenty of water and watching my daily intake of food. Because of my discipline, I was successful and lost the weight I needed. My focus was on daily proportions in order to be what I wanted to be. Minimum daily requirements became a way of life.

Daily requirements are important for our health, so shouldn't they be equally important for our spiritual life? As a pastor I am asked how much bible should one read daily, how long should one pray daily, how much money should one put in the offering plate, how often should one go to church and the list goes on and on. Seems some are concerned about minimum daily requirements when it comes to God and being a Christian.

Jesus called His disciples by simply saying "Follow me". His invitation, as simple as it was, was more than just getting up from what they were doing and walking with Him. His call to "Follow me" was also to learn from Him, follow His examples and to be like Him in everything we do.

Paul is saying that it is because God loves us that He saves us. Because of God's mercy and grace we are His children and there is nothing required of us but to follow Jesus. Paul is telling us that if it was a requirement for us to do something, *"we'd probably go around bragging that we'd done the whole thing!"*

Our "following" frees us from minimum daily requirements, yet teaches us to be like Jesus. The definition of "Christian" is "Christ like". If we are following His lead, we will learn the need to open our bibles regularly, pray often, give to the church and less fortunate and serve those around us. Isn't that what Jesus did? Isn't that what Jesus teaches?

So, when it comes to your spiritual life, your minimum daily requirements are between you and Jesus. Each of us will be different and God will lead each of us according to His purpose for us. All we need to do is follow Him and He will tell each of us what we need, how much we need and how often we need it.

August 24

"Be imitators of God, therefore, as dearly loved children and live a life of love, just as Christ loved us and gave himself up for us as a fragrant offering and sacrifice to God." (Ephesians 5:1-2)

A group of traveling salesmen assured their wives that they would be home in plenty of time for dinner. With tickets and briefcases, one of these salesmen inadvertently kicked over a display of apples. Apples flew everywhere. Without stopping or looking back, they all managed to reach the plane in time for their nearly missed boarding. ALL BUT ONE!!! He paused, took a deep breath, and with compassion for the girl whose apple stand had been overturned, he went back.

He told his buddies to go on without him, told one of them to call his wife and explain he was taking a later flight. He then returned to where the apples were all over the terminal floor. He was glad he did.

The girl was blind. She was crying and helplessly groping for her apples. No one stopped, no one cared about her plight. The salesman knelt on the floor with her, gathered up the apples, and put them back on the table. He helped organize her display and as he did, he noticed many were bruised. He set them aside.

When the task was done, he said to here, "Please let me pay for the damage we did. Are you okay?" She nodded yes. He continued "I hope we didn't spoil your day." As he started to walk away, the blind girl asked him, "Mister…" He paused, she continued, "Are you Jesus?" He slowly made his way to catch the later flight with that question burning and bouncing about in his soul: 'Are you Jesus?'

Do people mistake you for Jesus? That's our destiny, is it not? To be so much like Jesus that people cannot tell the difference as we live and interact with a world that is blind to His love, life and grace. If we claim to know Him, we should live, walk and act as He would. Knowing Him is more than simply quoting Scripture and going to church. It's actually living the Word as life unfolds day to day.

We are the apple of His eye even though we, too, have been bruised by a fall. He stopped what He was doing and picked you and me up on a hill called Calvary and paid in full for our damaged fruit.

Too many Christians are no longer fishers of men, but keepers of the aquarium. When was the last time you were mistaken for Jesus?

August 25

"Therefore, if anyone is in Christ, the new creation has come: The old has gone, the new is here!"(2 Corinthians 5:17)

We live in a world where everyone wants new and improved, the latest and greatest. Did you know that advertisers use these words to entice and attract people to buy that in which they really don't need? "New and improved" sells. Why? People are attracted to something billed as new, bigger and better.

What this reveals about people is that everyone has a deep longing for something new. This goes beyond the things we buy. People desire new; a new life, a new hairstyle, a new love, etc. They know that the old way doesn't satisfy. They feel that the old is broken and that "new and improved" will provide them a new start.

We see it in in every aspect of life. People move from church to church, relationship to relationship, job to job. It is a human need that most people search to fulfill, and most are looking in the wrong places. They need to realize it's a hole that can only be filled one way.

That need that people try so hard to fill can only be filled with a personal relationship with Jesus Christ. When we accept His love, mercy and grace, old things are gone and forgotten, and everything is made new. And here is the part that I like, the newness isn't superficial, it isn't a gadget that will wear out, it isn't another place that gets old. It is new every day. It is different every day. There is no "plan" to pay for; the price is free, by grace through faith in Jesus. He gives it away free of charge, each day to those who want it.

How can this change us and make us new? Jesus gives us a new outlook, new perspective. With Jesus we have new desires and wants. We have new motives and motivations. We think differently, we have new purpose and direction. And most importantly, we have a new destination.

Jesus Christ offers a new life that far exceeds a new phone or anything else this world could ever offer. It is something that never grows old, never wears out and never lets you down. So what are you waiting for? New can be yours without waiting in line or waiting until your current contract expires. New can be yours for the asking.....

August 26

"But thanks be to God! He gives us the victory through our Lord Jesus Christ." (1 Corinthians 15:37)

You think you have it tough? Life isn't fair sometimes and often we can make mistakes that take us where we don't want to be. But what we do in those circumstances can define us. Last night I met a man that was just released from jail. He was testifying how his life has changed and how he is living a new life, in spite of just being released from jail and having a record. He testified as to how he came to know Christ, and as to why he was at our church.

He told a story of how he met a guy in jail who has a connection with our church. This guy he met is in jail for a long time, yet while inside, he has made a choice to live a life for Christ. He started a bible study and is leading men to Christ. Several of these men have visited our church since getting out. They are bound and determined to live a new life, one for Christ.

The kicker to this story is that the parents of the guy doing the bible study are connecting with these men when they get out. They are helping these guys and they were present last night. I watched as the parents cried like babies, knowing their son is living for the Lord and leading people to Christ.

You see, we all make mistakes, but what we choose to do afterwards matters. Even in a bad situation, we can turn it around and live a Godly life. Even when things are tough, you have a choice to make and you can turn it into something positive, with God. But you must make a choice.

As Christ followers we can have victory as our focus verse tells us, even in bad situations and tough times. The bible teaches us that *"in all things God works for the good of those who love him, who have been called according to his purpose."* (Romans 8:28) But we must choose to live our lives for and pleasing to God.

August 27

"I am the way and the truth and the life. No one comes to the Father except through me." (John 14:6)

Have you ever heard the saying "You can't get there from here"? Well I experienced a real life occurrence of this at Sturgis. We left Sturgis, SD on our way to Devil's Tower. Our instructions were to cross into Montana and turn left onto Route something or other. As we crossed into Montana we saw a homemade sign that stated "Short cut to Devil's Tower" and it pointed down a two-lane road. It didn't look like a road that led to a major attraction so we kept going.

Some 30 miles later we pulled over knowing that we missed something. All that was around was an old building that looked deserted. I opened the door and found myself in a small town Post Office/home.

I asked the Post Master for directions to Devil's Tower. He told me to go back to that homemade sign and take that road. I told him that didn't look like the right road in which he said "I don't care what it looks like, you can't get there any other way." So basically he told us "you can't get there from here, so you need to change directions."

What a life lesson. In a society where people think there are many ways to heaven, at times we can find ourselves on a road that just doesn't get us there. Some try to be good, and we know from experience and the lessons of the bible that being good isn't enough. Some say all they need to do is merely believe in God and they are going, but we know that there is more to it than that. Other people follow other "religions" and I believe they find themselves missing out and on the wrong road, going in the wrong direction.

In our focus verse, Jesus gives us a pretty clear road map on how to get to where we all want to go. It isn't hard; we just need to follow Him and His instructions. Stay on the path He sets before us, obey His word and you can get to where you need and want to be.

We saddled back up on our Harleys and followed the old guy's instructions to the letter. Pretty soon we were standing at the base of Devil's Tower in awe. By following Jesus, we could one day be doing the same thing at the gates of Heaven.

August 28

"My grace is sufficient for you, for my power is made perfect in weakness."
(2 Corinthians 12:8)

One night as Joy and I set out to go to our bible study, she rolled her motorcycle out the garage, turned the switch and hit the starter. It clicked and went dead. Nothing, no sound, no lights, no gauges, it was dead. So I told her to roll it down to the street. Well if you have ever been to our house, we sit on top of a pretty good sized hill. Not the best driveway for motorcycle owners, but we have made it work for many years.

Once the bike was on level ground, I looked at the battery. Shame on me, I found corrosion. I got a wrench, loosened the terminals, cleaned them up and the tightened them. She tried to start it, still nothing. I got out the jumper cables, brought the truck down to jump it, and still nothing. It wasn't going anywhere.

So needing to get going, I told Joy to push while I pushed and steered the bike. We turned it around, pointed it towards the garage and off we went. Well we got about 5 feet up that drive and it came to a stop. We couldn't move it beyond that point.

Have you ever hit one of those points that, under your own power and your own strength, you just couldn't move? Sometimes we hit a wall and nothing we do will move it or get us through it. Too often we try to do things on our own that are beyond our strength, only to fail.

You have heard it said, He is strong when we are weak. Too often we try to accomplish the things we have no power over. If we allow Jesus to handle those things, our lives would be much simpler.

Well I would like to say we prayed and that bike went up that hill, but it didn't work that way. What we did realize is that the bike could stay where it was for now. We had a place to be and God's word to discuss. So we headed out leaving that bike right where it was. It still sits there as I write this, and in my weakness to push that bike up a hill, God gave me the wisdom not to kill myself.

August 29

"...the whole crowd of disciples began joyfully to praise God in loud voices..."
(Luke 19:37)

I love it when I see a group of people around motorcycles. People are awed at the look of them. I love to see the look in their eyes. I also love to see the reactions as the bikes come to life. There is normally a mixed reaction, some shield their ears, others marvel at the rich sound, and then there are those that walk away in disgust because of the loudness, just wanting it to stop or go away.

Our focus verse tells of a time when Jesus entered into Jerusalem. The crowd that gathered had a mixed reaction as well. They got loud and shouted praises to their King, their Messiah, and their Savior. But not everyone was pleased with the noise.

Just as is the case with the reactions when those bikes come to life; people also have mixed feelings about the noise Christians make towards their Savior. Some love to hear the praises and want to join in. Others walk away in disgust because of the noise. The Pharisees wanted Jesus to make them stop; they wanted the disciples to be quiet.

Jesus said that *"if they keep quiet, the stones will cry out."* He told them that even if the people don't praise Him, the stones would. Jesus will be praised, nothing will ever stop that. We are called as Christians to praise Him and to do so willingly and joyfully. This concept may not fit the unbelieving world that expects us to keep our beliefs to ourselves or at least be quiet about it. But we are to praise Him none the less.

Just as the bikers don't conform to the "norm" of this world, Christians aren't to live according to the world's expectations. We are called to live according to God's ways, not the worlds. As Christians we are called to live lives pleasing to Christ. I want everyone to hear me when I praise my God and I make no attempts to compromise that praise or to be quiet about it. I want people to look at me as being different from the rest of the world.

They already do because I am a one of those "noisy bikers". I also want them to know I am one of those "noisy Christians". I will continue to ruffle feathers, both on my bike and off, because I am pursuing God with my daily devotion, praise, worship and every fiber of my body.

So if you believe in God, and are one of His disciples, make some noise!

August 30

"The thief comes only to steal, kill and destroy. I have come that they may have life, and have it to the full." (John 10:10)

I have been seeing a lot in the news lately about terrorists. Every time I watch the news it seems there is another story about some form of terrorist and an evil act they are committing. Seems evil is running rampant in our world.

Did you know Satan is a terrorist? And like most modern day terrorists, it is impossible to negotiate with him. His will is to hijack us while on the path God has placed us on. His mission is to steal our joy, terminate our lives and degrade our relationship with God the Father and he is very aggressive about it.

Our focus verse warns us of Satan's plan. It helps us to see we must be observant and aware. We must keep our eyes open.

As a believer, we must fix our eyes on God. We must embed His word on our hearts. We must remain unswerving in devotion to Jesus. When we abide in fellowship with Him, we will be tempted by the enemy to resort to human wisdom rather than Godly guidance.

Has a relationship drained you of the energy God has given you to serve Him? Are you accused of weaknesses that urge you to deny your usefulness to God? The enemy's tactics are limitless, but his intention is plain: get the Christian off track! He wants us to mistrust Jesus and start making decisions based on fear and anxiety.

But we must remember Jesus' mission is to give us abundant life. It may not be easy or comfortable, but it will be good and founded on His joy. When we are confident that it's God's will and the circumstances arise that seem to contradict His will, we must know where they come from and cling to God. Do not negotiate with the terrorist when he threatens. If we let circumstances constrain us, Satan wins. God's voice must be the only one we hear and our faith must be fixed on Jesus and not waver; it's the key to abundant life.

August 31

"When I came to you, brothers, I did not come with eloquence or superior wisdom as I proclaimed to you the testimony about God. For I resolved to know nothing while I was with you except Jesus Christ and Him crucified. I came to you in weakness and fear, and with much trembling. My message and my preaching were not with wise and persuasive words, but with a demonstration of the Spirit's power, so that your faith might not rest on men's wisdom, but on God's power." (1 Corinthians 2:1-5)

As I write these thoughts and observations, I want to make one thing clear, these aren't written in order to show how smart or knowledgeable I am. They are written merely because I have felt God tell me to use them to spread His word to others. I, like Paul in our focus verse, want to share the Spirit's power working through me.

God gives me the power to be bold and speak when others may be quiet. God gives me the power to speak when others may think it to be offensive. I know not everyone will agree with what I write, some may even think I am being overbearing and pushy, but I feel God telling me to write, so write I will.

People can think what they want of me, but I am driven by God and I will be obedient at all cost. I take the Great Commission of Matthew 28 seriously. We are called to tell the world about Jesus and to baptize and disciple, so that is what I will do, with the help of God.

We must accept the truth that not everyone will understand or agree with us as we carry out that calling. But we must do as we are commissioned and spread the Gospel to as many as we can. Even Jesus told His disciples to go and tell, and if people wouldn't listen to them, "shake the dust off your feet when you leave."

So speak up if you are a Christian. Be bold to speak the truth no matter what others may think. Write, preach, sing, and shout if that is what God calls you to do. Take your role as a disciple of Christ serious and get busy. The kingdom is near, tell others about the greatest gift you have ever received, Salvation!

September 1

"Suppose one of you has a friend, and he goes to him at midnight and says, 'Friend, lend me three loaves of bread, because a friend of mine on a journey has come to me, and I have nothing to set before him." (Luke 11:5-6)

When my son was little he had a way of driving me crazy. If he saw something on TV and wanted it, he would ask for it nonstop. When he got up, when he was sitting at the dinner table, before he went to bed. He was relentless.

Have you ever wanted something so bad but were afraid to ask for it? As a Christ follower, that is called a worthless prayer. You know, one of those prayers that you thought was too big to pray? What about a prayer that you asked once and didn't want to bother God with it anymore? We all have prayers that seem to be inappropriate, too large, or the initial answer is no. True prayer means desperation outweighs protocol.

Our focus verse is Jesus' way of teaching us that a true prayer worth praying requires persistence. Jesus tells us that with boldness and persistence to ask, and keep asking. He even goes on to tell us to ask in order to receive, seek to find and knock for the door to be opened.

Most of us pray for a period of time, and then when we have not heard from God, we give up, assume it wasn't His will or He is too busy. Scripture never gives us permission to drop a request because we don't get an immediate response. We are to have a never quit asking attitude to our prayers. In fact, 1 Thessalonians tells us to "pray continuously".

So I say to you… pray with confidence and persistence. Declare His will in a situation and expect His response to your request. While we should always be open for Him to redirect our prayers, or even say "no", we should never assume that a slow answer, according to our standards, is a non-answer. Like the farmer who waits for the harvest, we are to wait for His answers. Jesus is very clear so keep on asking!

September 2

"No one knows about that day or hour, not even the angels in heaven, nor the Son, but only the Father. Be on guard! Be alert! You do not know when that time will come." (Mark 13:32-33)

I went to the funeral of a 49 year old woman, a biker, and a friend. The family was in a natural state of grief, they were also in a state of shock, because she was so young and her death was so sudden. No one expects to die that young, or that sudden, but the bible tells us that we don't know the time of our demise.

We learn from our focus verse that the time of our death is not known by anyone but God. He and He alone holds that time secret and it isn't revealed until His purpose is to be accomplished. Scripture also tells us to be ready and to be alert. What does this mean? If we don't know when we are going to die, what do we prepare for, what are we on guard for?

We are to be prepared for the day our soul enters into eternity. The reality is we all will spend eternity in one of two places, heaven or hell. Both places are real and both places are forever. We must prepare ourselves now for that reality. We can't put it off until later, because later is not guaranteed.

The hardest part of a funeral for me is the not knowing. Oh, if I attend a funeral of someone I know for a fact had a relationship with Jesus, I can celebrate knowing that they have entered the gates of heaven. But if I attend a funeral of one who no one is really quite sure, that is hard. To not know their eternal state is a tough one. It is difficult for the family. On one hand they want to believe that they are "in a better place", but are they? I think the lesson here is to know without a shadow of doubt and to make sure your family and loved ones know as well.

What is the status of your eternal soul? Have you made the decision about where you will spend eternity? If you haven't, or you aren't sure, you need to know. Salvation is easy, ask God into your heart, believe He is your Lord and Savior and then start following His commands, ways and teachings. If you want to talk, I am always available, just call me....

246

September 3

"Compromise your beliefs, or die!" (Daniel 3:17-18)

These days the news seems to be filled with the evidence of a declining and dying world. The media pushes the filth of this world down our throats and fill the airways and papers with what this world views as "must know" news and decaying morals. Most people I have talked to dismiss bad behaviors as "only being human". We must be reminded that "only being human" is what made us sinners to start with.

A long time ago a man and woman were given everything they could ask for with only one rule and they failed miserably. They could have been excused because they were "only being human" but God created us in His image; pure, righteous, and holy. God held them to a standard and because they failed, He expelled them from the Garden of Eden. We too are faced with a standard of living and in order to live that way we have choices to make.

Our focus verse refers to three men who were faced with an ultimatum. They were told to bow and worship the image of a man, but they refused. They could have found a variety of excuses for compromise, but they chose to place their faith in God and worship only Him.

Very few of us will ever face a "compromise or die!" ultimatum. Almost all of us will be tempted to compromise our convictions and bow to things like financial gain, physical pleasure, personal recognition, or the fear of conflict. We are constantly tempted with the entertainment we watch, listen to, and read, the web sites we go to and sometimes the company that we keep. Standing firm to our beliefs requires a determined effort to remain solidly on God's path.

Hearing God's direction for our life can be difficult; but one truth remains - God never asks us to compromise His standard in order to follow His path...NEVER! We can therefore be assured that ANY compromise represents a deviation from His plan.

We need to strengthen the convictions God has already placed on our heart and we don't need to be ashamed of, or fear, what we know is His true calling on our lives. We need to conduct ourselves daily, in public and private, so that what we believe in is reflected in the way we live our lives. Let's take a stand and live a God-honoring life...without compromise.

247

September 4

"I am Jesus whom you are persecuting" (Acts 9:5)

The Apostle Paul was once a persecutor of Christians. He went from house to house and dragged believers off to prison (Acts 8:3). Paul set off for Damascus in order to rid the land of these "misguided" Christian troublemakers, however, Jesus had other plans!

Although Paul was persecuting those who believed in Jesus, and as our focus verse tells us, Jesus knew it. Jesus still revealed Himself to Paul in such a magnificent manner that there was no doubt as to the truth of the Gospel. Paul encountered Christ and was blinded by the light and his life was changed forever.

Most of us will never encounter Jesus in such a dramatic way as Paul did. One day, without any lights, voices, or great fanfare, Jesus simply meets us where we are and forever changes the course of our life. And just as Paul was called to follow Jesus, we are called to follow and be obedient.

When we encounter Jesus, truly encounter Jesus, our lives can never be the same. We are new creatures, changed forever for God's purpose. Our attitudes, actions, and way of living should change. There should be evidence of that change in our lives that others can see. Just as a pregnant woman starts showing the signs of a baby in the womb around month 3 or 4, the new Christian should start showing signs of being born again soon after conversion. The change can come in drastic ways, but can also be subtle. The way we talk, the way we act, how we carry ourselves, the company we keep, we realize the old habits aren't becoming of the Godly life we are called to live.

Change and transformation are an important part of the Christian life. We are promised a transformation, to be more like Christ and as we serve Jesus in our everyday lives, we are gradually changed to be more Christ-like in our thoughts and actions.

What actions, behaviors, or worldly ways do you still possess that you know would not be welcomed in Christ's body? As you grow in Christ, look at your life and ask God to change those things that aren't Christ-like. He will give you the power to change.

September 5

"God overlooks it as long as you don't know any better—but that time is past. The unknown is now known, and he's calling for a radical life-change."
(Acts 17:30 MSG

When my son was very young, he was a Magic Johnson fan. He loved watching Magic play and I often heard him outside doing a play by play as he dribbled and shot. He was always Magic and he always drained the winning shot.

We had the chance to go on a trip to Mexico around that same time. As we walked the streets we came on a vendor selling NBA jerseys and wouldn't you know it, there hung a Magic Johnson jersey. So I bought him one. He was so excited, but I made him leave it in the package until we got home. When he finally opened it he was not very happy. The name on the back of the jersey was misspelled and read JONHSON.

Cheap knock-offs are deceiving, but when you look real close, you can tell they aren't the real deal. The same can be said about our spiritual lives. Those of us who believe and say we are Christ followers are called to "be like Christ", to "be holy" because He is holy. We are called to be changed people, different from those who continue to walk in sin. But for many, they are as easily spotted as the misspelling on that jersey.

So what about you? Are you the genuine article when bearing Jesus' name, or are you a "in name only" believer? Does your life reflect true change, complete change, or is your life the same as it was before you believed?

My prayer is that you are the real deal, because the end is coming. We live in a very dark world and I want to remind you that we (true Christ followers) aren't of this world. The world we belong to is the kingdom of heaven and it's only open to those who are for real. So be for real....

September 6

"Andrew, Simon Peter's brother, was one of the two who heard what John had said and who had followed Jesus. The first thing Andrew did was to find his brother Simon and tell him, 'We have found the Messiah" (that is, the Christ). And he brought him to Jesus.'" (John 1:40-42)

I bought a new lawn mower, but I kept the old one. I just couldn't throw it out. Whenever the new one gave me trouble, out would come the "old reliable" one. The bible talks to us about people who were just like my old mower, constant and predictable. Their work isn't affected by moods, cloudy days or rocky trails. They aren't addicted to pats on the back, attention, or applause. They focus on the task at hand and are as faithful in dark prisons as in the lime light.

Andrew...he wasn't a preacher, never stood on stage, and may never have been on a planning committee. But if it weren't for him, Peter would have stayed a fisherman. Andrew was constantly telling someone about Jesus.

Then there was Epaphroditus. Most of us have never heard of him, but Paul knew him well. Paul called him "brother, fellow worker, fellow soldier and messenger." Paul paid him praise when he wrote *"he almost died for the gospel."*

These accolades don't come by simply attending Sunday service. You don't earn these accolades by occasional attending small group or the church picnic. They are earned over time and by getting your hands dirty, rolling up your sleeves, getting to know people and letting them know you. You get accolades like the ones Paul used by being there when needed and staying until the job is done.

Reliable servants are the binding of the bible. Most never made the headlines and their names aren't used often in sermons, but if it weren't for them and their devotion to God, many events we read about would never have happened. Their examples should be as important as any written on the pages of the bible.

Reliable - "re" over and over again and "liable" means responsible. Dependable means to be trustworthy. To be reliable and dependable takes time and is earned. Just as my old mower has earned the title "old reliable", through time and service to God and the body of Christ, you too can become reliable and dependable, a vital part of the kingdom of God here on earth.

September 7

"... because of the man's boldness he will get up and give him as much as he needs. So I say to you: Ask and it will be given to you; seek and you will find; knock and the door will be opened to you. For everyone who asks receives; he who seeks finds; and to him who knocks, the door will be opened." (Luke 11:8-10)

In our house we have a rule. If the porch light is on we welcome visitors, but when the light goes out, we are either in bed or want to discourage guests. This is a custom handed down to us from our parents. But with that said, we have also made it clear to those that know us, if there is a true need, you are welcomed into our home. We turn no one away, no matter the time, or even if the light is on or not.

In our focus verses we read about a man who seeks help from a neighbor because he has unexpected visitors late at night. It was late, an inconvenient time to go to the neighbor for help, but the need was there. And even though it wasn't the best time, the man was persistent and the neighbor answered the knock at the door.

This is how the Father is to be sought, with persistence. His nature is to meet needs. If we are zealous to have others' needs met, certainly He is even more zealous to meet these needs.

How persistent are you seeking God's help for the needs of others? When we are told to *"bear one another's burdens"* (Colossians 3:13), do we interpret that as a brief mention in our daily prayer? Or are we zealous and bold in our approach to God? This boldness pleases God. In this story it is almost as if God is begging to be pestered.

Does our zealous approach to God on behalf of others equal the boldness of this persistent neighbor? Are we persistent in helping our brothers and sisters meet their needs, physically and spiritually? We need to go before God with persistence and intercession for others.

September 8

"The dead man came out, his hands and feet wrapped with strips of linen, and a cloth around his face." (John 11:44)

The phrase "out with the old, in with the new" reminds me of a new year's resolution. New Year's resolutions are always about bringing in the new and disposing of the old. For most people, it is about making a resolution to become a better person, begin an exercise regimen, get healthy, or to make a change in our life. It is about ridding oneself of the old and becoming a new person.

In our focus verse we read of a man who has died and was buried. His family grieves over his death. Jesus performs a miracle that demonstrates His power and deity. He calls Lazarus out of the grave, yet he was still bound.

Jesus tells those around him to free him from what bounds him. Jesus is telling us that it is hard for someone alive because of Jesus to move, act, or do while bound with the very things that bind them when they were dead. In order to be fully alive in Jesus, one must shed the grave clothes of the old self.

As I thought of this I decided to apply this to my Christian walk. It has become a desire of mine to rid myself of anything that may cause me to stumble or constrains me from being what Jesus wants me to be. I want to rid myself of anything that doesn't align itself with Jesus, His ways and His will on my life. Negativity, worry, procrastination to name a few things has to go, because it isn't conducive to my spiritual growth. It's time to allow God to handle those things that I worry about. It's time to be more positive and stop allowing negativity to get in the way of the things God wants of me. It is time to stop blaming a perceived lack of time and start reading my bible more, praying more and doing the things God wants me to do.

If I want my Christian walk to be everything that Jesus wants it to be, I need to shed the things that restrict, bind and hinder. If I want to be the man that Jesus wants me to be, I need to shed the old for the new. In order to fulfill Jesus will and purpose for my life, it is "out with the old (self), in with the new (self)."

252

September 9

"The apostles and the brothers throughout Judea heard that the Gentiles also had received the word of God. So when Peter went up to Jerusalem, the circumcised believers criticized him and said, 'You went into the house of uncircumcised men and ate with them.'" (Acts 11:1-3)

I have often been criticized for going places and associating with people most "Christians" feel I shouldn't. They mean well, but I think they miss the point of outreach ministry. They didn't understand, at first.

In our focus verses above, we notice that Peter has pretty much the same thing happen to him. He received a vision from God, he got an invitation from some guy to go preach the gospel in the most unlikely place, and he went. Because of his actions, people came to know Jesus and were saved. But the people inside the church were not happy about it. The Message tells it like this: *"What do you think you're doing rubbing shoulders with that crowd, eating what is prohibited and ruining our good name?"*

Jesus heard the same thing when He went to eat with Matthew and his sinners and tax collector friends. (Mark 2:15-16) Too often those inside the church forget that they were once outside the church and someone came to them to tell them about Jesus. Otherwise they would still be outside the church. When one begins to grasp that, they buy into the concept of outreach.

Well-meaning people, who love me, expressed concern that I may be influenced. They warned *"bad company corrupts good character."* (1 Corinthians 5:33) They are right to a degree, but they needed a gentle reminder that we as Christ followers are called to "go" to every nook and cranny, "tell" everyone we can of the good news of Jesus Christ, and "teach" people how to live a life far different than the one they are living. I can't do that unless I go outside the walls of the church.

I am thankful someone did that for me. When I needed it most, someone left the safe confines of the church building and entered into a friendship with a sinner such as I and led me straight to the arms of Jesus. Once we, as Christ followers, understand that and do that, the world as we know it can change. The world needs more followers willing to go where others won't and share what God is doing in their lives, so more can come to know the saving grace of Jesus. So let them talk, and they will, just go and tell.

September 10

"Boldly and without hindrance he preached the kingdom of God and taught about the Lord Jesus Christ." (Acts 28:31)

My main focus in ministry is to tell others about the Gospel and what Jesus is doing in my life. I know that I am empowered by Jesus to do His work that He calls me to do.

As Christians, these things should not be new to us. We also should know that this isn't a new concept. The disciples did just this. They went and told others, they lived lives that others saw as different and they were empowered by the Holy Spirit.

Jesus called Paul into His ministry and sent him on numerous mission trips to spread the good news. Paul was equipped by the Holy Spirit for what he would face and who he would come in contact with. Our focus verse tells us that Paul did just that. This is Outreach Ministry 101. Go, tell, teach, and win souls for God's kingdom.

Jesus doesn't call us to do the same thing we've always done in the same ways we've always done them. He calls us to go further and deeper, go to places where we can't depend on our own experience and abilities. Do things that we can't depend on our own experience and abilities. He puts us in places where we must depend entirely on Him.

He has given us the Holy Spirit as our guide, our teacher and our counselor. We have to learn how to rely on Him in every situation. His power, through us, will help us to reach people, speak boldly, and be our strength even when we feel weak. "The Holy Spirit may call us into some very unlikely places, with effective witness to some very unlikely people." (Bruce Paul)

The next time you step out, try to share your faith, and when you feel helpless and know you're in over your head…just remember that God placed you there. Outreach can be scary but we can't avoid it and be obedient to Jesus at the same time. This is the way to bear fruit in His kingdom. Jesus knows what it takes to bear fruit, and it always involves going beyond our own expertise, our limited vision, and our resources. He calls us to step out into places and with people where we have no choice but to depend on His instructions and His power.

"God doesn't call people who are qualified. He calls people who are willing and then He qualifies them." (Richard Parker)

254

September 11

"Do not let your hearts be troubled. You believe in God, believe also in me." (John 14:1)

9/11 - I woke to the news that one of the twin towers in NYC had been hit. As I watched the news, one tower smoking, I see an airplane come into view. At first I thought it was a replay of what happened earlier, but then realize that the one tower was already smoking. I see with my own eyes the second plane slam into the second tower, practically going through it. I sat in disbelief.

As I watched throughout the day, I saw something that will be forever etched in my mind. I watched in disbelief as the towers crumbled, collapsed and fell. With sorrow in my heart I cried that day. I didn't know a soul that lived there; my heart was heavy and went out to those that lost their lives. My prayers went out to their families and for those watching this life changing event.

As I recall that day, I turn to the one thing that has become a constant in my life, my bible. Jesus said in our focus verse, "Do not be troubled…" and I believe He meant it. We also read in scripture about things getting far worse.

We hear of wars and rumors of wars. We are frightened when we see falling towers and biological pathogens killing hundreds. But Jesus says our hearts should not be troubled.

For those who are Christ followers, even if all hell breaks loose around us, (and it quite literally is), there is a place of safety beneath the surface of troubled waters. Jesus dwells there and we are allowed to dwell with Him.

The world cannot touch the one who rests in Jesus' care. It may threaten, but it can never harm those who seek rest with Jesus. He is our Refuge, our Shield, and our Provider and He tells us not to worry. He can be trusted, the Rock of Ages does not move.

So as times get tough, when the world seems to be falling apart and when your heart is heavy, remember the words of Proverbs 3:5; "Trust in the Lord with all your heart and lean not on your own understanding…"

September 12

"LORD, there is no one like you to help the powerless against the mighty. Help us, O LORD our God, for we rely on you..." (2 Chronicles 14:11)

On a recent trip, we visited a place called Hopewell Rocks in New Brunswick, Canada. At low tide you can walk on the ocean floor. The rock formations loom overhead, an amazing sight, one that everyone should experience.

While walking around I looked up and noticed in several places, small trees growing out of the rocks. They seemed to be hanging on for dear life. How can a tree grow out of a rock? Tree roots need dirt to grow, but it's a rock, yet they seem to be just fine.

This got me to thinking, how often do we seem to be just hanging on? You know, life gets overwhelming at times and we feel like we are clinging by our finger tips. How many times have you just felt like letting go?

Those trees are a picture defying what we think is normal. They rely on God to provide what they need to survive. With little dirt to grow its roots, it gets its nutrients from other sources. It gets light from the sun, which God created. It gets water from the ocean spray and the rain that falls, which is given by the hand of God. It grows because God wants it to grow.

We can survive even the most difficult times when we rely on God to give us what we need to get through life. We can actually overcome the difficult times when we put our lives in God's hand, allow Him to provide us with what we need to make it through. We can even grow through the provisions provided by God, even when the world sees us in a difficult position. So no matter what you face today, hold on, God can rescue you. Call upon Him for help, and He will provide.

September 13

"In fact, everyone who wants to live a godly life in Christ Jesus will be persecuted." (2 Timothy 3:12)

I have been doing ministry for a while now and over the years have seen the good and bad in people. I have learned some hard lessons and have had my share of ups and downs. Life as a Christian comes with a certain amount of rejection and that's not always easy to take. People can be harsh and some will try to hurt you for the way you choose to live.

We call that persecution. It comes when you are living a lifestyle totally opposite of the lifestyle the world expects of you. Many places in scripture we are told straight up that when we live as Christ commands us to live; we will be persecuted, even hated by some.

I was talking to a friend and I found myself lecturing him on where to go and what to do as a Christian. I felt bad afterwards and thought I was out of line. I asked that friend for forgiveness although I had done what I did out of love. You see, I was reminded that there are some that will try to pull you down when you are trying to stand tall. It is easier to be pulled down than to lift someone up.

My young friend is an on fire Christ follower, wanting to do great things for the kingdom, but often as Christ followers we need to remember this tough lesson, not everyone wants what you have. Not everyone wants you around to share your faith with them; they want you around to pull you back into that darkness that you came from.

We learn three lessons about persecution. We must expect it, endure it and embrace it. This may be tough but we are told that *"Blessed are those who are persecuted because of righteousness, for theirs is the kingdom of heaven. Blessed are you when people insult you, persecute you and falsely say all kinds of evil against you because of Me. Rejoice and be glad, because great is your reward in heaven..."* (Matthew 5:10-12)

Rejoice when you are persecuted and worry if you aren't. When you aren't persecuted, you may not be living as Christ wants you to...

September 14

"Remember this: Whoever sows sparingly will also reap sparingly, and whoever sows generously will also reap generously." (2 Corinthians 9:6)

I have a habit of never spending my loose change. I save it until I get home and then drop it in a jar we keep for just this. Our intent is to fill it, then cash it in.

I read a story about a little boy who had a dad that did the same. He put all his change in a jar and was determined that the contents of that jar would provide a better life for his son.

Well, the years passed and the boy went to college and got a job in another town. Once when visiting dad, the son checked and the jar his father kept was gone. It had served its purpose and wasn't needed any longer.

The son got married and had a child. He had told his wife of the pickle jar and how it played a role in the life he now lives. He spoke of the life lessons he learned from his father because of that jar.

The son took his wife and child home for a visit and one night after dinner my wife took the baby into his parents' room for a diaper change. She returned with tears in her eyes. She handed the baby to its grandfather and took her husband by the hand.

"Look" she said and directed his attention to the spot beside the dresser. There sat the pickle jar as if it had never been moved. The bottom already covered with coins. As the son looked up, he noticed his dad standing there with baby in his arms.

I shared this story with you because as I read it for the first time, God spoke to me about its meaning. I too am a father, one that loves my son and would do anything for him. I too sacrificed and provided for my son, in order for him to have a better life than me.

But this story spoke far greater truths into my heart. I recalled after reading this story the truth of a Father who poured into my life. He poured into me a means that changed my life, shaped my future and gave me the life I could have never had on my own.

That Father I am referring to is naturally God. Most of us know the biblical truths of why God sent His son, Jesus Christ. Jesus' coming was so we would never feel the pain He felt on that cross. His purpose was to give each of us a better way of life, much like the father in the above story. So now it's your turn, pour into others' lives so they too can know what you know and live the life God wants them to live.

September 15

"Remember this: Whoever sows sparingly will also reap sparingly, and whoever sows generously will also reap generously. " (2 Corinthians 9:6)

Since I didn't grow up in church, there were several things that I had to learn through time. One of them was the concept of tithing. I didn't understand the whole thing of giving away my money. I didn't understand if you give the percentage you make before taxes or after. I am being honest; I was lost when it came to these things.

Then I heard about giving of your "first fruits", your offering to God. It was explained to me in a way I understood and then, and only then did I begin tithing. But something happened, I wanted to give more. I wanted to help others so I gave extra, and then something else happened. It was as if I never gave enough.

Many of us have heard it said that you can't out give God. Our mind always thinks in terms of money and monetary gain. Give your tithe, God gives us more money. Well, maybe that is true, but not always. God asks us to give of our time and energy as well as our money, and when we do, He blesses that too.

What God promises is that you give and He blesses. God loves a "cheerful giver". God doesn't need our money, so it doesn't imply that you give to God and He is happy. No, what it means is that He loves to see a Christian who is so filled with the joy of the Lord that we want to share what we have with others.

I know sharing is hard and we are often rejected. I know we get tired and feel we are wasting our time. But we are told to share, go and tell. So, don't give up, give out of your abundance.

So I challenge you to look for opportunities to share God with others. Look for opportunities to give the gift of the good news of Jesus Christ to people that need to hear it. Look for opportunities to give God's love for everyone to everyone you meet.

September 16

"A Canaanite woman from that vicinity came to him, crying out, 'Lord, Son of David, have mercy on me! My daughter is suffering terribly from demon-possession.' Jesus did not answer a word." (Matthew 15:22-23)

My dog Ziggy loves cereal. Bring out the container and she comes running. I normally do not give her "people" food, but every now and then I "drop" a piece for her. She quickly grabs it and runs to a safe spot to eat her treat.

Jesus is confronted by a woman who wants healing for her daughter, yet Jesus ignores her at first and then pretty much calls her a dog. He withholds His healing because she isn't worthy of it. I have to admit, I have read this passage many times, but today it seemed to bother me.

Why would the Savior of the world withhold that in which He came to give? So I went digging and what I found was very interesting and gave me hope. You see, Jesus came for the Israelites, God's chosen people. This woman along with most of us reading this, do not fit into that group. She was pretty much an outcast and, to the Jews, considered lower than a dog.

Was Jesus really going to withhold His power to one who asked, simply because of her social status? If He did then where would that leave us? Or was Jesus testing her? I believe He wanted to see if she would acknowledge her unworthiness to receive His healing. And if we read the entire passage, we see that she agreed with His description completely.

Agreeing she was an unworthy Gentile, like you and I, she asked for His mercy, love, and grace. She basically said, "You're right, I am not worthy but I notice that crumbs sometimes fall from the table to the floor. Can't I at least have a crumb?

Jesus was amazed at her great faith, and her daughter was healed. Often those that think they are the closest to Him have no hunger for what Jesus offers, yet we learn that a self-confessed "doggie" cries out for it. And that cry was rewarded.

So are we like Ziggy, patiently waiting for something to fall, or are we standing at Jesus feet begging for what we want? I think Jesus wants us to come to Him and ask, no matter how unworthy we may seem. He honors the wishes of those who truly want the gifts He gives. But we have to go to Him with faith that we will receive.

260

September 17

"From this time many of his disciples turned back and no longer followed him" (John 6:66)

Sometimes you can say things and know that you will get a certain reaction. I remember when I tried out for football in high school. The first day with over 100 guys on the field, out walked the coach. With clip board in hand, he announced that starting that very day there would be two practices every day and each one would be one and a half hours long. I watched as the coach marked out names of those who walked off the field.

I believe Jesus made statements to intentionally thin out the ranks as well. While Jesus was going around performing miracles, the number of followers rose. Then one day while teaching, Jesus spoke some pretty tough things and as our focus verse says, some walked away.

Now, I may be wrong, but I think Jesus wanted to rid himself of fair-weather followers. Jesus knew there were some that hung around just for the show, while others truly believed that he was the Messiah. And while I'm sure Jesus was sorry to see them go, I believe he preferred having a few true believers around him to a throng of fans who said they believed but did little to change their lives.

I believe the same is true today. Jesus wants followers who are willing to stick around for the hard stuff. He wants true believers, ones who will do whatever it takes to serve, to go and to tell. Being a follower of Jesus is not easy, but the rewards are great. So, will you stick around?

September 18

"I tell you the truth, anyone who has faith in me will do what I have been doing. He will do even greater things than these, because I am going to the Father." (John 14:12)

Ever see something and immediately a thought is planted in your mind? While sitting in a bible study once, I happened to look across the room and saw "Found people find people. Saved people serve people. Growing people change. You can't do life alone" written on the wall.

Simple words but for me they became a powerful reminder. I really like the book of Acts. For me it is how the church was born and how the church should operate today. It doesn't take long reading the book of Acts to see that the people who initially followed Jesus finally got it. After all the lessons, parables and rebukes by Jesus, the men and women that followed Jesus up to the cross got it.

Think about it, they were lost; Jesus found them and gave them a better way of life. They waited for the very thing Jesus promised, the Holy Spirit, and in the upper room it came to them. They immediately began to find others who were lost and bring them into the family. They began to serve other's needs, bringing more into the family. They began to change, to be transformed in the way they acted, thought, and dealt with others. The old ways were gone; the new life Jesus talked about was evident. And what inspires me most is that they began to do life together as likeminded people.

What if the church today were like that? Oh, I don't mean church as a building, I mean the church as in the people who believe in, follow, live for and obey the word of God? What if we were to live as the disciples did in the book of Acts? What would happen in this world? How would this world be changed?

We look for politicians to change the world. But I believe we, the Christ followers, could have the most impact on the world if we only live up to our potential.

Think about it, with faith in Jesus and the Holy Spirit within us, we can do anything. Remember Peter, the guy who denied Jesus, well we are told in Acts that his shadow healed people. Peter did nothing but believed and lived as Jesus commanded and power came out of him. What could we do? Think about it....

September 19

"I pray that out of his glorious riches He may strengthen you with power through His Spirit in your inner being, so that Christ may dwell in your hearts through faith. And I pray that you, being rooted and established in love, may have power, together with all the saints, to grasp how wide and long and high and deep is the love of Christ, and to know this love that surpasses knowledge—that you may be filled to the measure of all the fullness of God."
(Ephesians 3:16-19)

While traveling across the U.S. heading to the Grand Canyon, we made a fuel stop. We were about to head into what is known as the "High Desert", so we wanted a full tank of diesel to get us over the mountains. Shortly after getting back on the road, we noticed the RV struggling to climb the elevation.

We were losing power and our speed was declining. We struggled to keep up to the speed limit and it wasn't getting any better. What could be wrong? We had plenty of fuel and it wasn't like this before we stopped. Could it have been bad fuel? It didn't take long before we saw a warning light on the dash. That was our signal to get help.

I don't know about you, but at times my spiritual life can be like this. I read my bible and attend church to fill my "tank", yet at times I seem to lose power. At times I find it difficult to climb the mountains of life. That's when I know it's time to find help.

Our focus verses tell us that God strengthens us with His power and fills us with His fullness. We get our power from God and not ourselves. Through God's love and a connection with Him, we can have the power necessary to do anything, even climb the mountains of life.

We stopped at a "power train" specialty shop. With a little diagnosis, they changed a few filters and we were on our way. We hit the road under full power.

There is more to having or being filled with power than just going through the motions of the "tank filling" rituals of attending church or reading a bible. We need to diagnosis ourselves to see what needs changed in order to have the power that comes from God. Sometimes it's just a minor adjustment and sometimes it takes a little more. But, until we stop and take appropriate measures, we will sputter and lack the power necessary to get through life.

263

September 20

"'Is it true, Shadrach, Meshach and Abednego, that you do not serve my gods or worship the image of gold I have set up?" "Shadrach, Meshach and Abednego replied to the king, 'O Nebuchadnezzar, we do not need to defend ourselves before you in this matter. If we are thrown into the blazing furnace, the God we serve is able to save us from it, and he will rescue us from your hand, O king. But even if he does not, we want you to know, O king, that we will not serve your gods or worship the image of gold you have set up.'" (Daniel 3:14, 16-18)

Revelation 3:14-22 makes it clear that John was writing to those in the church. John is saying that God prefers hot followers. That means going against the normal and putting off the old self.

Our focus verses show us three guys who were examples of hot Christians. Faced with doing something that went against their belief, they chose to stand firm. When the king demanded, they refused. They would not compromise. They knew it came with serious ramifications.

They knew who they served. They knew who would protect them. And even if they died, they were not willing to compromise what and who they stood for, for anything. So off to the furnace they went. The rest of the story real fast; the furnace was heated to 7 times hotter than normal. The guys who tied them up and threw them in died because it was so hot. The ropes burned off them, but yet they walked around. A fourth person joined them and when called, they walked out, not a hair or piece of clothing burnt.

They were thrown into the fire for what they believed in, for not compromising their faith. But, they walked out unharmed. These guys stood their ground for what they believed in. They went against the grain of a dark society that worships any and everything. They went into the furnace and walked out leading the king to the God they serve! Can I hear a halleluiah!

When you take a stand for what you believe in, no matter the heat, you can withstand it. When you are willing to give everything for the God you serve, He protects and brings you out victorious. But, you must be willing to take that stand.

That is a "hot" Christian, one willing to stand up to the heat of opposition, ridicule, and persecution. Do you really care that your so called friends talk about you because you are different? I bet when they see you come through the fire, they too will start to praise God's name. So, turn up the heat!

September 21

"I will show you what he is like who comes to me and hears my words and puts them into practice. He is like a man who building a house, who dug down deep and laid the foundation on rock. When a flood came, the torrent struck that house but could not shake it, because it was well built." (Luke 6:47-48)

I remember the greatest receiver to play the game, Jerry Rice. It was reported he showed up an hour early to run patterns and catch balls. Jerry Rice is an example of what practice can do. He participated in 20 seasons; 13 Pro Bowls; won 3 Super Bowl Rings and is a Hall of Famer. Christians can take a few lessons from this. He had a play book and he studied it. We have a play book, it's called the Bible and we should be studying it daily. We should run this thing we call life according to the play book, over and over again until we know it by heart. Practice makes perfect.

Jerry Rice listened to his coach. He took instruction from the coach and the coach was always right. We too have a coach, His name is Jesus. He calls the plays, He directs our steps, He is always right, He sees the entire field and He knows the game better than we do. We should practice listening and taking instructions from Him. Practice makes perfect.

In our focus verses Jesus is teaching that practice makes perfect. He guides, we listen. He calls the plays, we follow His call. By following His teachings, we can be the people He intends us to be. Practice makes perfect.

I once read a church sign that said "Practice makes perfect, just be careful what you practice." What if Jerry Rice would have studied another team's play book? How would that have affected his game? If he practiced the wrong plays, would he have had the same impact on the game of football?

Be very careful what you practice. If practice makes perfect, then practicing the wrong things can lead to destruction. *"But the one who hears my words and does not put them into practice is like a man who builds a house on the ground without a foundation. The moment the torrent struck that house, it collapsed and its destruction was complete."* (Luke 6:49)

What are you practicing? Are they the things of God? Will your practice habits define you as a Christian? The choice is yours because practice does make perfect, one way or the other.

September 22

"Why are you down in the dumps, dear soul? Why are you crying the blues?
Fix my eyes on God - soon I'll be praising again. He puts a smile on my face.
He's my God." (Psalm 43:5 MSG)

The Christian life can be a series of "hills and valleys"; times we
are on the hills of delight and then times we are in the valley of
depression. Life can be filled with ups and downs, like a spiritual
rollercoaster. Life can be depressing at times, and for some this can be
a physical reaction to a chemical imbalance, but to most of us it's often
self-induced. The fact is, no matter where you are in life, you can
choose to praise or to pout.

The reason I say this can be seen by taking a closer look at our
focus verse. In five verses, the use of personal pronouns like "I", "me"
and "my" are used seventeen times. One reason we can be so
depressed is having an unhealthy fixation on ourselves; *my* problems,
my feelings, *my* needs, *me, me, me...* If we look at it this way, we see
not only the problem but the cure.

The psalmist, who went from a plea in the valley to praising God on
the hills, came to realize that an attitude change was in order. It's not
about me; it's about God. It's not about your weakness, but God's
strength. Focus on God, not your shortcomings and you can be an over
comer. When we begin to think about God instead of ourselves, we can
enjoy the life God has planned for us, no matter if you are on a hilltop,
or deep within the valley.

Let me give you an example. There is this lady named Linda, who
has had every imaginable form of cancer. She has had treatments,
surgeries, experimental drugs, even the newest technologies, yet the
cancer keeps comes back. But through it all she remains focused on
God and His purpose for her life. She stands strong and is determined
to live her life for God. She smiles when she is sick, praises God when
she is weak, and never have I heard her pout about "why me?" She
chooses to praise God and He still has His hand on her. I don't know
what God has in store for Linda, she doesn't know either, but she does
know He has a plan and she is going to stand firm in following that
plan, no matter what. That, my friends is real faith! She could pout
about her situation, but instead she praises God's name and her face
always has a smile on it.

September 23

"Delight yourself in the LORD and he will give you the desires of your heart." (Psalm 37:4)

As we rode the train to the Grand Canyon, the weather wasn't being very cooperative. It was raining, snowing, sleeting and cold. We were told the fog had settled in and the chances of seeing the bottom of the canyon were doubtful. As we stepped off the train you could see the fog, thick as pea soup and hanging just below the lip of the canyon.

Joy and I had seen the Grand Canyon before, but our friends Dennis and Laurie hadn't. We wanted them to see the beauty, but with the fog, chances are they wouldn't. Little did we know that each of us had been praying the same prayer, "Lord, just let them see what you've created." We also didn't know that as Laurie stepped to the rim, she too prayed that God would give her a glimpse of the canyon floor.

As Laurie opened her eyes, the fog started to separate. The sun started to shine down and light the canyon up. In just a moment or two the floor was visible, the light reflected off the floor and walls to reveal the most magnificent sight we could imagine. I looked over at Laurie and she stood there weeping. Tears ran down her face; she stood with a look of awe on her face. I couldn't help but cry myself.

Never think for one minute your prayers go unnoticed by God. We are told God hears our prayers before they even leave our lips. We are told that God will give us whatever we ask for in His name. We are told that God will give us the desires of our heart. And we are told we have not because we ask not. Laurie, Dennis, Joy and I asked for a glimpse of one of the most spectacular sights I have ever seen, and God delivered. So, what are you waiting for, ask and receive....

September 24

"But He's already made it plain how to live, what to do, what God is looking for in men and women."(Micah 6:8 MSG)

My wife and I love to spend time talking with each other. We actually have an open conversation that has been going on for 20 plus years. When we talk, we learn more and more about each other. We learn the other's likes, dislikes, feelings, emotions, needs and wants. Our conversations have built the relationship that we have, and with each talk, we grow closer to each other.

Prayer is talking to God. As a Christ follower, we should have an open conversation with God. With prayer, God learns our likes, dislikes, needs and wants. But it requires time and energy of us to have this conversation. Are you too busy to pray? I believe the greatest motivator to pray is seeing answered prayers. But if we are too busy to pray, then we may never know that.

In our focus verse we learn what it means to have a daily relationship with God. We need to spend time with Him in order for us to know Him and for Him to know us. A relationship takes time and commitment. A relationship with God takes prayer.

Ponder on this for a moment. If you only pray when you need something or when times are tough, do you really have a relationship with God? Isaiah 59:2 tells us *"But your iniquities have separated you from your God; your sins have hidden His face from you, so that He will not hear."* So if you are living a life of sin, or there is unconfessed sin in your life, scripture tells us God doesn't hear us. *We know that God does not listen to sinners. He listens to the godly person who does His will."* (John 9:31)

So, if you have a relationship with God and you spend time daily making that relationship stronger, He hears and He answers the prayers of your heart. For me, nothing motivates me more to develop my prayer life than answered prayers. I can attest, I have had many prayers answered, because my God tells me *"ask and you shall receive."* (Matthew 7:7)

September 25

"...in all things God works for the good of those who love Him." (Romans 8:28)

I am praying these days for a friend who is battling cancer. My heart goes out to him, his family and his friends. We have sat and talked about what may happen and he has made some plans, while not giving up hope for a miracle. I know He can even use an illness for His glory.

I pray that his family and friends learn a lesson from my friend. He has always been the strong one, yet now he is frail and weak, facing a tragic illness and his future is uncertain. I pray they evaluate their eternal status. No one is immortal. Everyone has to face death one day. It's a reality that no one wants to think of, much less face.

One thing I have learned in ministry is that those that know their eternal fate seem to take life threatening issues much easier. When you know without a shadow of doubt where you will end up, it makes leaving that much easier. An eternal resting place in heaven takes more than just being a good person. You can't buy your way in; you can't do enough good deeds, you must have a relationship with Jesus Christ.

In Luke 18:18-27, we read about a rich young man who had it all, yet he himself felt like there was something missing. He found Jesus and asked Him what he needed to do to ensure his spot in heaven for eternity. The answer he received wasn't what he expected.

The answer he received was not what he expected to hear. He was very rich and valued his wealth. He was holding on tight to the one thing that he cherished the most, and he wasn't about to let go. Seeing his reaction, Jesus let him go.

Jesus gives the answer that is hard to swallow for those who are self-sufficient. For those that think they can do it on their own, they go away sad because of what they have to give up. Jesus wants our heart, mind, and soul. He wants us to rely on Him, not our own sufficiency. He wants us to give up the things we think bring us happiness and put our trust in Him.

I pray that those that know my friend realize that it takes giving up the things of this world that they cling to so they can take hold of the things of God that matter. I feel my friend has done this and take great comfort in that. I pray that those his life has impacted do the same.

September 26

"I give you this charge: Preach the Word; be prepared in season and out of season; correct, rebuke and encourage - with great patience and careful instruction. "(2 Timothy 4:1-2)

Timothy is a book of encouragement to a young preacher. Timothy was about to take over for Paul. Paul knew the hard times, discouragement and rejection he would face. Paul's advice: stand firm to his true calling. Paul's words echo today, to everyone who walks with God.

Paul says we must *"Preach the Word."* Use it to correct, reprimand and lift up those around you. But he also instructed that before we can preach the word, we must study the word and apply it to our lives. Then we "preach" or speak the truths we have learned from the Word of God.

Paul warns that we must preach truths. His words in verse 3 tell us that some may preach to suit people's ears. In other words, they may distort the Word of God. Some may try to make it say or mean what they want it to. Some try to remove the "tough or hard" teachings to suit their lifestyles. Some even remove the sufficiency of the Cross or the necessity of a repentant heart. The world rewards those who dilute the truth of Christ. But God doesn't.

Unfortunately, false teachers will continue to be around us and will always have an audience. But we must refuse to compromise our belief. We have been given the Word of God, the truth that can change the world and we must live by it. And while the Word of God is a wonderful blessing, it also carries a responsibility. We are to know the Word of God and apply its principles, teachings, directions and life changing lessons to our lives and live a life transformed from our "old selves" to the "new creation" God wants us to be. And then, after we have been *"born again in His likeness"* we must share His message with others at every opportunity.

A life dedicated to standing up to this charge from Paul can be rewarding, a blessing and life altering. When we stay aligned with the Word of God, when we learn from it, when we let it change our lives and then we go tell others about it, the rewards for us and others last an eternity and we live lives the way God created us to live. Let's accept the charge today to stand firm and Preach the Word of God!

September 27

"So if you're serious about living this new resurrection life with Christ, act like it. Pursue the things over which Christ presides. Don't shuffle along, eyes to the ground, absorbed with the things right in front of you. Look up, and be alert to what is going on around Christ—that's where the action is. See things from his perspective. Your old life is dead. Your new life, which is your real life—even though invisible to spectators—is with Christ in God. He is your life."(Colossians 3:1-3 MSG)

After retirement I tried to sleep in, since I really had no place to go. That didn't work out well for me. I love mornings. I love to get up early, read, reflect and often write. But after retirement, something has changed. Instead of coffee, bible, notebook and pen, I start with coffee and social media.

As a result, my devotions, bible reading, prayer time and writing suffered. And my day suffers. So I asked myself "Is that feeding my mind and spirit with proper preparation and spiritual nutrition my day?

Our focus verse gives us a glimpse of how to live and what to focus on. We need to re-calibrate how we think and reestablish the correct vision for our day. And for me it starts in the morning. We should start each day by focusing on Jesus and "pursue the things over which Christ presides", as top priority. After all, it's a privilege to meet with the Creator of the universe, Savior of our souls and Lord of life.

So how are we going to do this? First, when we wake up, we need to develop a ravishing hunger and thirst for God. Our morning diet should consist of the breakfast of champions. *"Then Jesus declared, "I am the bread of life. Whoever comes to me will never go hungry, and whoever believes in me will never be thirsty." (John 6:35).*

We all know that breakfast is the most important meal of the day. So why shouldn't our diet consist of the things of God. *"Let me hear in the morning of your steadfast love, for in you I trust. Make me know the way I should go, for to you I lift up my soul." (Psalm 143:8).* A morning started this way re-calibrates and prepares us for the battles ahead and for a future in heaven.

So, if we don't "like" that post first thing in the morning, it's because we are busy with God. He comes first. I challenge each of you to change your morning routine. I bet your day, and mine, will be a better one.

September 28

"Therefore I tell you, whatever you ask for in prayer, believe that you have received it, and it will be yours." (Mark 11:24)

I really like Amazon and it's the first place I go to when I need something. No matter what I need, it provides me with many options, right at my fingertips. I type in just what it is I need and a list appears for me to choose from. I pick what I want and bam, it gets delivered.

Well I had an interesting thought the other day. How many of us treat God like He is Amazon? I know, sounds strange, so let me explain myself.

Our focus verse says to some "whatever I want I can ask God for it and it's mine." I just call it out, even give Him a list of exactly what it is, what color, how much, etc. and He delivers it. We treat God as a source to fulfill our wants, desires and wishes. But is that truly what that passage means?

I believe God isn't a "source" in which we can pick and choose from. God isn't something we go to only when we need something. God isn't something that provides a list of options in which we can pick what we want and don't want. God is our provider, one who gives us the things He desires for us.

Jeremiah 29: 11-13 tells us *"'For I know the plans I have for you,' declares the LORD, 'plans to prosper you and not to harm you, plans to give you hope and a future. Then you will call upon me and come and pray to me, and I will listen to you. You will seek me and find me when you seek me with all your heart.'"*

God listens to those who pray with right motives. He answers prayers of those to fulfill needs, not necessary wants. He listens to those who seek Him with their hearts, not their thirst for "things". He listens to those who seek His will on their lives; even if it goes against the things we want or have planned. God is far greater than Amazon, because the things He offers will last. So try calling on Him to pour out His will on your life and then sit back and wait to see what He delivers.

September 29

"Therefore, if you are offering your gift at the altar and there remember that your brother has something against you, leave your gift there in front of the altar. First go and be reconciled to your brother; then come and offer your gift."(Matthew 5:23-24)

Have you ever lived out a passage of scripture? Well I did just yesterday. You see, a friend and I had been feeling like there may be an issue between us. Both of us were concerned, yet to be honest, I did nothing about it. But he did. He picked up the phone (only because a face to face was impossible at the time) and he confronted the situation.

We talked, we cleared the air, and we ended the conversation closer than before. That is what friends and brothers in Christ do. Face to face, or at least voice to voice, not via text messages, social media, email, etc. A lot can get lost in the translation and emotions can't be properly expressed that way.

The bible teaches us that when we have issue with someone, we are to go to that person and reconcile the issue promptly. Our focus verses go as far as saying we should do so before we offer our worship to God.

First, the matter should be handled privately between the two parties. If not, we hold it in and that causes us to get even angrier. We gossip to others about it and that causes others to look at that person differently. We allow the problem to divide the friendship, eventually ending it.

I am glad my friend loves me enough to discuss the issue and clear it up. I am glad that the issue is resolved and laid to rest. Yeah, it is over and done with. We can now move forward, growing closer as brothers.

So, do you have an issue with someone? Maybe it's time to make a call, go visit, talk, and clear the air. I believe if we all did this, we would have less tension, less hatred and less division in this world. Give it a try and you will feel better when it's done. I do!

273

September 30

"No one sews a patch of unshrunk cloth on an old garment. If he does, the new piece will pull away from the old, making the tear worse. And no one pours new wine into old wineskins. If he does, the wine will burst the skins, and both the wine and the wineskins will be ruined. No, he pours new wine into new wineskins." (Mark 2:21-22)

I recently bought a new cell phone. I didn't really want to, but the old one wasn't working too well. So after much research and price comparison, I bought a replacement that was advertised to be of similar size. My thought was I could use the same case and things I bought for the old one.

But once the new phone arrived, I noticed that the new phone didn't fit into the old case. They were not compatible. Seems the manufacture was a little sneaky, even though they advertised it as similar in size, it was off just enough to make you buy new cases and carriers. So it was off to the store for me.

The same is true with our walk with Jesus. We come to Jesus because the life we were living just wasn't working too well. We accept the new life, yet often try to fit it into our old lifestyle. They are incompatible. They may look alike, but we soon find out the new things don't fit well with the old things. So change is required.

Jesus used the wine and wineskin example to illustrate this very point. Old and new do not mix. It's a recipe for disaster. The new life with Christ (wine) needs to be placed in a new creation (wineskin). Jesus makes us a new creation and a new life begins. A life with Christ helps us to live a life filled with joy and peace. A new life in Christ helps us overcome old ways and live the life He wants for us.

But we must be willing to throw away the old. Something that for some is hard to do. I know because my old phone and case still sit on my desk. But with Jesus' help, we can shed the old for the new and live a new, better life. Give it a try....

October 1

"Jesus bent down and wrote with his finger in the dirt. They kept at him, badgering him. He straightened up and said, "The sinless one among you, go first: Throw the stone." (John 8:6-7)

I see so many people doing dumb things and making bad decisions. Upon seeing them, my first reaction is shock. It takes me a minute to think back and realize that I have done some pretty stupid things in my life as well. If we are honest with ourselves, every one of us would agree, none of us are perfect.

Recently I ran across this statement: "Another reason we should not be quick to condemn people is the fact that we are usually guilty of the very thing that we are condemning. Bad traits always seem to look a lot worse on other people than they do on ourselves." (Cleve Walker) Too often we are quick to condemn or judge others, while we too are guilty of the same thing, or something worst.

Jesus taught on this very subject in our focus verses. In fact, if you read the entire thing, the men who caught this woman wanted to stone her to death for her wrong. Jesus didn't agree, nor disagree, with the punishment, He merely stated that those who have never sinned be the first the throw a stone. Pretty tough to follow that up with a good slider or curve.

Upon reading further on, we find out that they all just dropped their stone and walked away. For you see, we are all guilty of one sin or another.

Jesus' lesson is clear, if you are innocent of any wrong, then you have the right to condemn and judge. So the next time you see something and get upset, ask yourself if you have ever done the same thing. I think you will find that we are all guilty as charged. If so, then cut them some slack, encourage them to do better.

October 2

"For it is by grace you have been saved, through faith and this is not from yourselves, it is the gift of God..." (Ephesians 2:8)

Before I was saved, I met Leanne. I once saw this lady go into diabetic shock and come out of it praising God. How can one who just went through a life threatening event praise God? I didn't understand anything about God or the bible, so this behavior was foreign to me.

Then that changed. I accepted Jesus. I came to understand how we think isn't how He thinks. Take healing for an example. Me, I would simply snap my fingers and all disease and suffering would be gone. But Jesus heals in a variety of ways. He can heal with a touch, with words; He sent a healing ahead, once He spit to heal. His ways aren't our ways and often it is hard for us to comprehend.

A friend of mine fell down a flight of steps. She was banged up, yet she praised God for protection. See, she thought in God terms and realized that her fall could have been worse; she chose to believe God put His hand out and saved her from serious injury.

Another friend helped his elderly neighbor fix her leaf blower. Seems the woman got her scarf sucked up by the blower. After taking the blower apart, he realized that God protected the lady. Seems the scarf, much longer than the woman was tall, was wrapped around the lady's neck at the time the fan of the blower sucked in the scarf. Only God could have unwrapped the scarf fast enough to keep the woman from getting strangled.

When we are so caught up in thinking that God has to do things in certain ways, we may miss out on the miracles that happen all around us. We must open our eyes and our hearts to God and realize that His love goes so deep for us that He will go to any extreme for us. Even in the things we see as bad, if we are open to God, we will find that His ways far exceed our ways, and His hand reaches farther than we can ever imagine.

Leanne knew her life could have ended, my friend's fall could have killed her, and that little old lady could have been strangled by her own scarf. Yet the hand of God, the very God that created us, saved them for another day. These people now sing God's praises because they know they were saved and they know their life is in His hands. So the next time something happens, take a moment before reacting, you just may find a reason to praise.

October 3

"Yet a time is coming and has now come when the true worshipers will worship the Father in the Spirit and in truth, for they are the kind of worshipers the Father seeks." (John 4:23)

I used to go to church and feel like there was something missing. I enjoyed the music, I enjoyed the prayers, I even sat on the edge of my seat during the Pastor's sermon, but I left feeling like there still should be more. I never truly understood what was missing until one day it came to me, I was just there. I wasn't participating, I was merely receiving.

I started to think about how we approach other aspects of life. We go to football games and dress up in our team colors, yell at the top of our lungs until we lose our voices, and even strip nearly naked and paint our bodies. But when we go into worship we sit still, reserved and calm. We feel like we must stay still, remain silent and be entertained.

One day that changed for me. I realized that God wants my worship, and He wants me to be happy to worship Him. If I can get into *worshiping* a bunch of guys chasing a ball, why not demonstrate that same enthusiasm to a God, who saves, forgives, heals and blesses. So I now approach worship differently.

I give God my undivided attention during worship; even to the point of asking what more can I offer Him to demonstrate my love and devotion to Him. I sing, making a joyful noise, even if it offends the person in front, behind or beside me. I lift my hands, jump or shout praises, because I want God to know I love Him.

"Blessed is the worshiper who can truthfully and with pleasure say to the Lord. What can I do for You? You name it, it's Yours. Whatever I can offer You, pleases let me." (Chris Tiegreen)

God wants total surrender, without reservation. He wants us to come to Him in reckless abandonment, and to worship in Spirit and in Truth. I now approach worship asking God, how can I worship You in a way that says, I want You to know I love you and am thankful for all You have done for me.

October 4

"Rejoice in the Lord always. I will say it again: Rejoice! Let your gentleness be evident to all. The Lord is near. Do not be anxious about anything, but in every situation, by prayer and petition, with thanksgiving, present your requests to God. And the peace of God, which transcends all understanding, will guard your hearts and your minds in Christ Jesus." (Philippians 4:4-7)

I have met people that no matter what they are going through, nothing seems to shake them. They are never worried, never upset, and never really get stressed out. They are cool under pressure and always seem to look at the situation positively.

No matter what you are facing or going through, there is a way to go through it without being anxious. A Christ follower should always be able to rejoice in the Lord. Christian joy is a mood independent of our circumstances or surroundings. It is a frame of mind that most non-believers can't understand.

How can we have joy when one day we are celebrating a promotion, then the next we are being laid off? The secret is *"The Lord is near."* Jesus is not a friend that only comes when things are good. He is there through every situation. Jesus is with me all my days, and at times He holds me up, cries with me, cheers me on and rejoices with me. He is no fair weather friend, He is my constant companion. How can I not rejoice?

When the Creator of the world, the Savior, the Counselor, the Healer, the Provider, the Prince of Peace is with me, I am not anxious about anything. If I truly believe He is who He says He is and I walk in His ways, there is nothing this world can hand me that I can't handle.

So whatever you are facing, have you handed it over to Jesus? He can take your cares and ease your troubles. Jesus is a friend that stands with you through thick and thin, but without a relationship with Him you will never know this joy I speak about. So, what are you waiting for? He is only a prayer away! Rejoice!

October 5

"For we must all appear before the judgment seat of Christ, that everyone may receive what is due them for the things done while in the body, whether good or bad" (2 Cor. 5:10 TNIV).

I remember the days when I played sports. Those who won got trophies, those who didn't win, they got nothing. Times have changed. One of my favorite commercials shows a dad walking with his son who is holding a trophy. Dad takes the trophy, reads the inscription "Participant" and then goes into action. He rips the plaque off, turns it over and writes "Winner" on it. Dads don't want participant trophies for their sons and daughters.

The same is true with Christianity. Only winners get into heaven; not everyone. It is a false hope to think that every single person who dies goes directly to heaven. It just isn't so. That is a "participant" mindset. Live your life, die and go to heaven. Why, because I lived.

The reality is that we will receive rewards based on what we do in life. Those who obey and follow Jesus, do His work, are His hands and feet will receive crowns (1 Corinthians 9:25 and 2 Timothy 4:8) for their labor. These crowns we will lay at the feet of Jesus for the price He paid for our salvation.

At the judgment seat of Christ, He will want to know what you did with your time, resources, and opportunities with the gospel with which you were entrusted. I'm not talking about earning your place in heaven or working for the best reward. On the contrary, this reward system is based on humble service given out of the right motive for the Lord. So the question to those who proclaim to be Christians, what will be your reward?

279

October 6

"May the God of hope fill you with all joy and peace as you trust in him, so that you may overflow with hope by the power of the Holy Spirit." (Romans 15:13)

A Sunday school teacher invited her class to write down the questions that they would like to ask God. This one is priceless: "Did you mean for the giraffe to look like that, or was it an accident?" The kids also included a few comments and complaints, like: "I bet it is very hard for you to love all of everybody in the world. There are only four people in our family and I can never do it."

God expects questions and a reading of the bible tells us He has fielded His share of comments and complaints as well. Jesus also asks a few questions of us. Jesus meets two guys in John 5:1-8 and Luke 18:35-43. He basically asks them the same question. He gets two different replies.

In Luke, we meet a beggar who was blind and hears that Jesus is in the area and wants Jesus to notice Him. Once he has Jesus' attention, he is asked "What do you want me to do for you?" "Lord, I want to see," he replied. Jesus asked him a question and he was direct and sincere. He received just what he asked for.

Then there is the guy in John. He meets Jesus and is asked "Do you want to get well?" What followed was a complaint. He made excuses; he played the victim and never really answered Jesus.

The difference here is one knew that Jesus could and would heal him, so he answered the question with a direct request. The other, he was in the presence of Jesus and still thought his only hope was the pool that has been of no help for 38 years. How often do we complain as the verses ask? Jesus wants us to ask for what we want. And Jesus wants honest, direct answers to the questions He asks us. So, ask away, but also listen for the question from Jesus. What is it you want?

October 7

"Respect everyone, and love your Christian brothers and sisters. Fear God, and respect the king." (1 Peter 2:17 NLT)

I actually like Motown music. There is something about that music that bridged the culture gaps. I listen to all sorts of music, and blended in are the likes of Sly and the Family Stone and Aretha Franklin. One of my favorite songs was "Respect".

Our focus verse speaks on the concept of respect. The word respect is defined in Webster's dictionary as "to take notice of; to regard with special attention." Peter challenges us to *"to take notice of everyone."* To respect is to give care. It is to see in others the image of Christ and to treat others with dignity, value, and human decency. It is perhaps to live by a Golden Rule ethic in which we view others, not as objects of disdain, but as people made in the image of God.

Long before Aretha Franklin belted out the words to her hit song calling for a little respect, God's Word challenged us to do the same. I believe that to offer respect is one of the basic and fundamental distinguishing characteristics of the Christian faith. To respect is to value the lives of others —to treat others with common decency, civility, and grace. I wonder how well we "take notice of everyone." Do we really see the people around us, or look beyond them to see those whom we deem to have greater worth? Do we see the needs of others? Do we treat others as human beings who have quality and worth in the eyes of God?

To respect is to acknowledge others and to extend consideration and courtesy in their direction. To respect others is to see them through the eyes of Christ and not through our jaded and prejudicial eyes of human nature. It takes a special maturity of faith, but I challenge you to look at others differently, especially those who have been marginalized by society and quickly cast aside. Look at them, not through the lens of your experience, your biases, or even your politics. Look at those in need as opportunities God has placed in your journey to teach you about grace, acceptance, and respect. What if the homeless man, or the poor, single Hispanic mother, or the immigrant who can't speak the language is more than someone for you to hate? What if they are tests of faith that challenges the depth of your Christian maturity? Will your response in any way match the response of Christ in the life of that person? Can we use the title "Christian" if we refuse to offer simple respect?

281

October 8

"May the God of hope fill you with all joy and peace as you trust in him, so that you may overflow with hope by the power of the Holy Spirit." (Romans 15:13)

A Sunday school teacher invited her class to write down the questions that they would ask God. This one is priceless: "Did you mean for the giraffe to look like that, or was it an accident?" The kids also included a few comments and complaints, like: "I bet it is very hard for you to love all of everybody in the world. There are only four people in our family and I can never do it."

God expects questions, and a reading of the bible tells us He has fielded His share of comments and complaints as well. Jesus also asks a few questions of us. Jesus meets two guys in John 5:1-8 and Luke 18:35-43. He basically asks them the same question. He gets two different replies.

In Luke we meet a beggar who was blind, learns Jesus is in the area and wants Jesus to notice Him. Once he has Jesus attention, he is asked "What do you want me to do for you?" "Lord, I want to see," he replied. Jesus asked him a question and he was direct and sincere. He received just what he asked for.

Then there is the guy in John. He meets Jesus and is asked "Do you want to get well?" What followed was a complaint. He made excuses. He played the victim, and never really answered Jesus.

The difference here is one knew that Jesus could and would heal him, so he answered the question with a direct request. The other guy was in the presence of Jesus and still thought his only hope was the pool that has been of no help for 38 years. How often do we complain when asked what these verses ask? Jesus wants us to ask for what we want. And Jesus wants honest, direct answers to the questions He asks us. So, ask away, but also listen for the question from Jesus. What is it you want?

October 9

"I am the way and the truth and the life. No one comes to the Father except through me." (John 14:6)

This world loves a scandal. We read and hear of them daily. The biggest scandal in history is the scandal Jesus created. The scandal of the gospel of Jesus Christ is that Jesus didn't merely come to teach about God. He didn't come to present His take on scripture. He didn't come just to present a simple way to God. No the scandal that upset the Jewish leaders, Roman authorities, a mob that begged for His crucifixion, and is still upsetting people today, is that Jesus is the only way to God.

A great number of people know of Jesus but don't really want Him to be Lord over their lives. The other day I used a Christmas gift as an illustration to represent the gift of salvation Jesus offers. One person told me they were offered that gift early in their life but refused it because they knew it came with conditions and expectations.

People tend to accept the truth that Jesus saves without accepting the truth of Jesus as Lord over their lives. Think about this, how many lords do we have in our life? Are they our careers, relationships, or our lifestyles? They have more control over us than Jesus has. In order to be saved, one must allow Jesus ownership of their lives. You can't have one without the other. Romans 1:21 says *"For although they knew God, they neither glorified him as God nor gave thanks to him, but their thinking became futile and their foolish hearts were darkened."*

There is a saying "everyone wants to go to heaven, but no one wants to die." Well, in order to get to heaven, our old ways, thinking, attitudes and lords must die. We must surrender our hearts, minds, body and soul to Jesus in order to reach the final destination we so desperately want. So, embrace the scandal of the gospel and start living the good life....

283

October 10

"So he got up and went to his father. But while he was still a long way off, his father saw him and was filled with compassion for him; he ran to his son, threw his arms around him and kissed him." (Luke 15:20)

There once was young man who left home and set out to live his own life free from his father. He took his inheritance, his worldly belongings and lived a life filled with sin. His new life was filled with wild parties, wild living and squandering every cent he had.

His new life, the one he chose to live away from his father, landed him in a worthless job, hungry for something better and desperately wanting what his old life offered. He realized that the way he was living went against the standards set by his father, yet here he was. "What can I do?" he must have thought. "How do I get out of this mess?" he must have wondered.

I too lived a life that went against the way I was brought up. I squandered my young life with parties, drugs, alcohol and wild living. I made mistake after mistake, until one day I realized that the life I had chosen for myself wasn't the life that I wanted anymore. I wanted more.

Both this young man and I decided to turn back. The young man went home, back to his father. I, went to the father I never knew, but heard about so many times. We both rehearsed what we would say. We both went to the father in hopes of some sort of reconciliation, but received far more.

The father, our Heavenly Father, watched from afar. He waited for us to come to Him. He saw us, He ran to us, and He embraced us with love. He lavished us with gifts of forgiveness, mercy and grace, the very things we needed, but didn't deserve.

I want to say to you today, no matter what you have done, how you have lived your life, or how bad you think you are your Heaven Father awaits your return. He stands ready to accept you into the family with open arms. He asks no questions, He holds nothing against you; He only wants His children back home.

So if you are tired of living your life away from the Father, pack up and go home. Make the first steps towards God and He will meet you right where you are. His ways are best and He empowers us to live a far greater life than we can ever imagine. Don't hesitate, get moving. He waits for you.

October 11

"Peter walked on the water to Jesus. [30] But when he looked down at the waves churning beneath his feet, he lost his nerve and started to sink."(Matthew 14:29-30)

As I rode through a gorge on I15 from Mesquite, NV to Springdale, UT, the ground seemed to move skyward. Large rock formations were on both sides of the road. I was surrounded by them, large ones in my rear view mirror, both sides of the road loomed upward and in front of me, yes even more. They were everywhere, varying shapes, sizes, and colors.

As I drove through I noticed a sign on the side of the road proclaiming "Watch for Rocks". My first thought was, "Really?" What else is there to look at? Then it occurred to me that there was a road before me that I needed to concentrate on. The sign is a reminder to watch for "rocks" that may be in the path I was traveling.

God gave us those rock formations to look at, yet He puts a safe path before us as well. As pretty as the rocks were, taking my eyes off the path I was on could result in hitting a rock that may have rolled into the road. Hitting something in my path could have been tragic.

Sometimes we can get so focused on the things around us we lose sight of God and His purpose for us. The bible tells us to keep our eyes on Jesus and the path He sets before us, not looking to the left or right. I recall a story where Jesus calls Peter out onto the water. Peter gets out of the boat, walks toward Jesus on top of the water. It was all going well until Peter looked at the waves and water, taking his eyes of Jesus. The result...Jesus had to save him.

I was reminded that as much as I admired the rocks, I needed to keep my eyes on the path before me in order to get to my destination. Oh, my peripheral vision took in the beauty, but my mind stayed focused on the road. As it turned out, we were met with even more of God's splendor in Zion National Park.

Lord, help me to stay focused on you in all I do....

October 12

"...anyone who competes as an athlete does not receive the victor's crown except by competing according to the rules." (2 Timothy 2:5)

A friend said once, "Just because you don't read the rule book doesn't mean they don't apply." My dad taught me how to play baseball, but first he made read the rule book. He wanted me to know what I could and couldn't do.   My dad must have thought that way because he stressed the rules, me knowing them and he demanded I follow them.

Over the past few years we have seen some big names in sports fall. The reason is because they weren't playing by the rules. It amazes me how they could jeopardize their life, reputation and livelihood so easily. They forfeit everything because they chose to ignore the rules.

People fall every day because they ignore the rules. They have affairs or cheat on their taxes. They use "things" to enhance and satisfy. Some even forfeit their eternal life for what is called "the good life". Some, even professed followers of Christ, choose to ignore the word of God in order to keep living by the standards of the world, and simply because they feel living by God's rules are too hard. How many fall out before they reach the finish line, disqualified because they did not maintain an unquestionable obedience to the word of God.

When we live by our own set of rules and standards, we will fail. Rules are tough, they restrict at times, but they are designed for a purpose. Rules of the road for instance, are designed for safety and to keep traffic moving. God's rules set a standard of living that is pleasing to God and, if followed, ensures a blessed life and eternal resting place. This is not to say that every now and then we won't face a traffic jam or difficult situation in our life, but they will smooth out if we obey the rules and keep moving.

A player on a team must play by the rules at all the time. The rule book must be kept intact and complete. A Christ follower must obey the ways of God completely and constantly to maintain that relationship. A spare time Christian is a contradiction in terms. If you are a true Christ follower you must live every moment and every situation as one, obeying His commands completely.

So, pick up the rule book, read it and follow it. I am living proof that it works. Following God's rule book is the best thing I can do. I plan on receiving the victor's crown one day, and wearing it proudly!

October 13

"Don't store up treasures here on earth, where moths eat them and rust destroys them, and where thieves break in and steal. Store your treasures in heaven, where moths and rust cannot destroy, and thieves do not break in and steal. Wherever your treasure is, there the desires of your heart will also be." (Matthew 6:19-21 NLT)

Well, Joy and I took a big step and purchased an RV. One day, in the near future, we plan on retiring and when we do, we want to do some traveling. We have been planning our retirement for a long time and it seems to be closer than we ever thought.

But I have to say, as hard as we planned for retirement; we never failed to invest in what truly matters, our eternal life. We may have reached the point where we can retire here on earth, but not at the expense of our eternal resting place. We didn't obsess about the things that are temporary. We did plan, but the main focus has been towards our place in heaven. This RV will one day wear out and rust away, but our souls will live on forever.

The best investment we have ever made is to invest in our eternity. We have been faithful followers of Jesus Christ. We have lived our life for God and we have sacrificed our time, money and energy every time God has called us to because we believe in what the bible teaches. Our biggest investment focus has always been to obtain what the bible promises, eternity with God the Father!

Sure the RV is nice, but it isn't the mansion in heaven the bible speaks of. We are going to have a lot of fun traveling and chilling in the comforts of this vehicle, but one day we will give it all up to sit at God's feet and worship and praise Him all day long. Because we have planned for our future, the future that really matters, I can honestly say, our future looks bright. The radiance of the Lord will be so bright; we will need sunglasses in order to look at Him. I look forward to those raccoon eyes....

October 14

"And we pray this in order that you may live a life worthy of the Lord and may please him in every way: bearing fruit in every good work, growing in the knowledge of God, being strengthened with all power according to his glorious might so that you may have great endurance and patience, and joyfully giving thanks to the Father, who has qualified you to share in the inheritance of the saints in the kingdom of light." (Colossians 1:10-12)

While traveling I stopped to use the "facilities" and saw a sign telling people how to flush a toilet. It dawned on me that we have become an automated society. Seems more and more things are done for us. Think about it; automatic toilets, paper towel dispensers, door openers, and the list goes on. We have become so used to things being done for us we expect it, to the point we have to be told to "push the handle".

We can become that complacent in our walk with Christ. We can expect Him to do everything for us, while we just sit back and enjoy the fruits of His labor. If you need something, just ask Him. Are things going bad? Just ask Him for help or blame Him when it doesn't work out. Ask some people and they think salvation is automatic, say a word or two and you are heaven bound.

But if we think about this for a few seconds, we know that really isn't the case. God did create us for fellowship with Him. He created the world for us to enjoy. He has a purpose for us, but He wants willing partners and people who are not afraid of a little work. Look through your bible and you will see the word "work" a lot. We are created to work, not to be saved, but because we are saved.

The passage says that we must live a life worthy of Him and to please Him by bearing "fruit" for Him by "our" work. We aren't to sit back and wait; we are to do and receive. That is how we "share in the inheritance", by being active, productive and a vital part of the kingdom.

So, the next time you feel like God isn't present or hearing your prayers, ask yourself if you have done your part? Have you been active? Have you spent time talking, listening and obeying? Have you done that "work" He has asked you to do? Or are you just sitting back in "automatic" mode waiting, expecting or demanding? Maybe that is your sign!

October 15

"I have learned the secret of being content in any and every situation..."
(Philippians 4:12)

During our annual camping trip to James Island with friends, one of the things we do is spend a day at Splash Zone, a water park within the camp ground. It is designed primarily for the younger kids, no major water slides and such, just plenty of water to cool off in.

We enjoy the "Lazy River" as a group. We all grab a tube and relax as the current takes us along the river. At one point along the way there is a waterfall that douses us with cold water.

This year was a little different. The waterfall wasn't working. The "lazy river" became uneventful, yet still relaxing. There was nothing to look forward to, just go around and around, until...

In our unique style, we decided to make our own waterfall. As we neared the Boulder, we grouped together and kicked and splashed as much water as we could, dousing each other and anyone around us. The "lazy river" became fun again, and each time we kicked and splashed even harder, and laughed as hard.

Paul wrote the book of Philippians from jail, yet he tells us in our focus verse that he has learned to be content in any situation. That is a hard lesson to learn and even a harder thing to put into practice. But that is what we demonstrated in the "lazy river". We could have let the lack of a waterfall ruin our fun. We could have demanded our money back. Or we could have been content with what we had and just create our own. We chose the latter.

I think what Paul was teaching was that wherever he was, or in whatever circumstances he found himself, he was there by divine appointment. If he was hungry, it was because God wanted him to be hungry. If he was full, it was because God so planned it.

If we walk with Christ, we too should enjoy what we have and be thankful. Life is so much better when we live that way. When we stop focusing on what we don't have and thank God for what we do, life can be enjoyed to the fullest.

October 16

"Therefore everyone who hears these words of mine and puts them into practice is like a wise man who built his house on the rock."(Matthew 7:24)

My very first "motorcycle" experience was a mini bike. Remember those things? You pulled a rope to start it; you climbed on, twisted the throttle and held on. When I was a kid, going 5 mph felt like I was flying. But in reality, those things were pretty slow. The engine was a lawn mower motor and not really designed to pull the weight of the frame, much less the weight of a person as well.

The motor is the essential part of a motorcycle, designed to propel the bike and passenger. It is the foundation of the bike and everything else is designed around it. When you see a bike, one of the first questions asked is "what size motor is that?" The motor is the heart of the machine, its foundation.

Just as a motorcycle needs a strong foundation, we too need a strong foundation in our lives. Our focus verse speaks about building a house on a strong foundation, a rock. Jesus uses that to illustrate the necessity of building our spiritual foundation on solid ground. We must not only hear God's word, but put it into action in our lives, if we are to have a solid foundation, one that withstands the test of time and the pitfalls of life.

This principle also works in the concept of the motorcycle. No one would build a custom motorcycle and put a mini bike engine on it. So why try to build a solid life without God's word not only in our ears, but in our hearts and lives as well? In order to have the life God intended, we must have a life built on the things of God, the teachings of God and the example of Jesus Christ. Everyone needs a strong foundation, one that is evident in our lives, attitudes, habits, time and relationships.

Imagine this: You hire Orange County Choppers to build you a bike without a motor. It may look good, but if you never put a motor on it, it won't take you anywhere. The same is true with your life. You can do all you want to make your life look good and profess to be a Christian, but if your engine/heart (foundation) isn't right, where are you going? You want a life that takes you to great heights, one that propels you to your eternal reward; make sure your foundation is on solid ground.

October 17

"Rejoice always, pray continually, give thanks in all circumstances; for this is God's will for you in Christ Jesus." (1 Thessalonians 5:16-18)

On a recent motorcycle trip to Indianapolis a good day turned bad fast. Just outside of Knoxville, TN at a rest stop, my primary belt broke and it was clear, we weren't going anywhere. There we sat, the trip was on hold.

How we handle the events of a day like this tells a lot about us. I had a choice to make, I could get upset, or I could face it and look on the bright side. I chose the latter. Our focus verses just happen to also be my life verses. On this particular day I had the opportunity to put that truth into practice. Let me explain.

As I do always, I said a small prayer as I got on my bike. I asked for protection, safety and most importantly that I represent Him in everything I do. Just prior to that stop, we were traveling 75 on the interstate. Looking in my mirror, I saw a tractor trailer pushing me down a hill. God kept that belt together long enough for me to pull into that rest stop. You see, the belt broke while standing still.

We met some good people while we waited. One of them was Rick, the tow truck operator, who came to pick up my bike. I rode back to Knoxville and was able to share Jesus with him. He shared with me how proud he was of his son who was serving in the Army. Another person was Chuck, the service rep at Knoxville Harley Davidson. He had the parts needed to fix my bike and had a mechanic waiting to work on my bike the minute I arrived. They were friendly, polite and extremely dedicated to get me back on the road as fast as possible and they didn't take advantage of me. I am thankful that God placed guys like this in my path; it was an honor to have met them.

Lastly, I am grateful for a God that reveals Himself in every circumstance. I know that the events of that day were God's will on my life. I only hope that I represented Him in an appropriate manner. I know I tried hard to be thankful, joyful and grateful, even if the day didn't turn out quite like I had planned.

You see, God's plans outweigh ours and as long as we stay in His will, we win. So the next time life falls apart, remember that you can choose how to handle it. I hope you choose to see God and His will for you.

October 18

"If you knew the gift of God and who it is that asks you for a drink, you would have asked him and he would have given you living water." (John 4:7-8, 10)

Ever get more than you bargained for? I did at a fireworks store prior to New Year's. I picked out my favorites and as I was checking out, I asked the lady if she gave a Military discount. She told me no, but I will put a few extras in your bag. That was unexpected.

When Jesus and a Samaritan woman had an encounter, she got more than she ever wanted. As she drew water from the well, Jesus asked for a drink. At first she was a little taken that He would talk to her and even asks her for anything. Then she brought to His attention He had nothing to draw water with.

What pursued was a remarkable conversation. Jesus and His men stopped at a place where Samaritan's lived and we know that the Jews viewed them as less than equal. But once alone, Jesus, a Jewish man actually starts a conversation with a Samaritan woman, unheard of.

Jesus didn't see people as the world sees them. He looked past where she was from and I think He used the woman's task of drawing water to teach an object lesson. Let's face it, Jesus was capable of making water come out of a rock, so He didn't really need her help. He wanted to offer her more than what she came for.

As Jesus continues to talk, He reveals that He could provide a different kind of water, water that satisfies more than just thirst. Jesus calls it "living water." Jesus knew of her spiritual thirst and her need. Jesus knew this woman had tried to quench that "thirst" with relationships.

How often do we do the same thing? We have a thirst that we just don't know how to quench. We thirst for attention, approval, worth, pleasure, etc. So we go to whatever source we can find, hoping that it will quench, but it doesn't.

We also have the "living water" available to us. Jesus offers it freely, just for the asking. He wants us to have it and it will never, I mean never, run dry. The source will continue to flow for eternity, if we accept it. So, what thirst have you grown tired of? What thirst is in need of filling? Are you ready for the living water? You too can get more than you bargained for from Jesus, but you have to want it and ask for it. So I ask, do you thirst for it? Go to the well, drink and be filled.

October 19

"In this way the word of the Lord spread widely and grew in power." (Acts 19:20)

I have been told that I use social media as a platform, a place to preach the Word of God and share my views about the God I serve. Some of those that have told me that aren't speaking favorably, some are. I have been de-friended due to my postings and have gotten into a few heated discussions about my views. But that is okay, I use every means possible to spread the Gospel, at all cost. I also understand that not all my "friends" will accept my views, like what I say or agree with my opinions, but that's okay too. I speak the truth that my God gives me.

In years gone by people like the Apostle Paul didn't have the modern means available to spread the Gospel. Back then the Gospel was spread by word of mouth or by traveling preachers, as Paul was, in order to introduce people to the message of God. Yet the Word was getting out.

The church grew as the Word spread. New believers were being added at a staggering count. The Gospel was gaining power with frequent telling. The impact was awesome and proves that the more the Word of God spreads, the more it grows in power. It did then and it can today, if we continue to spread the Gospel.

With all the means of messaging today; email, texting, social media, blogs, chat, to just name a few, the Word of God could and should spread like wild fire. Christians today have more available means of spreading the Gospel to more people than ever in history. We should be using these modern means of communication to tell people about the life changing impact God has had on their lives. But I am afraid some Christians are afraid of who they may offend.

Have you done enough to spread the Word of God with all the means at your disposal? If not, what's holding you back? If word of mouth was so effective for the Apostles, we should be even more effective at spreading the Word today.

"I love to tell the story, for some have never heard, the message of salvation, from God's own holy Word." (Katherine Hankey)

October 20

"Let your eyes look straight ahead, fix your gaze directly before you. Make level paths for your feet and take only ways that are firm. Do not swerve to the right or the left; keep your foot from evil." (Proverbs 4:25-27)

My mother used to tell me I was as stubborn as a mule. In fact, if you asked my wife she would agree that I never really out grew that stubborn streak. In my younger days I thought being referred to as a mule was a bad thing, but then I learned some interesting facts about mules.

Did you know that the old wives tale of mules being stubborn is actually a sign of their intelligence? The truth is, because of where mules originated from, steep and rough mountains, they are actually very keen on self-preservation. A mule walks with its head down and will only make a step if it considers it a good step. The mule is very cautious and will look the situation over and determine the best approach before proceeding. And if it isn't, the mule will put up a fight to keep from going in that direction.

We can learn a lot from a mule. How often do we rush forward, only to get ourselves in trouble? How many times have we stepped out into something only to find ourselves out on a ledge, so to speak, without a way out? Well I can't answer for you, but I have been there and done that.

Our focus verses gives us clear instructions on how to be like a mule. As we walk with Christ we need to stay focused, keep our eyes on the straight and narrow path, do not waver or veer off course. In doing so we will avoid the pitfalls of life that can cause harm or get us in trouble. It may be slow, but it is a sure way to reach the destination we all want, a godly life and the reward of heaven.

So my advice is to be as stubborn as a mule in your Christian walk. Slow and steady, be sure of your footing and always stay on the safe path. Remember Peter, as long as he kept his eyes on Jesus he did the impossible, he walked on water. It was only when he looked away that he began to sink. So keep your head down and your eyes on Jesus.

October 21

"The wind blows wherever it pleases. You hear its sound, but you cannot tell where it comes from or where it is going. So it is with everyone born of the Spirit" (John 3:8)

On a recent trip to Oak Island, NC, we sat on the porch overlooking the coastal water way and enjoyed our morning coffee. It was an unseasonable warm morning for December, temperatures in the 60's with a nice ocean breeze. While sitting on the porch that morning I read an article about a town that had been hit hard by a storm all night long. In the morning, the residents of the town were amazed to find a common, plastic drinking straw driven deep into a telephone pole by the powerful winds of the night before.

What an amazing story that was. I was driving to our trip to Oak Island the night before and was seeing large piles of sand some two streets over from the beach. A hurricane earlier had hit the island and moved the sand from the beach that far back. The wind has amazing power, yet we can't see it and often don't really know where it comes from.

Our focus verse comes from a conversation between Jesus and Nicodemus. Nicodemus is having a hard time understanding the whole "born again" concept and the thought of a "Holy Spirit". And let's face it, often so do we. It is hard to comprehend the thought of what it means to be filled with the Holy Spirit. We can't see it or touch it, yet we are to accept it as fact. How do we know?

Jesus is basically saying, "Can you see the wind, Nicodemus?" "No." "But do you see its effect?" "Yes." "That is what it means to be born of the Spirit." Jesus is saying that we can't see the Holy Spirit with our eyes, but we can see the work of God that takes place in the human heart. When one is saved and has truly given their heart to God, they are different, clearly and visibly.

We may not see the wind, but we can see its effect, like what happened to that straw and the piles of sand. The same is true when you have been born from above by the Holy Spirit. The clear effects of the new person can only be explained by the thing you cannot see, but you know is there. So, are you filled with the Holy Spirit?

October 22

"Because of the increase of wickedness, the love of most will grow cold, but he who stands firm to the end will be saved." (Matthew 24:12-13)

As we read the paper, watch the news and hear of the events happening around the world, it sounds so much like Matthew 24 that it's scary, or is it?

Jesus tells us in this chapter about the events leading up to the end of time, the time He tells us He will return. It stands as a warning to those of us who claim to be followers of Christ that bad things will happen to good people. But when they do, we have one of two choices to make. We can fall away from that which we profess and suffer now and through eternity or we can stand firm in our faith and be rewarded in the end. The beauty of God's design, we get to pick which one.

As I hear about this ISIS thing going on I can't help but think about this chapter. These wicked men are grabbing Christ followers and torturing and killing them. As tragic as it is, the fact that none of these people are denouncing their belief in Jesus Christ and that ISIS can still find believers tells me that the Word of God is being stood on in that part of the world.

As sad as it makes me to hear about Christ followers suffering, it gives me hope that there are people who are willing to be true Christ followers even if it means death. You see, if any of those people who are or were taken had denounced their faith, we would have heard about it. The enemy likes to brag, and the fact that they are still killing, as harsh as that is, tells me that God is alive in their hearts up to the end.

How about you? Would you stand firm, right up to the minute you die? Would you proclaim Jesus Christ is Lord in your life, no matter the consequences? You see, we all know Jesus is Lord, but is He your Lord? Does His word ring in your ears even when bad things happen? I pray I too would be strong enough to face the enemy and stand firm.

My prayer is "Lord, strengthen me so that I too can and will face the enemy and be strong to the end."

October 23

"Just as Moses lifted up the snake in the desert, so the Son of Man must be lifted up, that everyone who believes in him may have eternal life" (John 3:14–15)

One day my dad sat me on his tractor and told me to plow the field. My rows weren't as straight as his when he plowed. He stood on the back of the tractor, told me to pick a spot ahead and focus on it. As long as I focused on that spot the rows were straight.

Our focus verse is often overlooked, because of John 3:16. Everyone can quote that one, yet the verses before are overlooked, their meaning lost. In Numbers 21 we are told that the Israelites were complaining. Because of their constant grumbling, God sent venomous snakes to bite them. They quickly went to Moses for help. God told Moses to erect a pole with a serpent of brass on it. Whoever looked at that serpent on the pole was healed of his or her snakebite. God did everything he could do. The Israelites simply had to look at that pole in order to save their life.

That is the picture of Jesus on the cross. This is the meaning of John 3:16, God loved us and sent Jesus, and those who keep their eyes on Him will live. Jesus came to save those who have been bitten by the snake (Satan) and are in need of saving our lives. If we look to Jesus and keep our eyes focused on Him, our lives are spared and we enjoy salvation. Just as I focused on that spot ahead and plowed straight furrows, when we focus on Jesus and keep our eyes on Him, our path is straight and leads to God. So keep your eyes on the one who provides the antidote to the poison this world spews, Jesus.

October 24

"But the fruit of the Spirit is love, joy, peace, patience, kindness, goodness, faithfulness, gentleness and self-control."(Galatians 5:22-23)

I want you to meet Paul. He is the service rep at the Sydney, Nova Scotia Harley Davidson dealership. Within thirty seconds of meeting Paul, I was sure that this encounter wouldn't end well.

My first impression of Paul was that he was what we in the south call your typical northerner. Paul was very short with my friend. He was rude, arrogant and abrasive; qualities in a person I find hard to handle.

Now meet my friend Dennis. He wasn't having a good day. He was 2000 miles away from home and his wife's motorcycle was making an awful sound. As he stood in front of Paul, with Paul's attitude, I was almost sure this would not be a pleasant visit to a Harley shop.

But Dennis taught me a lesson, and I think a few others as well that day. Instead of giving back that in which he was receiving, he was extremely polite and friendly. Something happened to Paul within seconds; Paul changed, he lightened up and he even smiled. Paul's whole attitude changed and within minutes the two were exchanging jokes, imitating each other's accents and acting as if they had been friends for years.

I wish I could tell you everything worked out perfectly, but I can't. The bike was shot and down for the remainder of this trip. But the encounter ended in laughter, kindness and even with Paul going out of his way to make it as pleasant as possible. What started out looking like a disaster, turned out to be an enjoyable trip to a Harley dealership in a land far, far away.

Our focus verse tells us the results of walking with Christ. We begin to show the characteristics of Jesus Himself and that can change a situation in a moment. It is amazing how one act of kindness can change everything. How we respond to people can make a difference. A lesson I received loud and clear, how about you?

October 25

"The Spirit of the Sovereign Lord is on me, because the Lord has anointed me to preach good news to the poor." (Isaiah 61:1)

Ever been to an Apple store? The people working there aren't sales people, they are people who know their stuff and want to lend their expertise for a few minutes for free. Now that is what I like, since I don't like sales people.

One of my favorite quotes is *"Preach the Gospel at all times and when necessary use words"* (Francis of Assisi) I believe Francis was like me; he didn't like sales people. He was aware of the look people get when they sense a 'preach' heading their way. You know it, the look some get when you say you are a Christian? He knew how people prepared themselves for the "Jesus" sales pitch.

No one likes to be preached at, no more than they like a sales pitch. I believe if you have really good news to share with someone – they can tell before you even open your mouth. It is difficult to hold good news in.

In the bible, we see that where ever Jesus went, people knew He was there. He didn't have a banner and there was no fanfare. Something about Jesus walking into a room brought pizzazz. He only had to invite people to follow Him and they left everything in an instant.

True preaching isn't about preaching with the use of words. It is about how you live your life, how you react to situations, it's about in whom you place your hope and trust. Your friends, who don't know God, know you. They can read you and your life. They watch you to see if you are real and if your faith is real. In order to reach them, they look to see if you love them or if they are just your evangelism project.

In order for those outside the Church (not the building but the body of Christ) to listen they must first know several things. First, are you for real? Second, has there been significant change in you that sets you apart from them? Lastly, do you really care about their eternal salvation? Jesus says in Matthew 12:34, *"out of the overflow of the heart the mouth speaks."* The connection between heart and mouth is vital in order to "preach" a good sermon.

The Hebrew word for preach is 'piel' which means to "bear news". Think about it this way. When you "bear" a child it's not just words; there is something to see. And it's pretty exciting stuff. So, to "preach" we should "bear" good news in our daily lives and speak when necessary.

299

October 26

"Without warning, a furious storm came up on the lake, so that the waves swept over the boat. But Jesus was sleeping. The disciples went and woke him, saying, 'Lord, save us! We're going to drown!'"(Matthew 8:24-25)

I attended a wedding some time back. It was a touching ceremony, picture perfect with laughter, family, friends and love. During the outdoor reception, the air was filled with more laughter, conversation and dancing. Then it happened.

A storm came up. Rain started to fall, the sky grew dark and it looked as if the party was over. But to my amazement, the people continued to laugh, talk, eat and enjoy themselves. They were okay just riding the storm out with as little cover as they could find. In a few moments the storm cleared, it seemed as if the clouds parted and the wind died down. The people present just kept going, the party went on.

How often do we let an unexpected storm stop us in our tracks? We are so worried about it that it seems to ruin everything. Even if we know it's only temporary, the storm still seems to get to us. That is what happened in our focus verse. The disciples were in a boat with Jesus yet the storm made them think they would drown. Really, when Jesus is with you, do you really think you will go down with the ship?

Later during the reception the storm came back, this time heavier. It was obvious that the storm was there to stay. What happened? They just moved the party indoors. It didn't stop the festivities. The storm was taken in stride....

When starting a new life, whether it is marriage or a new walk with Christ, know that storms will come and storms will go. Some may be light and others may be harder. How one responds to the storms is what matters.

When we walk with Christ and He is the center of our lives, storms are much easier to face. He calms the storms, quiets the wind and stops the rain. He also calms our lives, stills the troubles and allows us hope for a better day. So, when the storms come, let God handle them and just move out of its path.

October 27

"I have brought you glory on earth by completing the work you gave me to do." (John 17:4)

When my son was little he liked to help around the yard. He tried hard to please me and to make me proud of him in everything he did. When he was four, we had a small strawberry patch in the back yard. I took him to that patch, showed him the baby strawberries and taught him how to pick them when they were ripe. Every day that summer I came home to a little boy with strawberry stains on his mouth, who proudly told me he had made sure all the ripe strawberries had been picked that day. I never ate the first berry because not only did he pick them, he ate them all. He had become the best strawberry picker I could ask for.

Jesus, the Son of God came to earth for the purpose to do God's will. He was the Savior of the world, one who would lead us to the Father and live as an example of how we are to live. Before He would be arrested, beaten and hung on a cross, His prayer was simple, that His life had brought glorify to God. His prayer was that He had completed everything God had given Him to do and by doing so, God was pleased and glorified.

I do not think anything written in scripture should be taken lightly. There is a reason for that prayer, and I think it is for us to pray as well. What if everyone who professed to follow Jesus were to live their life to bring glory to God? What if everyone who professed to follow Jesus were to live their life to complete the work God has given us to do? If we lived our life with the sole intent to bring glory to God and to do His work, I think we would be living in a far different world that what we live in today.

Jesus fulfilled His call and the purpose of God. We are saved because of Him and for that I am thankful. His desire to please the Father has given those who believe and follow eternal life. When Jesus ascended to heaven I can only imagine how proud God was of Jesus. Just as I was proud of that little boy with strawberry stains on his mouth, God was proud of the way Jesus lived and completed His work on earth.

So my prayer today is that my life brings glory to God and that I live to complete the work God has given me to do. I pray that at the end of my life I hear God say, *"Well done, good and faithful servant! Come and share your master's happiness!"* (Matthew 23:21)

October 28

"But thanks be to God! He gives us the victory through our Lord Jesus Christ. Therefore, my dear brothers, stand firm. Let nothing move you. Always give yourselves fully to the work of the Lord, because you know that your labor in the Lord is not in vain."(1 Corinthians 15:57-58)

The song "Through the Fire" has always spoken to me and helped me weather many a storm. *"So many times I've questioned certain circumstances"* and *"Many times in trials, weakness blurs my vision"* are verses that speak to me. We have all been there, weighed down with the trials of life. It gets to us all from time to time.

But when this happens we need to know that *"I've never been forsaken... I've never had to stand the test alone...it's through the fire my weakness is made strong."* As children of God we aren't left on our own. He walks with us and He is in the boat with us during the storm. He is strongest when we are weak. His strength is what we need to get through.

Listen to the chorus of this song. *"He never promised that the cross would not get heavy, and the hill would not be hard to climb, He never offered our victories without fighting, but he said help would always come in time, Just remember when you're standing in the valley of decision and the adversary says give in, just hold on, our Lord will show up, and he will take you through the fire again."*

We are called to be immovable, always standing firm in God's work. We are to be consistent in our faith and not allow the events of the day to sway us. Too often we are moved by anything that happens in the world. We get a flat tire and let it ruin our day. We get depressed and ask "Where is God?" This passage tells us God is going to give us victory always, even when things look bad. God always leads us to triumph, that's the promise.

How do we have victory in God? If He is always going to give us triumph, then we can always be strong and unwavering. You can know that through every problem or obstacle, no matter how big or small, you are going to be led to victory. God wants us to become the person of dedication, always faithful. You have a God that is dedicated to you; so the least you can do is to stay dedicated to Him.

Just as the song states, *"...it's through the fire my weakness is made strong."* Let your strength come through weaknesses.

October 29

"As iron sharpens iron, so one man sharpens another." (Proverbs 27:17)

Whether on the road, over dinner or in social settings, my friends and I speak into each other's lives. We trust each other. We challenge each other. I am a better person because of my friends, because they speak with honesty and courage, because they are there for me, because they turn my heart toward God and His ways.

There is a depth to our friendship that makes me who I am. During these times together, we expose each other, we are vulnerable yet safe, we get into each other's grills about priorities, marriages, parenting, and ministry, our faith matters. We hold one another accountable. I can only speak for myself but I welcome this, in fact I need it.

We all need friends in our lives that love us enough to help us be a better person. We all need people in our lives that lift us up, make us stronger, encourage and strengthen us. We all need people in our lives that hold us accountable to God's standards and that make us better people and better Christ followers.

Our bible verse makes a compelling point about a friendship like this. It tells us that strong people make others strong. We should have friends who sharpen us, challenge us, and makes us wiser and better. We need people who ask tough questions, shares godly truths and confronts us when we need confronted.

If you have someone like that, thank God for them. If you don't, look for someone that can be that kind of friend. Once you find someone, give them permission to speak into your life and ask they allow you to do the same. Look for deeper relationships when selecting friends, not just a pool of shallow acquaintances. When we have friends that sharpen and we become a friend that sharpens, our lives are enriched.

Helen Keller said *"Walking with a friend in the dark is better than walking alone in the light."*

October 30

"And we know that in all things God works for the good of those who love him, who have been called according to his purpose." (Romans 8:28)

A couple suffers one of the most tragic things grandparents can live through; the death of an infant grandchild. Devastated, at a loss of words, they wonder why this happened. Why did a loving God take their baby from them? That was the question they had for the pastor at a nearby church. The pastor, with tears in his eyes simply said "I don't have an answer, but you have to trust in the Lord."

There is an age old question, "Why do bad things happen to good people?" This is hard to answer directly. And our focus verse says God can turn all things, in this case something bad, into good. How can this be? Let me see if I can paint a picture for you using more of their story.

The couple starts to "Trust in the Lord." They surrender their lives to Jesus. They begin to attend that very same church. The couple begins to serve, living out their faith in tangible ways. The man begins to write songs about his faith. He shares his musical talents and gives his testimony. Her father begins to attend the same church. He gets sick, people from the church show up, love on them, pray for him.

In a hospital room, late at night, the sick old man struggles for each breath. His four children surround him, pray with and for him. They share time together that is long overdue. They laugh together and share memories. For a brief moment in time they are a happy loving family, come together for the man they love.

These events and the results of those events clearly show that even through death, illness and pain, God can use it for good. The Message version of the bible uses this wording for our focus verse, *"That's why we can be so sure that every detail in our lives of love for God is worked into something good. God knew what he was doing from the very beginning."*

So never underestimate the power of God. He can turn any event; yes any event, into something that demonstrates His glory. Good can come of any event when God is in it. It may not seem so at the beginning, but in time, if you keep your eyes open and "Trust in the Lord", you will see it. People come to faith, overcome obstacles and lives are changed. God is at work, don't miss it.

October 31

"Even though I was once a blasphemer and a persecutor and a violent man, I was shown mercy because I acted in ignorance and unbelief. The grace of our Lord was poured out on me abundantly, along with the faith and love that are in Christ Jesus." (1Timothy 1:13-14)

Our church has an annual Trunk or Treat event. One year we loaded the bed of my truck full of the candy to be given out. What a sight; an abundance of sweets awaiting the kids. Often my mind goes back to that truck load of candy. I thought about God's abundance just waiting for someone to receive it. I thought about things like mercy, grace, love and forgiveness. I thought about how God gives, even though we don't deserve it at times. I thought about the people handing out candy last night, giving to each kid, no matter what they had done prior to arriving at their trunk. The gift was the same, each receiving freely.

In our focus verse, Paul writes about what he was before coming to know Christ. He was a man that spoke evil of Christ and those that followed Jesus. He was a man that hunted down and killed followers of Jesus. He carried out an evil plan once to rid the world of those walking in the "Way" of Jesus. Yet, a gift awaited him, one that was free and given in spite of the things he once did.

He tells us of this gift, given abundantly to him, even though he didn't see himself worthy of any such gift. He wrote "The grace of our Lord was poured out on me abundantly, along with the faith and love that are in Christ Jesus." Jesus met Paul while he was a blasphemer, persecutor and evil man, offered him the gift of salvation and freed him from the control of this world. He gave abundantly something that no human can ever earn.

I can't help but think about those children last night. They received abundant kindness which they did nothing to deserve or warrant. They merely showed up and received, and some I can tell you walked away with abundance. They left with more than bags of candy. Their smiles told a story, their eyes were awakened to the gift of love of Christ's people and they left happier than when they arrived.

November 1

"Jesus answered, 'I tell you, Peter, before the rooster crows today, you will deny three times that you know me.'" (Luke 22:34)

My Dad always said, "If it doesn't kill you it will make you stronger." As I have grown in my faith, I now think this is a biblical truth. Let me explain. In Luke 22 we read of a conversation between Peter and Jesus. Peter vows to go to his death for Jesus, yet Jesus knows Peter will deny Him. If we read on, we learn that is just what happened. Peter, out of fear for his life claimed he didn't know Jesus.

At first glance of our focus verse, we can almost hear Jesus' disappointment in one of His disciples. Peter is bold and strong, until he is faced with reality. Jesus knew that and He knew Peter would fail. It is sad, I have been there. I have experienced someone tell me they would die for me, only to abandon our friendship when the times get tough,

For a long time I read this passage as just that, Jesus predicting Peter's failure and that prediction coming true. But as I thought of my father's saying and then reading this again, I hear what Jesus is saying a little differently. What Jesus says is that Peter will fail, but once he realizes what he did and repents, he will use that to not only strengthen his own testimony, but to strengthen those around him. Read verse 32. Jesus says *"but when you have turned back..."* Not only does Jesus predict Peter's failure, He predicts Peter's repentance.

My father's saying rings true, what Peter did didn't kill him and he became stronger because of it. Think about what Peter did after that. Peter became the "Rock" that the church was built on. Peter ran to the tomb when the others didn't believe what the women reported, Peter was tasked by Jesus to feed Jesus' sheep, and Peter preached at Pentecost resulting in 3000 people coming to know Jesus that day. Peter was strengthened because of his failure and his repentance.

The good news for us is that we all fail, but have the ability to recover. Some of us think that our failures define us, they keep us from all God has to offer. But the truth is if we believe in and follow Jesus, those weaknesses can strengthen us to do Jesus' work here on earth. They don't disqualify us; they qualify us to be a part of God's family. Think about the stories in the bible, from failure to forgiveness, weakness to strength, death to life. That is God's way.

November 2

"Return home and tell how much God has done for you." So the man went away and told all over town how much Jesus had done for him. "(Luke 8:39)

When talking to Christians about sharing their faith I often hear "I don't know how..." "I don't know enough..." or "What if they don't listen..." These are common excuses. Have you ever heard of Penn and Teller? Did you know Penn Jillette is a well-known and outspoken atheist? A guy like that would be pretty tough to approach with the Gospel, right? So, what do you think happened when a Christian business man witnesses to Penn after one of his shows in Las Vegas?

Penn gave this analogy. He says if you and he were standing in the street and a truck was coming at him, at what point would you tackle him to get him out of harm's way? He said this because even though he doesn't believe in God, he feels it is a Christian's duty to share his or her faith. What he said was: *"I don't respect people who don't proselytize (evangelize). If you believe that there is a heaven or hell, or that people could be going to hell, or not get eternal life, and you think it's not really worth telling them this because it would make it socially awkward...and atheists think people shouldn't proselytize, just keep religion to yourself... how much do you have to hate somebody to not proselytize? How much do you have to hate somebody to believe that everlasting life is possible and not tell them that?"*

Let me remind you that these words came from an atheist! So if an atheist thinks that you should be tackling people left and right to warn them of the truck of death that is coming their way, then would you be willing to overcome your fear of social awkwardness and share your faith? Are you willing to fight against your fear of rejection in an attempt to save someone's soul?

Our focus verse comes after Jesus drives out a demon in a man. Jesus tells him to go and tell what Jesus did. He wants us to share with others what Jesus has done for us. Jesus told us that the greatest commandment is love. We are to love everyone, even our enemies. We are to love them like Christ loves them and that means doing what it takes to save their soul and eternal state. So, do you know someone who is in need of the Good News about Jesus Christ? If so, tackle that issue now and try and save them from pending doom.

November 3

"I have given them your word and the world has hated them, for they are not of the world any more than I am of the world. My prayer is not that you take them out of the world but that you protect them from the evil one." (John 17:14-15)

Since accepting Jesus, I make choices on the behaviors that I subject my eyes and ears to. I choose to be "in this world" and not "of this world". There is a big difference. Once Natalie Grant, a Christian artist nominated for a Grammy in the Best Gospel/Contemporary Christian Music category, walked out during the show because of behaviors she didn't want to be subjected to. Now she could have taken the stage, make a big public deal of it, but instead, she just chose to remove herself from the things that are obviously of this world.

Now I didn't watch the show and after reading a few things about it, I am glad I didn't. But I love how she handled the situation. She quietly removed herself from the ungodly behavior and some noticed. That's enough.

When we choose to live our life different from the world, people do notice. We don't have to beat them over the heads with our bibles. We don't have to preach to them, or even quote scripture, just live our life differently and it speaks volumes.

A friend of mine had a birthday party just the other day. I really wanted to go, I really think the world of this person, but just knew that there may be some things I didn't want to be around. I am not condemning, but it just isn't my thing. I apologized to my friend about missing the party and her response warmed my heart. She told me that wasn't the place for me and that I didn't need to be there. She understood that about me and I love her for it.

People have to make their own decisions in life, about how they want to live, what they want to believe in and how to conduct themselves. I choose to live according to the ways Jesus modeled while He walked this earth. Do I always get it right? No way, but I try. And when I do it makes me know I am pleasing God, especially when someone notices.

So, what about you? Do the things of this world go against your belief? If so, take a silent stand and walk away from those things. The world is watching and they do notice. Who knows, maybe someone will follow.....

November 4

"The Israelites ate manna forty years, until they came to a land that was settled; they ate manna until they reached the border of Canaan."(Exodus 16:35

Our dog Ziggy is blind in one eye. She suffered from glaucoma and she is now required to have drops put in her eye twice a day. It often takes a conscience effort to remember to apply her drops. I tend to forget. If she gets them she is okay, if not she suffers with swelling and pain. I don't want her to suffer, so I try real hard to remember.

It is expensive and it's a pain to keep giving her the drops. Day in and day out she is required to have the care that only we can give her. We love her, so no matter the cost or the effort, we will give her the drops for as long as she needs them.

We take for granted that God does the same for us. Our focus verse tells of the heavenly manna that God rained down every day (except on the Sabbath). For 40 years the wandering Israelites had food to eat, yet they still grumbled and complained. He knows what we need and He gives it to us. God loves us even more than I love my dog. He knows I need daily care, comfort and attention. God knows I need things like mercy, grace and forgiveness, even though at times I fight him.

God doesn't hesitate to care for our needs. No matter what we have done or how difficult we may be, God is there with exactly what we need, when we need it. The difference between us and Ziggy, she is happy to take her drops. She sits there patiently while we do it. When it's over she wags her tail because of the attention she just received or the treat I am about to give her. Us on the other hand, we wiggle, complain, fight and are, more often than not, ungrateful. We want more or something different.

We can learn a lot from a dog. Maybe our life would be much nicer if we just sit back and took what God gives us. Maybe life would be easier if we were just happy with what God wanted for us. So, the lesson I take from Ziggy is to sit back and let my Master take care of me. He knows what I need and will give it to me, without fail.

November 5

"...for all have sinned and fall short of the glory of God, and are justified freely by his grace through the redemption that came by Christ Jesus."
(Romans 3:23-24)

I attended a "March for Jesus" rally recently. Several thousand people attended proclaiming the name of Jesus. They stood as one, and then there stood Tara. Tara was gender confused and not a Christ follower. She was there to state her opinion that there was no God. She stood bravely, one in a sea of thousands, willing to take a stand.

Many Christ followers took a moment to talk to Tara. They showed love, in spite of what she believed. Some witnessed, showed compassion, one even openly stating their admiration of the bravery. They circled her and prayed. Then there were several "Christ followers" barking harsh comments. They told Tara she was "damned" and was going to hell. They showed no compassion, no love of Jesus.

I wondered how Tara may have viewed God after the entire encounter. What would she remember, love and compassion or hatred and judgmental voices.

In my past I stood against Christianity and opposed it. Our focus verse reminds us that we were sinners when we came to know Jesus. What led me to Christ were those who loved me in spite of my objections.

God's love goes beyond one's appearance, gender, color or sin. We all have sinned, meaning we have done something that goes against God's ways. Yet Jesus died for us, even while we were sinning and saved us from that sin so that we can be reconciled to Him. Because He loved us as we sinned, we are saved. So doesn't it stand to reason that even the Tara's of this world are afforded the same?

Think the next time you are faced with something that goes against what you believe to be right. Think before you speak and ask yourself, how Jesus would handle it. Chances are, if we do that, our actions may just very well reflect the very image of God.

I pray for the Taras of this world, because once I was a sinner, lost in this world on a path to hell. But someone loved instead of judged. Someone took interest instead of casting me into the lake of fire. Jesus told us to "love" as we want to be loved. Let's be more like Jesus....

310

November 6

"For God so loved the world that he gave his one and only Son,* that whoever believes in him shall not perish but have eternal life."(John 3:16)

I want to say up front that this is my opinion on the subject of Tattoos on Christians. Tattoos on Christians are an age old discussion and there are divided camps on the topic. People have their opinions and some will do anything to try to discredit a Christian who has a tattoo. Some of the strongest proponents against tattoos on Christians are other Christians. They typically have an opinion that is so deeply seated they can't let it go or move past it. I have tattoos and, as a Pastor, you can imagine the criticism and looks I receive.

With all that said, my belief is that having a tattoo will not keep anyone from serving the Lord. God can and will use anyone, tattooed or not. Having a tattoo will not keep us out of heaven either. God sent Jesus down to earth, to die on a cross and to rise from the grave, just as our focus verse tells us, for everyone. He didn't have disqualifiers; He loved the world and those in it.

Our actions as Christians should speak louder than any tattoo. I suggest that we focus more on the person than what they wear or have on their bodies. We need to move the focus away from the tattoos and onto God. Jesus loved those who the Pharisees disliked and it ticked them off. They thought Jesus to be a radical, when in reality they were the radicals. They didn't understand a God who loves so much He would sacrifice the one thing that meant the most to Him.

Not everyone will approve of tattoos, earrings, loud music or the like. I have heard of church splits because of carpet color. When we start to focus on the things that don't really matter, instead of the gospel, we do more harm to the church than good.

So let's start to look past the exterior and more towards the heart. Jesus spoke of this when He accused the Pharisees of washing the outside of the cup while leaving the inside dirty. In order to be a disciple of Jesus, we must look at people like He did, with compassion. Let's look at what Jesus looked at, people and their needs. The debate may continue, but I suggest focusing on the main thing, sharing the love of Christ to all.

November 7

"These words I speak to you are not incidental additions to your life... They are foundational words, words to build a life on."(Matthew 7:24 MSG)

I, like everyone else, have very little spare time on my hands. Seems my calendar is always full, free time is at a premium. I also know that I will take time to do what is important to me. I can always find time to do what I enjoy, what I get pleasure out of and what makes me happy.

I have heard people say they don't have time to do this or that. But when you listen to what they did do, they had plenty of time for what they were really interested in. Case in point, I used to play a lot of golf. I always found time for a round with my buddies. Sometimes we would play two rounds in one day.

During that time I know I must have said thousands of times, "I don't have time for..." I could find time to play golf, but the other things that could have been done, or maybe needed to be done went to the end of my "to do list".

So with that being said, I now make time to spend with God and study His word. It is a priority and something that not only needs to be done in order for my life with Christ to grow, but something I enjoy doing. And when I do, I want to make the time alone with God as meaningful as possible.

When I sit to read my bible I take my time with God seriously. I know that I need to take serious the things God's word teaches me, because that is what His word is for. The word "teaching" is used 35 times in the four gospels alone.

Jesus uses some very strong language about the importance of His teachings. Our focus verse reminds us that Jesus didn't teach for the sake of teaching; He taught lessons that are to be used to build our life on. His teachings are to strengthen us, help us to overcome the world and to grow closer to Him.

Jesus lived out what He taught, and He tells us to do the same. Every story of Jesus in the bible helps me to live a life worthy of Him. So, when time is limited I study His word with a mindset, "He said it, I believe it, so therefore I'll do it." If the Savior of the world lived out what He taught, then so will I.

November 8

"'Martha, Martha,'. the Lord answered, 'you are worried and upset about many things, but only one thing is needed. Mary has chosen what is better, and it will not be taken away from her.'" (Luke 10:41-42)

My dog Ziggy loves to sit in my lap and be petted. She is most comfortable when we are together. She is in our home for the sole purpose of companionship. We love her, she loves us, and we enjoy the time spent together.

We were created for the exact same purpose. Way back in the days of Genesis, God created man and woman for companionship. One of my favorite mind pictures of the Garden of Eden is God walking with Adam and Eve. The Bible is very clear. God made us for Himself and he enjoys spending time with us.

Jesus came to earth for the same reason, to spend time with us. Once when Jesus was visiting two sisters, one was so busy she was missing time with Jesus, while her sister sat leisurely at His feet. Jesus' words to Martha may seem strange to us. Why does someone who has called us to obedience tell His servant to stop working, sit down, and listen? The answer lies in God's priority for us.

Nowhere in the Bible are we told to serve Him at the expense of knowing Him. God's main desire is to spend time with us. Think of your son or daughter. Did you have them to wait on you, or to spend time with you? Do you want their labor, or their love? I hope the answer is to love them and spend time with them.

So it is with God. He is first and foremost a Father who enjoys His children. He wants you to be like my dog, to enjoy His presence and His touch. So slow down and spend that time with God, you will be better for it.

November 9

"He tells us "Do not work for food that spoils, but for food that endures to eternal life, which the Son of Man will give you. On him God the Father has placed his seal of approval."(John 6:27)

I like Thanksgiving. It is one holiday that hasn't been over commercialized. When I think of Thanksgiving I can't help but recall my mother in the kitchen baking. She loved to bake and I loved the fresh bread, the cakes and pies and I loved to watch her go about the process with a smile.

Thanksgiving means many things to many people. Let's face it, most of us think of Thanksgiving as friends, family, football and food. We get visions in our heads of all the people that we will surround ourselves with, the games on TV and mostly all the food that we will fix and eat. We look forward to the turkey, ham, sweet potatoes, pie and, well let me stop there because I am getting hungry.

The food we think of during Thanksgiving always seems so much better than normal every day food. Everything tastes better during Thanksgiving and we get to enjoy foods we don't get on a normal basis. Because of this, most of us eat entirely too much. We regret the second helpings after the fact, but it is so good at the time.

While Thanksgiving food is good and so filling, Jesus tells us that regular food will spoil and we are to focus on a food that has eternal ramifications. Jesus is telling us in our focus verse that He is the food that lasts an eternity. Strange thing to refer to Jesus as food, but Jesus offers us something that fills in an entirely different way.

Jesus said *"I am the bread of life. He who comes to me will never go hungry..."* Jesus is telling us that belief in Him and following His ways fills the void most of us hunger for and secures our eternal salvation. It is what sustains life, the life that matters.

Thanksgiving food can fill us, but sooner or later we get hungry again. We have to keep going back to fill that void, but the food Jesus offers fills us forever. Understanding that is key to being one with Christ. The bread of life is eternal, and that is so good!

314

November 10

"...that you may be filled to the measure of all the fullness of God."(Ephesians 3:19)

We have one of those beds where you can adjust the head and foot for a more comfortable night's sleep. We keep the foot raised slightly to help with my "restless leg syndrome." The head has a small lift, but for the most part that is it. Joy asked me a while back if she could adjust it and my comment was pretty much, whatever makes her happy.

The other night I woke to the whirl of the motor that drives the lift mechanism. The foot of the bed was rising. I thought it was going up a little high, but whatever my wife wanted was okay with me. I repositioned and off to sleep I went. Not long after, I woke to the whirl of the motor again. This time the head was going up. I looked over, saw the control lit up and remember mumbling something to my wife, but repositioned and fell asleep before I heard her reply.

The sight I saw when I woke up made me literally laugh out loud. The foot of the bed was up so high I couldn't see over it. The head was equally as high and there we both lay, curled up in balls in the fold of the mattress. It looked like one of those "half pipe" skate board ramps.

How often in life do we find ourselves in uncomfortable situations, yet do nothing about it? We just make an adjustment and live with it, no matter how uncomfortable we become.

God never intended for us to live this way. God wants control of our lives in order for us to overcome the bad situations. God offers a different way to live, but we must be willing to allow Him control of our lives, fully and without reservation. Our focus verse tells us that the more Jesus dwells in our hearts, the more we are filled with all the fullness of God.

What does that mean? It means we are empowered by God to overcome the things that cause us harm or discomfort. We live the life God wants for us, not the life we settle for.

By the way, my wife didn't make the adjustments to the bed that night. Her pillow did. In fact when she heard me laughing, she too woke up and joined in. Sometimes the situations are out of our control, but God can help us to see them for what they are, and help get us through them with a much better attitude. So call on Him, let Him control your life. It makes all the difference.

November 11

"So he went down and dipped himself in the Jordan seven times, as the man of God had told him, and his flesh was restored and became clean like that of a young boy. "(2 Kings 5:14)

While traveling we sometimes talk about what those early settlers must have thought. You know those brave men and women who packed everything they owned into wagons and went west. What drives someone to leave the known for the unknown? What kind of faith leads someone to risk it all?

I read a story called the *"Before Principle"* and I think it may help to explain that to have faith in something better or something we need takes the courage to just believe and throw caution in the air. Faith takes a person to new heights, believing that what they want will be delivered.

"A letter in a can tied to an old water pump on a trail across the Armargosa Desert read as follows: This pump is all right as of June 1932. Under the white rock I buried a bottle of water, out of the sun and cork end up. There's enough water in it to prime the pump, but not if you drink some first. The well has never run dry. Have faith. When you git watered up, fill the bottle and put it back like you found it for the next feller. Desert Pete P.S. Don't go drinking up the water first. Prime the pump with it and you'll get all you can hold."

If you were a traveler walking down a parched desert trail with your canteen bone-dry, would you trust this guy Desert Pete? There is no proof that his claim is true. Everything about this letter is a risk. What would you do?

We must trust those who came before us that the things we read in the bible are true. The experiences of those who walked before us are accurate. In Scripture, the "before principle" is repeated over and over. The Israelites had to march to the Red Sea before God parted it. Naaman had to wash seven times in the water before God cured him of leprosy. Peter had to obey Jesus' instruction to row out to deep water before he caught a boatload of fish.

The weary traveler reading Desert Pete's letter was put to the test in a way similar to how the Hebrew people at the Red Sea, Naaman, and Peter were put to the test. God honors radical, risk-taking faith. God relishes favoring people who apply the "before principle."

So what might God be calling you to do? Do you trust Him? Will you apply this principle to that call? Will you take the first step of faith? If you believe, take the risk and see just what God has in store.

November 12

"But now he has reconciled you by Christ's physical body through death to present you holy in his sight, without blemish..." (Colossians 1:22)

I love working with my hands. I like building things and seeing results. But, to be honest, I often try too hard at being a perfectionist. I want to do it right and I want to do it right the first time. That is how my dad taught me and how I have lived my life all these years.

I am in the process of building my wife a "she-shed" as she refers to it. It is a building in which she will use as she see fit. It has come along well and I am now in the final stages of finishing it. In order to do so, I am doing something I did years ago and at first hesitated to do it now. I am finishing the dry wall.

This is a process in which you use what is known as "mud" and "tape" to cover all the seams and blemishes after the install step. It's not hard, just time consuming. And for me, it drives me crazy. You see, it takes at least three steps to get a finished product. That is where I have an issue. I want each step to look like the finished product and no matter how hard I try, it doesn't.

The same is true in our walk with Christ. We often want to go from sinner, and in my case a really bad sinner, to a saint overnight. It doesn't work that way. We, in our own strength, can't make ourselves perfect. God calls us to Him, and then over time He cleanses us, washes us and takes away all the old attitudes, behaviors and thinking.

If we stay true to our faith and we allow God to work in our lives, He will smooth out the flaws, the wrinkles, and the blemishes that we see. He, in His perfect time, makes us clean, pure and as our focus verse says, *"Without blemish"* in His eyes. But we must allow Him the freedom to work on us.

My job is coming along, but there is more work to do. God's work in me is coming along but I know there is plenty more work to be done. I will just let Him smooth, clean and sand my rough edges as He sees fit. My prayer is that by the time I get to Heaven, He will see me without blemish and welcome me in. Only God can do that.....

November 13

"Be joyful always; pray continually; give thanks in all circumstances, for this is God's will for you in Christ Jesus." (1 Thessalonians 5:16-18)

"You have had a fire at your house!" Not something one wants to hear while away on a trip. But that was the news I received and there was no changing it. Seems the neighbor poured hot coals from his grill into a dry flower bed. The end result was a fire that burned a section of my fence and melted the siding from one end of my pool house.

Bad news comes and most times it is not at the most opportune time. It catches us off guard. That is life and it happens to us all. How we respond makes all the difference.

For me, some 2000 miles away, there was nothing I could do about it. I began to ask, was anyone hurt? The answer was no and that was a blessing. Was there any structural damage? The answer was no; another blessing. Is there any potential for further damage? The answer was no; yet another blessing. I breathed a sigh of relief and then the biggest blessing came; I talked to Jason, the neighbor I had never met.

Sometimes bad news can work out to be a blessing in disguise. For me it was a chance to meet Jason. I have now talked with him several times, something I failed to do for over a year. I found out a little about him and his family. Now I have a chance to work alongside him as we repair the damage the fire caused. I pray that this results in a new friendship and a chance to share with him what God is doing in my life.

How we respond to situations matters. I could have panicked and let the news ruin my trip. Or I could have looked for God's hand in a bad situation and counted my blessings. The latter is what I did and as it was, the blessings were many.

So the next time you get bad news, take a moment to ask yourself, could it have been worse? Chances are the answer is yes. If so, start counting your blessings and then give thanks to God.

November 14

"When they came to Jesus, they saw the man who had been possessed by the legion of demons, sitting there, dressed and in his right mind; and they were afraid. Those who had seen it told the people what had happened to the demon-possessed man, and told about the pigs as well. Then the people began to plead with Jesus to leave their region." (Mark 5:15-17)

When my wife made the Army promotion list I told her she would begin to see changes in how people treated her. I told her she would lose friends. She didn't agree, but I knew from experience. The same thing happened to me a year or two earlier. People change when you change. Get promoted and your co-workers treat you differently. Give your life to Jesus and start following His ways and watch how many of your friends aren't friends anymore. Why is this?

Mark 5:1-17 records a story of a demon possessed man who sees Jesus and goes to Him for help. This guy is mean; no one comes near him. He is cast out of the town to live in the tombs alone. Then Jesus comes along and casts out his demons. The man is transformed.

When the town's people came they saw the demon possessed man changed and in his right mind. He was no longer a threat to them yet they were afraid. Why? Was it the ex-demon possessed man they were afraid of, or was it the new man he had become?

I believe they focused on the dead pigs. They saw the cost of saving a man and that is what they were afraid of. Salvation comes with a cost, and to some, they aren't willing to pay it. The price for the man was a herd of pigs. Maybe the people were calculating the price it may cost them. I believe the reason they asked Jesus to leave was because Jesus was too costly a guest.

People fear Jesus because of the cost His presence may bring. His presence may cost friends, comforts, behaviors, attitudes, social status or even financial loss. Some aren't willing to pay that price for the promises of Jesus and the reward of eternal life. They would rather lose their soul instead of a few worldly things.

Know this: following Jesus Christ and calling Him Lord and Savior comes with a cost. You will change and not everyone you know will like it. You may have to give some things up, but the reward far outweighs the loss. So stand strong, be faithful and know that what you gain is greater than anything you may lose.

November 15

"Everything is permissible, but not everything is beneficial." (1 Corinthians 10:23)

My dog Ziggy loves to chase squirrels. It's a daily routine for her. She will stand at the back door, eyes glued to the yard and watch. She has done it so many times and she often gives the squirrel a little head start before she starts running.

She has chased squirrels in our back yard for about 7 years now. She is a pro at it. But the other day, the unexpected happened. She chased a squirrel up the hill until it jumped up on top of the fence, out of harm's way. Ziggy, feeling triumphant turned towards the house, her back to her prey, and started back home. But the squirrel did the unexpected; he started after Ziggy. The squirrel came up behind Ziggy, startling her, making her do a back flip. It was obvious she didn't see that coming.

Often we chase things in life over and over again. We do it so often that we think we are in control, that we have mastered it. Often the chase can become just a routine, going through the motions, not even realizing what we are doing. And when we get complacent, the unexpected happens. If we aren't careful, the thing we have been chasing can sneak up and grab us from behind.

Our focus verse tells us that everything is permissible, but not beneficial. The world tells us that everything can be ours, but what it fails to tell us is that not everything is good for us. There are things of this world, although they are legal, they can cause us eternal ramifications.

I often wonder what would happen if Ziggy ever catches a squirrel. Will she get hurt? Will she get bit? Get rabies? The outcome of that chase may not be favorable. The same applies to us. We can chase things that can end up biting us and causing us more harm than good.

Trust me when I say if you chase something long enough, someone gets hurt. So think before you go. Some things are better just left alone.

November 16

"Cleanse me… and I will be clean; wash me, and I will be whiter than snow." (Psalms 51:7)

Sad to say, I have a dark past. I came to know Jesus just shy of my 44th birthday. God has radically transformed my life since then. Because of where I came from, I relate most to Saul/Paul in the book of Acts.

Paul wastes no time getting busy for Jesus. He starts preaching, teaching and writing almost immediately. His zeal against the church had been reversed and he does all he can do for the church of Jesus Christ. It is as if his past was wiped away, in the blink of an eye.

Stuff happens and if you are like me, the minute you put on a white shirt, boom…a stain appears. There is a new invention that can help with the stain problem. It is called a stain stick. One swipe and the stain is gone.

Now, I am not comparing Jesus to a stain stick, but the principle is the same. We all have pasts, things we aren't proud of. We all have habits, hurts and hang-ups that we know needs some attention. In our own power we scrub and scrub and that stain never goes away. But the power of Jesus to remove stains is out of this world. Jesus can remove any stain, if we let Him

Paul tells of his conversion in Acts 22. He is visited by a man named Ananias, a messenger sent by God, to pray for Paul. Ananias prays, and then tells Paul what God's plan is for him. I bet Paul was a little confused and maybe hesitated, trying to figure out what was going on. Ananias looked at Paul and asked him *"…what are you waiting for? Get up, be baptized and wash your sins away, calling on His name."*

Just like that, Paul was cleansed. The stains of his life were removed. Our focus verse tells us God's forgiveness turns our dirty selves into something that resembles fresh, untouched snow. Isn't that a great picture?

Do you have a stain in your life that needs removed? Is there something you have tried to clean yourself of and it just never seems to go away? Or, in a lot of cases, when we try to clean that stain, it grows, spreads and gets worse. Well I know a stain remover that you need to use. Call on the name of Jesus and that stain will vanish. Jesus has the power to remove whatever is in your life that needs to be cleansed, but just like the stain stick, if you don't use it, it is worthless.

November 17

"Come! Whoever is thirsty, let him come; and whoever wishes, let him take the free gift of the water of life." (Revelation 22:17)

I like to give gifts and I won't lie, I like to receive them too. A friend of mine once gave me a gift out of the blue. He told me that he normally doesn't buy gifts for others, but he saw this coffee mug and thought of me. I was thrilled, not only to receive it, but that he thought enough of me to buy it.

Now, you may think, what is so special about a coffee mug. Well I like my coffee and I like cool looking mugs to drink my coffee from. I have a small collection and each one means something special to me, to include this one. Coffee isn't just a morning thing; I can drink it all day. It quenches my thirst.

We all thirst. We have a physical thirst, one that needs liquid to quench. A cool glass of water does a lot for that thirst. It provides moisture; it whets a dry, parched throat.

But there is a spiritual thirst as well. We all long for something. Our hearts are dehydrated, we worry, and we suffer from guilt, fear, loneliness, irritability and sleeplessness. God never intended for us to live this way.

A story in John tells of a woman who has an encounter with Jesus. She is thirsty, so she goes to a well. But there is more to her thirst. Her soul longs for something and she is desperately searching in all the wrong places. Then Jesus offers her *"living water"* that will quench that thirst and never run out. What is He talking about? It's called grace.

Unmerited favor offered as a free gift from the only one who can give it, Jesus. It is the gift that saves, and it's free for the taking. When we drink of that grace, it does what nothing else can; it quenches that spiritual thirst. But we must accept it and, like the woman, we must go to the well often and drink deeply of it.

Jesus says in our focus verse to come and take the gift He offers, the water of life. I refused that gift for the biggest part of my life, but once I took it, I never want to live without it. It's like coffee; I can't imagine a day without it. What about you? Are you thirsty? Have you been searching? Find what you need with Jesus and never thirst again.

November 18

"Jesus declared. 'Go now and leave your life of sin.'"(John 8:11)

Have you ever seen a mole? You know, one of those critters that dig up your yard. Once they invaded my yard and turned it into what looked like a mine field. They came and went before I had the pleasure of catching them.

Things can threaten that in which we build up. The biggest threat to the church can be from within. Some who appear loyal to the church can, in fact, be undermining it.

The sin of tolerance: "I know what I am doing is wrong, but I will do it anyway. It's my life." The sin of selective authority: "Who are you to tell me what to do? I'm a member and pay my tithe." The sin of catered needs: "The church is to look after me and to take care of my wants." How about the sin of being inward focused, "Before we go out to bring new people in we need to take care of our own." My pet peeve: the sin of limited evangelism: "That person seated there is not our kind."

When we allow the very things Jesus taught as being wrong infiltrate our church and the body of believers in which make up the church, it does more harm than good. Turning a blind eye to sin in fear of rocking the boat does no one any good. We must lift each other up, we must hold each other accountable and we must do all we can to make Christ look appealing to others. If our lives look no different than those in the world, then how can we expect people to come to walk with Jesus?

Jesus told us to be *"new creations"*, set apart from those who don't believe, don't profess or walk with Christ. In our focus verse, he told the woman caught in her sin, to leave that old life of sin. He repeatedly told people *"sin no more"* fully meaning just that. Stop what you are doing and change. We have the power to overcome sin; it's called the Holy Spirit. But the Holy Spirit can't and won't live in a worldly vessel.

If you have sin in your life and you are okay with it, chances are the Holy Spirit has moved out. If you want Him back, clean up your act. Let's lift others up and help them be who they profess. Keep one another accountable for their actions. Keep me and other professing Christ followers on the narrow path. One day they will thank you for it.....

November 19

"Blessed are the poor in spirit, for theirs is the kingdom of heaven."
(Matthew 5:3)

A man was mowing his yard with an old beat up mower. The mower would run for a minute, then quit. When it did run, it coughed black smoke, spit and sputtered.

An older homeless man happened by. He said "I can fix that." The man told him to go ahead. The homeless guy flipped the mower over, kicked it a few times, flipped it back over and told the guy to start it up. It ran perfectly.

Well, as I was mowing my yard, wouldn't you know it, my mower started to do the same thing. I have two mowers so I went and got the second one. It did the same thing. The more I tried, the less they ran. So, thinking about the story, I flipped the mower over, gave it a few kicks and tried it again. What could it hurt?

Sometimes our spiritual walk can be like those mowers. We spit and sputter. We struggle to keep running this thing Paul calls a race. It begins to look hopeless, all odds against us. We have everything we need, our salvation, the bible, the knowledge that we are God's child, yet we still have a hard time. Why?

Our focus verse calls us the *"poor in spirit"*. What does that mean? The poor in spirit are those who need help, the help that can only come from Jesus. Take Peter, who when walking on the water, takes his eyes off Jesus and begins to sink. He then understands he is in need and cries out desperately, *"Lord, save me."*

The poor in spirit, realizing their need for God's help, cry out, *"Lord, help me."* Can you imagine the number of problems that would be solved if people would seek help? Many of us spit and sputter along the way, all the while Jesus is right there to figuratively give us a kick to get us running again. Some would rather stay in the ruts of life because they are unwilling to cry out for help. God is willing and wants to help. All we need to do is ask.

Well to end my story, one of the mowers did begin to run the way it was supposed to. It took me longer to mow my yard than normal, but only because it took me too long to give it a kick. The next time you begin to spit and sputter in your walk, ask God for a kick. It may hurt but it will get you up and running smoothly.

November 20

"The LORD himself goes before you and will be with you; he will never leave you nor forsake you. Do not be afraid; do not be discouraged."(Deuteronomy 31:8)

How many of you remember the old Motel 6 catch phrase? Just in case you don't it was: *"we'll leave the light on for you."* Every time I heard that I thought of my dad. Let me explain.

When I was growing up my dad had a routine. Just before dark he would turn the porch light on. Then just before going to bed he would turn it off. I asked him once why he did this and the answer I got made sense and has been my practice my entire adult life. What he said was *"When the porch light is on it means anyone is welcomed to drop in. When the light is out, only someone with an emergency should knock on the door."*

So I guess that concept was what Motel 6 was implying. The light is always on so you are always welcomed. This got me to thinking, who else leaves the light on constantly and welcomes us always? Well the answer is God! His light always shines and He always has open arms for anyone who stops by.

Our focus verse tells us He is always there, always available, never to leave or forsake us. His presence is constant, as long as we are walking with Him. No matter the time, no matter the circumstance, God is ready and willing to hear from you. You won't wake Him nor interrupt Him. His light is always on and we all should know that.

So what are you facing today? What is going on in your world that you need help with? God is there and He is ready to help out, but you have to stop by. Give it a try and go to a friend that waits for you and never grows tired of waiting for you. And He is a friend that will help out and never condemn you. God leaves the light on and it shines on the path that leads to Him.

November 21

"Submit yourselves, then, to God. Resist the devil, and he will flee from you."
(James 4:7)

I used to own a very small pop-up camper. The refrigerator was so tiny it was pretty much worthless, so we bought a 100 quart cooler. Once while we were camping in the Redwood Forest we wedged the cooler under the tongue of the camper to keep it safe from all the critters.

Late that night I heard something that sounded like my cooler being drug out. I grabbed the flashlight and out the door I went. Standing in my underwear, I spotted the bandit. A very large raccoon had his paws on the handle of my cooler and he was dragging it off.

Remembering the instructions the Park Ranger had given us about encountering wild animals, I tried to make myself look bigger. I raised my arms over my head and began to yell, hoping to frighten him. I think I heard that critter laugh at me. There I stood, trying to look bigger than a raccoon in my underwear. He wasn't having it. He had my cooler and he was taking it home. I was powerless to scare him.

So I told my wife to throw me the broom. I cracked him on his nose, not hard, but with enough force to let him know I was serious. Nothing, he kept dragging. So I did it again, and then again. Finally, he let go. He climbed a nearby tree hissing and giving me dirty looks as we locked the cooler in our truck.

Satan will come *"to steal and kill and destroy"* and we are powerless to fight him on our own. I was powerless to fight my little thief, and it wasn't until I realized it and relied on a higher power did he flee.

When Satan comes at us, he wants to drag away the things than mean the most to us and the only way to fight him is to follow the instructions of our focus verse. Submit to God, rely on His power working through you, and then Satan will flee.

November 22

"When Jesus had entered Capernaum, a centurion came to him, asking for help."(Matthew 8:5)

I like to travel. My wife and I, along with our best friends, travel a lot together. Our thinking is that the more places we can see the better. I believe God created this world for us to explore, so when we travel that is exactly what we do. We try to take it all in, leaving nothing to regret once we leave. We go where most tourists won't or don't. We immerge ourselves into the area.

We have been known to get lost (or turned around as I like to call it) occasionally. To some that may be a distraction from the journey, to me, it's merely a part of the fun. Most times we see some pretty cool stuff when lost or off the beaten path.

We find things along the way. We meet people and see unique things along the way, and most of the times it leads to more adventure and discovery. We always find something that wasn't in the guide book. Getting lost is an opportunity for exploration.

If we read the life and times of Jesus we will find He did most of His healings and other miracles along the way. What most would think of as a distraction was ministry to Jesus. In the three years Jesus traveled to the cross, He was sidetracked a lot of times.

If you profess to be a Christ follower then you too are called to minister. We are called to "be like" Jesus Christ and to walk in His footsteps. We minister through our wandering and the workings of our daily life. Those people and places God puts in our path aren't distractions but chances to share His love, mercy and grace.

And who knows, somewhere along the way you may wander into a situation where the power of Jesus is just what was needed. So enjoy the journey, no matter where it takes you. Enjoy the journey, no matter what Jesus puts in your path, and share what He is doing in your life.

November 23

"The Son reflects the glory of God and shows exactly what God is like. He holds everything together with His powerful word. When the Son made people clean from their sins, He sat down at the right side of God, the Great One in heaven." (Hebrews 1:3)

When I was little, I went everywhere and tried to do everything my father did. I wanted to be just like him. In fact, his friends called us Pete (his name) and Re-Pete, a little carbon copy of him. I didn't mind the nickname since to me it meant I was like my dad.

I see a lot of people trying to be like someone else, and for the most part, they fail. We were made in our unique way by the creator of everything. God made us in His image (see Gen 1:27). Now we can't be God, but we, as followers, are called to "imitate" and reflect Him.

The writer of the passage above equates the nature of Jesus with the nature of God. Not only does he say that Jesus reflects the glory of God, but check out the next part... *"..and (He) shows exactly what God is like."* What he is saying is that Jesus is an exact representation, or mirror image of God. What that implies is that by following Jesus, we should reflect the image of Jesus.

Have you heard the phrase, "he is the spitting image of his father"? It is believed to have come from another phrase, "splitting image", which refers to the splitting of a plank of wood into two separate pieces whose grain patterns match exactly. As a woodworker, I have seen this and tried very hard on several projects to make this work. Another belief is that the phrase means that the father could have "spit him out of his own mouth". Either implies that the one is an exact replica of the other.

Here is the difficult question, "Do we that claim to be followers of Christ reflect Him accurately?" Are we the "spitting image" of God? Do we reflect accurately in word and deed? We should. We need to be conscious of the fact that some people will get their entire impression of God by looking only at our lives. Does that scare you? It should.

For those professing to be follower of Jesus Christ, we need to at least attempt to reflect His imagine in all we do and say. We need to be the image of Christ so that others can come to know Him, follow Him and receiver His mercy, grace and love. So, if you want to be like anyone, be like Jesus.

November 24

"…but if we walk in the light, as he is in the light, we have fellowship one with another and the blood of Jesus his Son cleanses us from all sin. If we say that we have no sin, we deceive ourselves, and the truth is not in us. If we confess our sins, he is faithful and righteous to forgive us our sins, and to cleanse us from all unrighteousness." (1 John 1:7-9 ASV)

Many years ago an unfortunate accident happened and the end result was a spot in our carpet that just won't go away. We have tried everything imaginable but nothing seems to get it out. We are just stuck with it. Every time I see that stain, it reminds me of that night.

When we sin, or fall short of expectations, the end result is normally something we aren't very proud of, a stain on our character or reputation. We are often the ones that remember those stains, even when others tend to forget. We can be our own worst enemy. Forgiveness comes hard for some. And once we have that stain, we try everything we can to wipe it clean, failing every time. Nothing we do can make it go away. We relive it in our minds, we try to rationalize and apologize. We try to overcome it by doing things to make up for it, but it remains. I had some of those stains once. I tried drowning them with liquor, piling stuff on top of them to hide them, and even attempting to make them seem less of a stain by creating new ones. But the stains remained.

I finally realized that I could never wash away my stains. I realized that I have no power to get rid of those stains. Only God can. The passage above tells us that if we walk in the light, with God, He can actually purge those stains out of our lives. He can rid our lives of those things that mark us as a failure.

God's forgiveness is based on the blood of His Son that was shed at Calvary. That blood provided God with a righteous basis on which He can forgive sins. It has lasting efficacy to cleanse us, it is better than Oxiclean. God guarantees to forgive and to forget. When we confess our sins, we must believe, on the authority of the word of God that He forgives us. And if He forgives us, we must be willing to forgive ourselves. That is when the stain finally disappears, never to be seen again.

November 25

"She will give birth to a son, and you are to give him the name Jesus, because he will save his people from their sins." (Matthew 1:21)

We don't get a lot of bad weather in South Carolina. But when we do, it normally takes its toll. My back yard is my refuge. I take great effort to make it a place for solitude and relaxation. My landscape reflects the south, sago palms and large palms trees.

As we suffered from another storm, the ice started to weigh down the branches of my palm trees. They looked as if they were about to break, so out I went, in freezing rain and ice, equipped with a broom to save and protect my trees. I took my time knocking the ice off each branch, until the tree branches started to spring back up. Why? Because I feel anything worth having is worth saving and protecting.

The bible tells us that we were created in God's image. He created us to have fellowship with Him. God takes great pleasure in His people. If you read Genesis 2 you will see that God met Adam and Eve in the garden, to walk and talk with them. Wow, wouldn't that be cool? But after the fall (Genesis 3) things changed. Mankind became a sinful people. We started to get weighed down with the things of the world, putting God off and turning our backs on Him. But, God still loves His people, no matter what.

God loves the things He feels are worth having. God so loves His people that He will go to great measure to save and protect them. He would even send a piece of Himself (Jesus) to this world in order to save and protect the very thing He created.

God had a plan to save His people. Our focus verse tells us God found a woman, a virgin, who was worthy to carry the savior of the world and a man that was worthy to raise that child. Think about it, God loves us so much, even when we are not worthy, to go to such extreme to save us. *"But God demonstrates his own love for us in this: While we were still sinners, Christ died for us".* (Romans 5:8)

God sent Jesus, to save and protect you and me. He did more than take a broom to some iced over branches, He came, He lived, He died and He rose, for you and me. He paid the price for our sins so we can live a better life. He felt us worthy enough to save us and protect us, even from ourselves, and to me that just takes my breath away. I feel special and want to praise His name!

November 26

"Then Jesus cried out, "Whoever believes in me does not believe in me only, but in the one who sent me. The one who looks at me is seeing the one who sent me. I have come into the world as a light, so that no one who believes in me should stay in darkness." (John 12:44-46)

Have you ever walked into a dark room, turned on the light and it was so bright that you had to shield your eyes or squint in order to block out some of that bright light? The same goes when we look into the sun or on coming headlights. Our eyes don't know how to handle all that light, so we shield them in order to see. It feels more comfortable when you block out some of that light.

Our focus verse tells us that Jesus is the light that was sent into this world to drive out darkness. This passage tells us that when we believe we aren't to stay in darkness, we are to come into the light. Yet sometimes people are more comfortable in that darkness, or at least in the shadows, half way between light and dark. People shield their eyes and lives from that light by hanging onto certain habits, lusts, worldly things. Some can't seem to accept all that light, they like the shadows, it is more comfortable there.

But God's word is clear. When you believe in Christ, the darkness must go. God spoke on day one of creation, "let there be light" and he pushed darkness away. Mankind brought darkness (sin) back into this world and for some people it's where they live. For some they like the middle ground, the shadows, saying they believe, yet still live in the darkness of this world.

In order to experience the fullness of Christ, we have to allow ourselves to grow accustomed to the light of Jesus. When we enter that room, our eyes soon adjust and we can stop shielding, squinting and fully open our eyes. We can get used to the brightness of that light, feel its warmth, its glow and find comfort in it.

True believers of Jesus Christ must get accustomed to the light of Jesus. We need to stop shielding our eyes and living in the shadows. We need to live like God created us to live, in the bright light that comes from Jesus Christ, our Lord and Savior. Don't be afraid of the bright light, be drawn to it.

November 27

"Whoever sows sparingly will also reap sparingly, and whoever sows generously will also reap generously" (2 Corinthians 9:6)

My dad was a farmer. He would prepare his land well in advance of the growing season, watch weather patterns and study his seeds, all in anticipation of a good crop. He would plant the seeds, water the land, keep the weeds pulled and tend the soil to promote growth, all in anticipation of the harvest that would come. His attention to detail and dedication to his planting always resulted in a bumper crop come harvest time. He always got more out of his garden than he put into it. He would not only feed us daily off this crop, but would provide vegetables to his neighbors.

My dad knew that a good crop provided not only for our immediate physical needs in the form of a harvest of crops for his daily use but also for his future needs in the form of seed for next year's planting. The general principle was the more he planted and harvested, the more he was able to use and give away.

We can learn a lot from my dad the farmer when it comes to sowing and harvesting. Preparation, determination, patience and study leads to a harvest that makes all the work worthwhile. We can also learn that the more we plant and the more we harvest, the more we have and the more we are able to give.

Our focus verse gives a clear lesson on reaping what we sow. This sowing and the harvest that comes from the planting are greater than vegetables and potatoes; it's souls for the kingdom. We harvest in proportion to our planting.

In order to sow we must trust in God for the seeds and in order to reap we must sow the seeds He gives us. As a Christian we have an obligation to sow the seeds, water them and wait for the harvest. Luke 10:2 states *"He told them, the harvest is plentiful, but the workers are few. Ask the Lord of the harvest, therefore, to send out workers into His harvest field."*

Are you a worker in the Lord's harvest field? Are you planting seeds in the form of the gospel? If not, take a lesson from a farmer son, get God's seeds in fertile grown, tend the garden and then wait for the harvest.

November 28

"All of them were filled with the Holy Spirit and began to speak in other tongues as the Spirit enabled them."(Acts 2:4)

As we traveled across the country, we jumped from one place to another. I found myself looking out the windshield of the RV for hours at a time. During one of those long stretches my mind went to a time when I traveled across country with my son. He was very young and didn't like to sit still for long periods of time. He would ask, over and over again "Are we there yet?" Sometimes he would change it up a little by asking "How much longer?" or "When are we going to get there?" I kind of chuckled to myself, because at that very moment in time I was thinking the same thing.

Sometimes we can be in such a hurry to get there that we may miss out on a blessing. We live in a society of instant gratification, yet in reality good things come to those who wait. Take the followers of Jesus. Just before He went up to Heaven, He told them to go to Jerusalem and wait. His instructions in Acts 1 were to "wait for the gift my Father promised". I bet that seemed like a long time to them. The results were more than they expected. Our focus verse records that the gift they received was the Holy Spirit. Their wait paid off with the greatest gift of all.

But what would have happened if they hadn't been so patient? What would have happened if they would have given up because it didn't come fast enough? Well, we will never know, but it would have changed history as we know it. The gift was worth the wait.

That thought brought me back to reality. The wait for what was next was going to be worth it. In fact, I started looking at the scenery that unfolded before my eyes and received gift after gift. I saw the sights of God's creation. I had rewarding conversations with close friends. I talked and listened to my Heavenly Father. Then, at the end of my wait, I received gift after gift of amazing things before my very eyes. Things I can share with pictures, and things I can't because I have no record, only the memory.

Sometimes we must wait for the things God wants to give us. The wait may seem long and too hard to bear, but I can promise the gifts are worth the wait and God never disappoints. So what are you waiting for? If you believe in God and are a follower of Jesus Christ, He has gifts for you, if you just wait on Him.

November 29

"I am the way and the truth and the life. No one comes to the Father except through me."(John 14:6)

There is a house in California called the Winchester Mystery House. It's beautiful on the outside, but once inside, tour guides must warn people not to stray from the group or they could get lost. Legend has it that Mrs. Winchester was afraid that the evil spirits of the people killed, by the guns her husband manufactured, were after her. She built the house to confuse them. It is a very strange house with many weird things, such as doors that go nowhere.

As I read our focus verse, I couldn't help but remember my tour of this house. The images of doors leading nowhere, or opening up to a view of the sky and a drop from the second story came to mind. My mind went to this world we live in, where everyone is trying to get somewhere, but under their own power. The world tells us there are many ways to get to heaven, but John 14 says otherwise.

Jesus tells His disciples that He is going to prepare a place for them and that He will return. They are confused. What Jesus is saying is that one can only get to the place He prepares (heaven) through Him.

By believing and living a life worthy of Jesus, we can go with Him when He returns. So what does this have to do with the Winchester House? That house represents this world. It's confusing; there are paths that go nowhere. There are doors that open to nothing, or open to clear danger. If we don't follow the guide (Jesus), we may be lost, and it will be for eternity. This world makes promises it can't keep.

Contrary to popular belief, not everyone who dies goes to heaven. Just being good, or being good at something, doesn't guarantee one a place in heaven any more than that house can ward off evil spirits. The only way to heaven, an eternity with Jesus Christ is through Him. He invites us to a better life and a promise He will keep, an eternal life that far exceeds anything this world offers.

So watch your step and pick your path wisely. Be careful of the doors you open and the stairs you climb. Jesus' path is straight and narrow, and He tells us only a "few" will enter the gate. Not sure about anyone else, but I am keeping my eyes on Jesus, because that is where I put my faith. I don't want to get lost and miss out.

November 30

"Then Jesus came to them and said, "All authority in heaven and on earth has been given to me. Therefore go and make disciples of all nations, baptizing them in the name of the Father and of the Son and of the Holy Spirit, and teaching them to obey everything I have commanded you. And surely I am with you always, to the very end of the age."(Matthew 28:18-20)

At a meeting for our motorcycle ministry, we discussed our vision, mission and goal and how we are to use every opportunity to witness to those we come in contact with. My heart has been burdened for those that do not know the love of Christ and who do not have a relationship with God. I believe we are to take serious the call God has on our lives to introduce people to God and make relationships within our community. I strongly believe in our focus verse, that we are called to be the tellers of the gospel.

God has been speaking to me about this for some time now on this topic and He continues to re-enforce the urgency we should have towards spreading the gospel. We are told in Matthew 9:37 that Jesus said *"The harvest is plentiful but the workers are few. Ask the Lord of the harvest, therefore, to send out workers into his harvest field."* We are those workers, the ones that are responsible to work the harvest field. Our harvest field is our own community. The work of the "Great Commission" is tremendous, but as Jesus says, the workers are few. I believe we are challenged to be among those few.

But in order to accomplish this task, we must grasp the greatness that the phrase *"All authority in heaven and on earth has been given to me."* implies. We need to step out of our comfort zone and believe that the greatness, the authority given us will equip us to reach people for Christ. The call of the Lord is great; we need to believe that greatness. We need to step out of our comfort zone and answer God's call. Dare to step out and serve greater. The harvest is great so go and be His faithful laborer.

December 1

"In your relationships with one another, have the same mindset as Christ Jesus." (Philippians 2:5)

I actually have a "catch phrase". When asked "How are you?" I reply "If life were any better I would have to hire someone to help me enjoy it". I try very hard to live life to the fullest. Happiness and joy in one's life makes this easier. I also think that positive thinking is a way to live life in abundance.

So with that said, meet a restaurant manager named Jeff. He too was known to have a catch phrase. When asked how he was doing, he would reply, "If I were any better, I'd be twins!" Every day it was the same. One day an employee asked "How do you do it? I don't get it. You can't be a positive person all of the time." Jeff just smiled and replied, "When I wake up each morning I have two choices today. When something bad happens, you can choose to be a victim, or you can choose to learn from it. I make the choice to learn from it. It's my choice how I will live life."

One day his positive choice was put to the test. He accidently left the back door to the restaurant open and was held at gunpoint by three robbers. As he tried to open the safe, shaking from nervousness, his hand slipped off the combination lock. One of the robbers panicked and shot him.

He was found and rushed to the hospital. Jeff read the eyes of the medical team as they examined him. He read in their eyes that they thought he was a dead man.

When asked if he had any allergies he replied "Yes, bullets!" The team couldn't help but laugh. Jeff looked up from the table and told them "I'm choosing to live. Treat me as if I'm alive, not dead." He did in fact live, thanks to the medical team and because of his positive attitude.

The Bible teaches that the way we think determines the way we feel, and the way we feel determines the way we act. So if you want to change your actions, change the way you think. If you want to change your attitudes, change the thoughts you put in your mind.

December 2

"I have set you an example that you should do as I have done for you."(John 13:15)

How many of you remember the song *"This is how you do it"*? An old song and one I never would have imagined being used as a sermon illustration. But that is what happened at a service I was privileged to attend recently. The pastor used that song title and the lesson from John 13:1-15 to teach about our purpose as Christ followers here on earth.

The story is about Jesus, who after a meal, took a basin of water and a towel and washed the disciple's feet. I know, not a favorite task for many of us, but Jesus did so to teach us a very valuable lesson. When He finished He basically said *"This is how you do it"* to His disciples. What He did for them was what He expected them, and us, to do for others.

Now that lesson used foot washing, but the lesson can be applied to anything that serves others. Jesus chose a group, they followed, and He taught them how to live differently in this world. We all have a purpose and, as this pastor said, "no one can sing your solo for you". Basically, you are meant to do something and only you can do it.

Jesus also equipped His disciples, which include us, to fulfill our purpose. He gives us the necessary tools through scripture, prayer, fasting and communication with Him. Everything we need, He provides, we just have to do it.

We are commissioned to serve others, to go tell others. Not to stay within the confines of our safe environments, but to go "fish" where the lost, the hurting, the sick are. That is exactly where Jesus found me, among the lost, the sick and the hurting and He lifted me up and set me on a path, His path for my life. That is what He commissions us to do; go fishing.

Our focus verse gives us the *"This is how you do it"* instructions. So, are you ready to get to work? We live in a world where people need the good news of Jesus Christ more now than ever. So, are you ready to obey your commission and do it? Follow Jesus' lead and you may never know whose life will be changed....

337

December 3

"Do not store up for yourselves treasures on earth, where moth and rust destroy, and where thieves break in and steal. But store up for yourselves treasures in heaven..." (Mark 6:19-20)

We all have things we treasure. For some its trinkets collected over the years. Some collect big items such as cars, motorcycles, etc. No matter what you collect, for some they cherish them more than anything. Ever see one of those people who love their stuff?

I like to watch the "American Pickers" show. I think that life would be cool, going from town to town looking through old barns and buildings. Sometimes those guys find great stuff, some they get to buy, some they don't. It intrigues me to hear how some of those people place such value on old rusty stuff.

We are told in our focus verse to prioritize our stuff, especially the stuff we put great value on. For some of us, we cling to the wrong things. Jesus taught that the things of this world, everything that we collect, will go away. What we should store up in our hearts are the things that last an eternity.

As we head into Christmas, it is very important to keep in mind what is really important in life. What catches our attention? What do we place value on and where will it be after we die?

We need to take an inventory of what we value, what we hold important in our lives. So as we make our lists for Christmas shopping, what is important to you and what is at the top of your list? Will it rust and rot? Maybe we can live without it in exchange for things that really matter.

December 4

"Every tree that does not bear good fruit is cut down and thrown into the fire."(Matthew 7:19)

I love to sit by a fire. There is something about watching the flames that mesmerizes me. Once I participated in a night out for the homeless. It was sponsored by a shelter and some of the men who lived in that shelter were present. We had a bonfire going and whenever it died down a young man would walk over to a pile of old, useless pallets, pick one up and throw it on the fire.

As I watched this our focus verse came to mind. We are told in scripture that we have a purpose. We are to spread the gospel, we are to love others as ourselves, and we are to be set apart from those of this world. But if we don't, we will be considered useless and thrown into the fire.

Also, as I watched this, the Jason Crabb song "Through the Fire" came to mind. As we walk with God, He may allow certain things to happen to us so He can teach us to be strong, to lean on Him and to become more like Him. He takes the old and useless, refines it to be beautiful, valuable and worthy. Like dirty ore, dug out of a mountain, it is put through a process to become silver: pure, valuable, and sought after. The refining process requires fire. Look at some of the lyrics from the song:

"He never promised that the cross would not get heavy and the hill would not be hard to climb. He never offered our victories without fighting but He said help would always come in time. So just remember when you're standing in the valley of decision and the adversary says give in. Just hold on, our Lord will show up and He will take you through the fire again."

Can you relate? Have you felt the heat from that fire? I have, and it hurts at first. But as we get through it, no, as God brings us through it, we grow stronger, better and rely more on God. So no matter what you are going through, rely on God to bring you through it and through the fire your weakness is made strong.

December 5

"If you, O LORD, kept a record of sins, O Lord, who could stand? But with you there is forgiveness..." (Psalm 130: 3-4)

"To err is human; to forgive, divine." (Alexander Pope) The meaning is that humans make mistakes, so we should forgive those that do, just as God shows his divine mercy in forgiving sinners. But are we, as humans, capable of that? How many of us forgive and then forget?

We've all done wrong and we've all held a wrong against someone. There is only one that can actually forgive and then "choose" to forget; God. We are told that if we ask for forgiveness and repent, God forgives and that's that.

Forgiveness of sins comes when we repent, turn from, and stop sinning. God says that He forgives everything. He will never utter a word about our past sins, but we must come out of them. We can't continue to sin.

But for some they would rather stay in the darkness (sin) because it is fun. They want to continue and ask for forgiveness as well. God's answer to that is NO! He won't forgive while we are continuing in that sin, He won't do that. It's a sin to keep on sinning, did you know that?

As a child of God we are afforded the privilege to be forgiven, no matter what mean, nasty, ugly things we have done. But if we continue to go on sinning, did we really repent? Are we really sorry we sinned in the first place? We all know what it is like to forgive someone who wronged us yet harbor that hurt. It is easy for us to say we forgive, but we are human, we never forget. But God can do both, but we must be willing to do our part.

I am so thankful for that truth. I have done many things in my life that I am truly sorry for. I have wronged people, I have committed some serious sins, but once I gave my life to God and repented of these things, I take great comfort that they are actually forgotten by the one that matters. God forgives me and I choose to live each day trying to live up to His standards, not the worlds.

How about you, what do you need to let go of? What sin in your life is keeping you from being the person God wants you to be? God can forgive, forget and bless, but you must do you part. Are you willing?

December 6

"Go and make a careful search for the child. As soon as you find him, report to me, so that I too may go and worship him." (Matthew 2:7)

Let me tell you a story about King Herod and the Wise Men. The story goes like this: The wise men heard of the birth of Jesus and went searching for Him. King Herod also heard and tried to trick the wise men into finding Jesus and giving him the location, so he could kill Jesus. Both had knowledge of Jesus, yet each had a different response.

The wise men went to great lengths to find Jesus and shower Him with gifts. They made finding and worshipping Jesus their number one priority. They wanted to give Jesus their very best and left everything behind for Jesus.

Herod was jealous. He wanted Jesus dead. He wanted to make himself number one. He wanted to use others for his own gain.

Have you ever heard of the Grinch who stole Christmas? You know the story, the Grinch hated Christmas and everything it stood for. He secretly tried to destroy it by taking the gifts, the food and even the decorations. He tried to make sure others couldn't enjoy it either.

Satan is the Grinch. He hates Jesus, Christmas and everything about that which is good. He will do anything to destroy joy, peace, love and happiness. He doesn't want you to have them.

But if you remember the stories, Herod doesn't win and either did the Grinch. Herod dies, Jesus lives and the Grinch, well he gets a dose of love and his heart was changed. No matter what they tried to do to destroy that which is good, good won out.

Whoville still celebrated Christmas in spite of what the Grinch did. Nothing could rob them of their joy, so the Grinch had a change of heart and he returned the gifts. If we celebrate in spite of the evil in this world, we too will win and nothing can take our joy.

As we near the busiest season of the year, I ask that you focus on what is really important. Set your priorities to reflect that which is the most meaningful to you. The greatest gift given was and still is the love of Jesus Christ. The greatest gift you can give yourself and your family and friends is the love that Jesus represents.

Put aside the worldly things our culture tells us is important. Set your priority to seek and worship the one true gift, Jesus. Share that love with those you love the most and I bet you will have the best Christmas ever.

341

December 7

"Those who obey His commands live in Him, and He in them. And this is how we know that He lives in us: We know it by the Spirit He gave us." (1 John 3:24)

We all know the story of Christmas. Baby Jesus was born in a stable to the Virgin Mary and her husband Joseph. The event changed the world and has the ability to change people's lives today. We celebrate the birth of Christ on Christmas day once a year, but have you ever thought about celebrating the birth of our Christ, our Savior everyday of your life?

Jesus was born to bring us hope, a future, and as an act of love beyond compare. Jesus was God's gift to the world, a piece of Himself. Jesus or Immanuel means *"God with us"*. He wasn't just born as a once in a lifetime gift, He was born to be the gift forever. God is with us because of the birth of His son. Jesus was born so we could have God in us, forever! There is a great implication to that reality. Jesus lives today as He lived then, He lives in His followers.

"Christ grew in Mary until he had to come out. Christ will grow in you until the same occurs. He will come out in your speech, in your actions, in your decisions. Every place you live will be a Bethlehem, and every day you live will be a Christmas. You, like Mary, will deliver Christ into the world. God in us!" (Max Lucado)

I was asked the other day what New Year resolutions I'll make. I didn't have an answer then, but I do now. My New Year's resolution will start today. I will make a resolution to live my life so that everyone that sees me, meets me or knows me will see Christ coming out of me. I will live my life so there is no doubt that Christ is in me and He comes out in all I do and all I am. My New Year's resolution starts today, the day after we celebrated the birth of this Christ that lives in me. What about you?

December 8

"I can do everything through Him who gives me strength." (Philippians 4:13)

Do you remember the super heroes of your past? You know, the ones that are coming back today like Spiderman, Superman, Batman, Iron Man, etc.? They were powerful, could do anything and nothing could stop them. They fought the forces of evil and always won. Not sure about you but I remember them well, I even acted out a few episodes in my back yard as a kid.

Today I know an even bigger, more powerful super hero than any of the ones I remember from my childhood. He is able to do amazing things; heal the sick and lame, raise people from the dead, change lives, give hope, promises eternal salvation and fights evil forces by just speaking. No evil force is powerful enough to fight against Him, and He is always on our side.

This super hero's name is Jesus and He can help us fight evil forces if we just let Him. Studies show that the effect of Jesus on people's lives stops crime; it actually lowers all the statistics. Jesus is the most powerful force against drugs, alcohol, violence, depression, illness, etc. He is the protection of individuals and families, if we simply believe and follow Him.

By being followers of Jesus we are called to be mini versions of Him. He is our super hero and we're to be little super heroes. The Superman of days past may have been powerful, but by being in the Spirit, we are even more powerful. We can move mountains, walk through walls, overcome addictions and change our lives. We need to believe that and live like that!

When it comes to our lives as believers of Jesus Christ, people should see that super hero in us and say, "Thank God he or she is here, they have come to save the day." Jesus means "God saves" and you have the power to save the day. You have the power of salvation through Jesus because you walk in the footsteps of Him. Who do you know that needs a super hero? Be a super hero to that person today and go out and save their day. You have the super power of the super hero of all super heroes, Jesus.

December 9

"When they had gone, an angel of the Lord appeared to Joseph in a dream.
'Get up,' he said, 'take the child and his mother and escape to Egypt. Stay
there until I tell you, for Herod is going to search for the child to kill him.'
So he got up, took the child and his mother during the night and left for
Egypt, where he stayed until the death of Herod. And so was fulfilled what
the Lord had said through the prophet: 'Out of Egypt I called my son.'"
(Matthew 2:13-15)

Have you ever experienced anything weird, out of the ordinary?
More than likely we all have, but what happens when we experience it
not once, but twice? Are we as quick to respond the second time
around?

During the Christmas season every church has some sort of
program depicting the birth of Jesus. But a little talked about fact is the
way this child came about. Seriously, an Angel spoke to Mary, telling
her she will get pregnant, even though she is a virgin. Then an Angel
goes to Joseph and tells him this child Mary carries is Jesus the
Messiah, and that he should accept the child as his own. That is weird,
yet they both obeyed and did as they were told.

To quote Paul Harvey: "now for the rest of the story." The baby is
born, visited by wise men and shepherds. Showered with gifts and
praise, Jesus is born, the Savior of the world. Then the weirdness hits
again. An Angel comes and tells Joseph to take the baby and run. And
the Angel tells him to go to Egypt, a place of oppression and slavery.
That is really weird.

What did Joseph think? We really don't know, but we do know
what he did. He obeyed. Because of his obedience, even in its
weirdness, baby Jesus escaped a sure death at the hands of King Herod.

It is easy to obey when we know it is God speaking. But how often
do we know or believe it's really Him? God speaks daily, through
scripture, the Holy Spirit and even "Angels", yet we often miss it or we
are so busy we don't hear. We can get so caught up in life that we miss
the things God is trying to bless us with or save us from.

Make a point to slow down and take a breath. Listen for God's
voice. He just may be trying to tell you something, give you some
direction or correction. If we are quiet and intentional in our listening,
we may hear the voice of God and that voice can change our lives
forever. So, I pray we all have Joseph like faith. When we hear God's
voice, we recognize it, obey it and get moving.

344

December 10

"But I trust in your unfailing love; my heart rejoices in your salvation. I will sing to the LORD, for he has been good to me." (Psalm 13:5-6)

I know a lot of people, and if asked, about every one of them would say they believe in and trust God. Today statistics claim that somewhere close to 80% of Americans believe in God or claim to be a Christian. I fit into that statistic. Yet everywhere we look we see people living contrary to the bible. We see people living defeated lives. Evil is among us and it keeps getting worse. If so many claim to believe, why do we live in a world controlled by Satan?

Consider this: A man goes on a mountain hike. He slips and falls off the edge and on the way down to what he thinks is a sure death, he grabs hold of a small sapling that is sticking out from between two rocks. He clings to the sapling for dear life and calls out to God "Help Me!"

He hears a voice from heaven ask him, "Do you trust me?" "Yes I trust you", the man replies. The voice answers, "Do you really trust me?" Dangling in midair he ponders this question and finally replies, "Yes I do trust you, and if you haven't noticed I don't have much choice in the matter right now." The heavenly voice said "If you trust me, let go!"

Here lays the heart of the matter with trust. It is easy to say "I trust you" until it's time to let go. That is when we really must ponder, can I; will I? What if there is no ledge for us to drop down on? What if the only thing under our feet is air, and a very hard landing?

You see, it is easy to trust when things are going well. But what if the answer to our question or problem isn't what I wanted? What if the healing never comes, we don't get the job, or it is our time to go to our eternal home?

Trust is hard. We love to say "Isn't God good" when everything works the way we want it to, but what about when it doesn't? Real trust comes when we let go and no matter what happens, we say "Isn't God good." Real trust is letting go and knowing God is good, even when the tears are running down our faces.

So pray today that God helps you put total trust in Him. No matter what and no matter the outcome, let us rejoice in Him and the salvation He promises. Let our voices proclaim "He has been good to me"!

345

December 11

""Lead us not into temptation."(Luke 11:4)

I, like many, struggle with my weight. Oh I know how to lose those extra pounds, I know the importance of exercise, but I also know that I like food.

Just yesterday afternoon I had told my wife that I wanted to lose a few pounds, but last night I found myself in a buffet line, loading a plate with all the wrong things. The more I looked, the more I saw and was tempted to eat.

Temptation is a struggle for all who have ever tried to live a healthy and godly life. A quick look around our world today reveals that living healthy and godly doesn't come naturally to us, and we are constantly tempted with what does: food, ambitions, lusts, bad habits, self-interest, conflict, and more.

Temptation is a hard thing to overcome on our own. Temptation leads to sin, because we do what we know we shouldn't. We try to starve the sinful nature, ignore it, talk back to the devil who feeds it, beat it into submission, and more. These can all be helpful and effective techniques, but only work for a while.

But there is another way. We should ask God to lead us away from tempting situations. We decide to break a habit of food or drink or other substance, but we don't rid our environment of the substance. Jesus said in our focus verse that He can help.

Jesus knew that the key to overcoming temptation was to ask God to lead us away from it. Jesus knew from experience that when faced with temptation we should ask God for the power to say "no". That is when we become overcomers.

So if you see me in a buffet line and I am just standing there, hopefully I am praying. Hopefully I am asking God to give me the strength to just say no, to head to the salad bar and to skip the ice cream.

December 12

"What a wretched man I am! Who will rescue me from this body that is subject to death? Thanks be to God, who delivers me through Jesus Christ our Lord!" (Romans 7:24-25)

A man owned two dogs, a white one and a black one, who fought constantly. A neighbor asked "which one wins", in which the man said, "The one who I feed the most." This is so true even in our lives.

The Apostle Paul wrote in Romans 7 about the war that wages within us; good vs. evil. Our nature is sinful; we are all born with it. We know right from wrong, but naturally we lean towards the wrong. We know what God calls "good" and we know the "ways" He wants us to live, but it goes against our nature, hence causing a war within.

The conflict wages and we must get a handle on it in order to defeat it. But the reality is, as Paul wrote about in this chapter, it is an everyday battle. An 85 year old Pastor/teacher, who teaches preaching to seminary students, is asked a very personal question. "Sir," the young man asks, "when do the lusts of the eyes and the temptations of the body stop?" The old man thought for a minute and then replied, "It is at least after the age of 85."

That war that wages against light and dark, good and evil, right and wrong, exists every day in a person's life. How we respond and what we do dictates which one wins. It is a never ending battle and one that we can't win on our own. The fight is won by the one we feed the most.

Paul wrote our focus verse to acknowledge that we are unable to deliver ourselves from the offensive, repulsive bondage of the human nature towards sin. We must ask for help, help that can only come from the one who said *"Blessed are the poor in spirit, for theirs is the kingdom of heaven."* (Matthew 5:3) Jesus was not referring to the material poor, but those who acknowledge their helplessness and rely on the Lord to help them overcome the world and sin. They know their need and find it supplied in Him.

So, which "dog" are you feeding? Do you feed the sinful nature or the Godly nature? Do you know that you can't win the battle without Jesus' help? If so, then call on His name and ask Him to become your strength, your counselor and your comforter. Once you have Jesus in your corner, there is no battle you can't win.

December 13

"Every good and perfect gift is from above, coming down from the Father of the heavenly lights..." (James 1:17)

My Uncle Nick would visit once a year. He came to take the kids shopping for Christmas. Uncle Nick had no kids, so he would load us up in his big car and off we would go. He would turn us loose and let us get whatever we wanted.

One year I was gone when Uncle Nick came. I was really disappointed because not only did I miss seeing him, I missed out on the gifts as well. My mom noticed my mood when she gave me the "present" Uncle Nick left. It was a flannel shirt. Are you kidding me, a shirt for a Christmas? She insisted I try it on. I noticed something in the pocket, which turned out to be a 100 dollar bill. Now that was a gift.

In 1977 I received yet a gift that topped that. My son was born. I couldn't help but wonder what did I ever do to deserve such a gift? In 1994, I received another great gift; my second wife. She was the woman of my dreams and, to be honest, I never thought I could top any of these three gifts; they were unbeatable, until December 9, 2000.

On that day, I finally decided to stop living for me and to surrender my life to God. I hit my knees and asked God to come into my heart and He gave me the gift of salvation. I received God's love, forgiveness and the gift of eternal life in heaven. The bible promises that those that repent and are baptized *"will receive the gift of the Holy Spirit."* (Acts 2:38) I received that gift and my life changed. Now that was the greatest gift of all.

I also realize now, that even though I wasn't living for God, He lavished me with gifts my whole life. You see, He created Uncle Nick who loved to give, He created that child that was born for me to love and He led me to my wife Joy. Those gifts came from Him, as our focus verse tells us. Most of the time we don't give God credit, but He loves us so much He gives to us even when we refuse to listen to Him, obey Him, or even acknowledge Him.

God is the greatest gift giver of all. His gifts are too numerous to count, just look around. He gives us life, breathe and our very existence. He gives His love to us even though we aren't worthy and He loves us even when we don't love Him. He gives us the opportunity to spend eternity with Him and that my friends, is the greatest gift of all time!

December 14

"...you do not even know what will happen tomorrow. What is your life? You are a mist that appears for a little while and then vanishes." (James 4:14)

I live in an area where the motorcycle community is very large. Unfortunately with so many motorcycles in one area, too often we suffer tragic loss. The passing of a loved one is hard. No words can be spoken that eases the pain, fills the void and make the tears of loved ones go away.

The one thing I am reminded of during times of loss is that life is short. There are no guarantees and no promises of another day. Our focus verse tells us that we are here one minute, gone the next, so what we do with this life matters.

I can't help but recall the funerals I have officiated. I don't know how many times I have stressed the importance of choices in life. The decisions we make and how we live our life really do matter. Contrary to popular belief, not everyone will go to heaven. Being a good person doesn't guarantee us a spot, but believing in Jesus, accepting His free offer of salvation and living a life pleasing to Him does.

Once I traveled to Baltimore for business. I booked my flight, rental car and hotel, boarded my plane and arrived in Baltimore. I strutted up to the rental car board expecting to see my name on the "Preferred" list, only to find it wasn't there. Upon checking, I discovered I had booked a car in Boston, not Baltimore. It didn't take long to fix, and soon I arrived at my hotel. Again I strutted up to the clerk only to find out, I had no room reserved, again. Yes I had done this before on another trip. I had booked a car and room for another city. This is a good lesson. Just because we think we have a reservation doesn't guarantee us one.

Let this lesson remind us that we need to take seriously our choices in where we spend eternity. We must, without a doubt, know where we will go when we leave this life. I would hate for someone to be turned away, because their reservation is for the wrong place. I promise you: that is embarrassing.

December 15

"And let us consider how we may spur one another on toward love and good deeds, not giving up meeting together, as some are in the habit of doing, but encouraging one another, and all the more as you see the Day approaching."
(Hebrews 10:24-25)

Have you ever wondered why geese fly in a V formation? Scientists discovered they could fly farther and longer by flying this way. In this formation the motion of the wings of the goose in front of each one provides an uplift that makes it easier for the following goose to fly.

Occasionally, an independent goose tries to go it alone, but soon tires and has to stop or fall hopelessly behind the rest. Christians are like that, too. On our own we soon grow faint, give in to temptation, or get too discouraged to go on. We really do need each other.

Now I know the next question: "What happens to the lead goose? He has no bird to provide the uplift for him." The answer is simple and practical. When the lead goose gets tired, it falls out and takes its place at the end of the formation where it is easier to fly. Another goose moves up and leads.

What a great example for those who profess to believe in Jesus Christ. Sometimes people think they can be a Christian without being involved in corporate worship or a small group. The Christian life was never meant to be solitary. Christianity is always referred to as a body, a flock, a building, and a holy nation. There are no "lone wolves" in Christianity. Without regular participation in corporate worship, one tends to drift spiritually, much like the lone goose who eventually will tire and fall away from the pack. To say you love Christ yet neglect His body is hypocritical.

We can learn a lot from geese. Alone we fade, fail and fall away. Together we strengthen, encourage and help each other. Together we can go further, do more and are stronger. Jesus said *"For where two or three gather in My name, there am I with them."* (Matthew 18:20) So take some advice, join a church and/or small group. As you learn, there is strength in numbers!

December 16

"For I know the plans I have for you, declares the Lord. Plans to prosper you and not to harm you, plans to give you hope and a future." (Jeremiah 29:11)

Standing on a large rock in what is known as the "Valley of Fire" in Nevada, I watched as a car came to a sudden stop. It sat between two pull offs, one it had already passed and another just ahead that obviously the driver hadn't seen. The driver, in his hast to find somewhere to park, backed up into the pull out behind him. I watched as he got out the car and walked around trying to catch a view of the valley and take his pictures.

From my vantage point, I noticed that if he had gone down the road a few more yards, he would have found a much better spot to park. And the spot down the road would have given him a much better view to take his pictures, with less energy spent. But instead, he settled for the first thing he saw.

I thought about how true this is in most of our lives. Often we see something and take it. We live in a world of instant gratification. We want what we want and we want it now. We are so set in getting whatever it is that we stop short or even back up, in order to fulfill our desires. We settle when just around the corner something God wants you to see may be waiting that is much better and will better meet our needs.

How often do we put a damper on God's plans because we stop short or even back up? When we rely on God and let Him lead us, His perfect plan for us works out to our favor. Let God lead and wait on Him. He knows what is ahead and He knows what is best for you.....

351

December 17

"For the wages of sin is death, but the gift of God is eternal life in Christ Jesus our Lord."(Romans 6:23)

John and Sally are committed to God. They want to do their part so they sell a piece of property and give the proceeds to the church. But before they gave, they conspire to keep some of the money.

John offers the money, making it appear that it is all of the sale price. He is asked, "Why have you lied?" They knew he had lied. John drops dead immediately.

Sally is called to the office. She is asked "Is what John offered the whole price of the land you sold?" In which she answered "Yes" and she too drops dead immediately.

Is this harsh and unfair? How is it that they offered a gift yet died in doing so? Well, the issue isn't with the gift, but the condition of their heart. You see, they intentionally lied, therefore sinned.

That makes me think about my own life. Am I giving my all to God, just as I say? Or am I holding back? The bible is very clear, when we profess with our mouths, we also must profess with our hearts, minds and body and soul. You can't be partially in; it's all or nothing.

And there are consequences for our actions. This story is actually found in Acts 5:1-11. Ananias and Sapphira let Satan tempt them to deceive, lie and cheat, while making themselves look holy. The punishment was death. What if the same happened to us when we say one thing yet do another? What if the consequences of our sin were as immediate as what happened to this couple?

Our focus verse says the wages of sin (wrongs, lies, deceits, cheating, and disobedience) is death. Now, we may not immediately drop dead, but we do risk that. Or at the time of our death on earth we face a fiery eternal death in hell verse eternal life in heaven. So why risk it?

Being who we say we are as Christ followers matters. Our hearts must be pure, our minds must be focused on pleasing God and our motivations must be Christ centered. Being who we say we are has eternal consequences. As a pastor friend of mine said once, "We must be all in, or we are all out." There is no middle ground, it's all or nothing and your life depends on it.

December 18

"But if we hope for what we do not yet have, we wait for it patiently."
(Romans 8:25)

As I headed to Yellowstone, I asked God to reveal His beauty to me. I asked Him to let me see His creation and the creatures He created in their natural habitat. I longed to see buffalo, elk, moose and whatever other wild animals lived there.

My first 4 or 5 miles in Yellowstone I was so eager to see something, I found myself scanning the shoulders of the road for animals. I was so focused on "seeing" what I had asked for that I was missing out on the beauty of the surroundings. It was about then I heard God say "just wait". I had prayed for what I hoped for, now I needed to wait for God to give it to me. No amount of scanning would bring about that which I wanted, only God could deliver what I wanted to see, when it was the appropriate time.

Too often I get in a rush to have what I want. It's like that commercial, "I want it now!" I get so keyed up and anxious, that I can't enjoy the wait. Or is it that I don't really believe that God will deliver so I have to? But, as it was on this trip, I sat back, waited and I got more than I asked for.

Our focus verse talks of patience and waiting for God's perfect timing. Nothing about that says we must go find, or seek out ourselves, it says "we wait for it patiently." That is hard for me. Maybe it is for you too? But in this case, the wait was worth it.

As we rode through the park, we came face to face with buffalo. We encountered not one but many herds of them. We saw a bear, some deer and elk, along with some of the most spectacular views imaginable. God delivered that in which I asked for, and then some more.

God knows the desires of our heart and when we ask, and then wait, He reveals those things to us. No matter how long I walk with God, He never disappoints. He is always there, always showing me new things and for some reason, always blessing me beyond my wildest dreams. I am so grateful He loves me. And He loves you too.

So what is it you desire? Ask, believe He hears you and then wait patiently. It's even okay to keep asking, the bible tells us to. But know this, if it is within His will for you to have what you ask for, He will deliver and deliver big. So ask....

December 19

"Let's go to Bethlehem and see this thing that has happened, which the Lord has told us about." (Luke 2:15)

It amazes me how commercialized this world has made Christmas. Think on this, the long awaited next episode of Star Wars is released just prior to Christmas. Why? It only takes one trip to any store to figure it out.

Everywhere you look you see Star Wars stuff. Clothes, toys, games, figurines, re-released DVDs of past episodes... One may think we are celebrating Star Wars, not the birth of Jesus.

Everywhere you look, people pushing, shoving, and fighting over the latest craze to hit our world. They are totally lost in their obsession to get the "newest" thing before supplies run out. The cash registers are ringing, while business executives are singing, 'tis the season to make money.

Well, it wasn't always that way. Three guys stood in a field, minding their own business, when suddenly they heard of great news. The announcement was big, they, like many others, had waited for this day to come. In their excitement they left everything to "see this thing that has happened."

Three other guys heard the same news. They saw the trailer, and in their excitement to see this "new" thing, they too traveled long and far. They were excited to see, even though it took them a while to get there.

But, instead of buying, they brought gifts. For these six, that first Christmas wasn't about buying the latest worldly craze, it was about seeing the long awaited Messiah, the Savior of the World.

As we celebrate this Christmas, let us ask ourselves, why is this day so important? Is it to get the perfect gift? Is it to buy and give the perfect gift? No! That gift has already been given, in the form of a baby in a manger, Jesus.

We don't need to purchase this gift, just merely accept it. Receive this gift of Jesus this Christmas. Give this gift of Jesus this Christmas. Celebrate His birth and celebrate His promise. Jesus came to give us the gift of His undying love and the promise of eternal life with Him. It's free and in a time where everyone is in a hurry to get somewhere, you can get this gift without leaving your chair.

December 20

"Blessed are those who wash their robes. They will be permitted to enter through the gates of the city and eat the fruit from the tree of life."
(Revelation 22:14)

As a kid we didn't have computers, iPads, cell phones and golf carts like kids have today. We played in the dirt, we swam in the creek, and we rode our bikes everywhere. By the time we were called home for dinner, we were filthy and the sweat rings around our wrists and necks were proof of our activities.

I remember my mom saying "Go wash up so you can eat." Sitting at the table dirty was not an option. She wanted you to clean up before partaking in the meal she had prepared. Dirty hands and momma's cooking didn't mix.

It's the same in our spiritual lives. No matter what we think of ourselves, we can't scrub enough to rid ourselves of the dirt and grime of this world. We are born sinful, destined for hell. Our sins, no matter how big or small, intentional or not, make us unfit or unclean to sit at God's table.

Our focus verse tells us that cleanliness is required to enter heaven. Now we can't do this like we did as a kid, by splashing water on our face and hands and wiping the dirt off with a towel. It takes more effort on our part. In order to *"wash our robes"* we must repent of all the things we have done wrong. That means to turn from them and not do them anymore. Don't miss that part.

We must see the things we do that go against God as God sees them. We must see the sin, shame, the dirt in our lives and know that such things aren't allowed at God's table. By confessing them and asking for forgiveness, God is faithful to make us clean. Then, and only then, are we presentable to sit at His table.

So why not do so now? If you have sin in your life and you are truly sorry, and you want to sit with God at His table in heaven, it's time to wash up. Ask for and receive forgiveness. Ask for and receive the mercy and grace that is yours for free. Before you go any further in your life, take the time to allow God to wash away your sins and make you as white as snow. The table is set, are you ready?

December 21

"...whoever drinks the water He gives them will never thirst again." (John 4:14)

As I took a cool morning motorcycle ride to the mountains, I pondered water. Of all things to think about while riding, water. I couldn't get it out of my head. It wasn't hot, I wasn't sweating, yet I had such a thirst for water.

As I drank the water I had purchased at a stop, it came to mind that even though I wasn't sweating, my body was using up the water it contained. Activity, motion, temperature and other factors contribute to dehydration. To function properly, you need to keep your body hydrated at all times. So even though I didn't think I needed water, I did and I couldn't get enough of it.

Jesus, being God clothed in flesh, knew the importance of water and used it to illustrate the necessity of staying connected to Him. When Jesus met the woman at the well, our focus verse tells us He offered her something that satisfied permanently. He knew the importance of hydration, He lived in a desert environment, and was speaking of hydrating ourselves with the blessings and mercies only He provides. The woman could relate since she lived in the same arid climate and was at the well to draw the day's supply of a much needed commodity.

Just as we need the natural water to keep our bodies functioning properly, we need *"living water"* in order to stay connected to Jesus. When we fill our lives with the word (bible), daily conversation with the Father (prayer), and allow the presence of the Holy Spirit to fill us, we become hydrated with the very thing that keeps us alive. It is a necessity and when it is absent we can feel it just as we feel thirst for natural water. We crave it, and if the craving isn't fulfilled, our lives start to reflect the lack of His very life giving commodity.

Jesus wants us to have the *"living water"* that not only quenches, but overflows as well. The benefit of the water He offers is not merely limited to here on earth, but will go on forever. Nothing in this world can offer us the fulfillment that Jesus' *"living water"* offers. Anything we fill our life with here on earth wears out, gets old, or will fall apart. But the things that Jesus offers last an eternity.

Do you crave something but you're not really sure what it is? Try the *"living water"* Jesus offers, it just may be the best thing you ever tried.

December 22

"All this took place to fulfill what the Lord had said through the prophet: The virgin will be with child and will give birth to a son, and they will call him Immanuel which means, God with us." (Matthew 1:23)

For some of us, Christmas is all about gifts, decorations and celebrating. People get wrapped up in the festivities, forgetting the true meaning. For those of us who call ourselves Christians, the true reason for this season is the coming of Jesus Christ. "God with us" is why we celebrate Christmas.

But what does that really mean? We know the story of baby Jesus being born of the virgin. We know about the wise men, the shepherds and the host of angels. We all know that Jesus came to save those who would accept Him from the evils of this world. But how many actually think about all that when celebrating the birth of Jesus?

Christmas isn't only about the birth of Jesus. Christmas is also about an event and subsequent events that changed the world and those who believe in that birth. Author David Wilkerson said *"The heart of Christ's message is extremely simple: an encounter with God, a real one, means change." "It is transformation. It is being born again to a new life."* That encounter could only happen with that birth in the manger. That birth gave each of us the opportunity for a better life, one that can last an eternity.

In the book *"The Cross and the Switchblade"* David Wilkerson uses this example. *His grandfather encountered a big snake, one that petrified him. He stood, unable to move as he watched the snake. But then it moved and he watched a miracle. The snake shed its skin and crawled away a new beautiful creature.*

Jesus came so we could shed the "sin-shell" of our old lives and leave it behind. He came so we could leave the old person behind and allow Him to transform us into the new person, one who can live in fellowship with Him. When we have a real, meaningful encounter with Jesus we can't help but to be changed. That is why Jesus came down from Heaven and laid in a manger, to change the likes of you and me. Embrace that change, accept the gift of Jesus and begin to live as a new creation.

December 23

"Never will I leave you; never will I forsake you." (Hebrews 13:5)

In the area I live there was a big ruckus about a manger. Some people have an objection to the placement of a tiny little manger scene in the back corner of a local library. The library was told to take it down because it "offended" someone. Can you imagine that? The scene of a baby's birth would be rejected and offend?

People around the world celebrate Christmas. They put up trees, buy gifts and eat large meals that day. I would guess the same people who objected to the manger scene probably had a tree with presents under it. Yet they reject to the "religious" implications. Why? Well, we may never know, but we do know that this rejection was foretold many years before the actual birth.

Jesus came even though He knew what would happen to Him. He came to save a people He knew would reject Him, would nail Him to a cross. Jesus never abandoned His mission to save the world, in spite of the fact that He knew some would reject Him, be offended by Him and want to kill Him. Instead, He came to love, to give mercy, to offer grace and to claim those that would accept Him as His very own.

I, for one, am thankful for the day that Jesus came to this world as a baby. I rejected Jesus for years. I scuffed at the idea of a Savior being born as a poor baby without a place to lay its head. Yet here I am today, bought and paid for by that baby's blood, not because of anything I have done, but because He came, He lived, He bore my penalty and He paid my price, because I couldn't.

He loved me even though I rejected Him. He claimed me even thought I laughed at Him. He promises me an eternal place with Him in Heaven, even though I do not deserve it. After Jesus came, knowing His fate, after paying the price, He gave us the promise found in our focus verse. And we know that He never breaks His promises.

So, some will reject Jesus and the manger. Some may not understand the birth of a baby in a manger that would save the world. Jesus knew that beforehand, yet came anyway. And by the way, those people are who Jesus came for. So pray for those who reject Jesus. Pray they receive the gift of Salvation this Christmas and come to know the one who was born, our Savior.

December 24

"The Word gave life to everything that was created, and His life brought light to everyone. The light shines in the darkness, and the darkness can never extinguish it." (John 1:4-5)

Growing up poor gave me an appreciation for the simple things. We never received much for Christmas, and what we did get, we appreciated. We did have a real tree, decorated with love. The whole family would have a hand at putting on the lights and ornaments. I never knew the origin of the tree, why people put them up, or what they meant, nor did I care, I just knew the tree signified Christmas was coming.

The tree meant more to us than gifts; it signified warmth, a time of family, friends, laughter and a feast on Christmas day. I wasn't raised in a home that spoke of God, Jesus, or anything religious, but Christmas was special to us. The tree signified a time of love and happiness and I have fond memories of Christmas' past.

I later learned that five hundred years ago a man named Martin Luther, a leader in the Protestant Reformation, began the custom of the Christmas tree as we know it. It is said that while he walked through the woods before Christmas Eve, he saw an evergreen tree illuminated by starlight. He was amazed at its beauty and was reminded of the night angels appeared to the shepherds in Bethlehem and announced the birth of Jesus Christ. Luther cut down a smaller tree, carried it home and decorated the tree with lit candles, telling his family they represented Christ as the light of the World.

The Christmas season is upon us. Trees are going up all over and I guess most of you are putting yours up as well. As you do, may it be more than merely a decoration. As you look at the tree, remember the symbol of God's light and love in a world that is still desperate for salvation, hope, mercy, and grace. As you look at the tree, think about Jesus Christ as the One who came to this world to bring God's light into a world of darkness. As you look at the tree, think more about the origin of the tree and not what's under it.

One of my wife's favorite things to do this time of year is decorate the tree, plug in the lights, turn off all the other lights in the house and stare at the tree. At first I thought that was crazy, but as I think about the tree in this context, I can't wait to put our tree up, plug it in and let it light up our house as a symbol of God's light that illuminates our life.

December 25

"When they saw the star, they were overjoyed. On coming to the house, they saw the child with his mother Mary, and they bowed down and worshiped him. Then they opened their treasures and presented him with gifts of gold and of incense and of myrrh." (Matthew 2:10-11)

Christmas day is really fun with a grandson. I watched my grandson, just shy of three, as he opened his gifts with the same reaction each time. His mouth would fly open, his eyes opened wide and he would yell out "Oh wow!" Every gift received the same reaction, he truly was grateful to receive each and every gift.

That morning reminded me of the very first Christmas in which I truly understood what the day represented. You see, prior to December 2000, I celebrated Christmas, but merely as a day to exchange gifts and eat a large meal. I never fully understood the Christmas story until December 9, 2000 in which I sat through my very first Christmas presentation. That night I heard and saw the story of Jesus unfolded before my eyes and I learned that Jesus came on Christmas day to save people just like me. That night, under my breathe I think I said "Oh wow" a hundred times.

That night, just like our focus verse says, I "bowed" and gave my heart to Jesus, the only thing I had to offer. That night I received the greatest gift ever, salvation. My life has been transformed since that day. On Christmas morning I was reminded of that gift that keeps on giving. Each day I live and walk with Jesus I should say "Oh wow", because it still amazes me that Jesus would love me so much that He did what He did.

This year, as we live out our lives, I pray we each have "Oh wow" moments. I pray we enjoy moments where we are amazed and reminded of His love, His forgiveness and His mercy and grace. May we have childlike excitement of serving a Lord that would go to great lengths for us. He would leave heaven, put on human skin, walk among the filth of this earth and bring us to Him, simply because He loves us.

So what about you? Did you celebrate His birthday like it deserves to be celebrated? Let us face each day with the words "Oh wow", and be excited to see the gift of salvation opened before us.

December 26

"Therefore, if anyone is in Christ, he is a new creation; the old has gone, the new has come!" (2 Corinthians 5:17)

There is nothing like a weekend with good friends, curvy roads and beautiful scenery. Needless to say, when we ride, we miss a turn or two every now and again. There have been times when we have had to make a few U-turns in order to get back on course. We rode one road once that the pavement just stopped, it became gravel and needless to say, motorcycles and gravel don't mix. So a U-turn was needed.

To me, this makes riding motorcycles exciting. But more often than not, we remember the mistakes, the U-turns and the bad roads more than we do the good ones. That just seems to be our nature.

In the book *"If"* by Mark Batterson, I read about what is called a "hard reset" in which a device is reset to its original settings. It will wipe the device clean and make it like brand new. That is what happens when you ask for Christ to come into your life and you receive His mercy and grace. You are reset and made new!

The trick is to act new. Be someone who has been reset. Think differently and act differently. Stop doing the things you needed forgiveness for to begin with. When you accept Christ as your Lord and Savior, He moves in. He lives in you and helps you overcome the things that caused you harm, trouble and pain.

The other trick is to forget the bad you did. Jesus did. Focus more on the good. Jesus remembers the good and He chooses to forget that in which He has forgiven you for. It is gone forever. Yet we tend to remember those mistakes. We find it hard to forgive ourselves. The inability to forget the sin we have confessed is actually part of our sin itself.

So, if you have made mistakes and are ready for a "new" life, you too can be reset. Just ask Jesus to come into your heart. That's it. He will give you the "hard reset", and He will make you like new. Then, with the power of the Holy Spirit, try to forgive yourself and forget the things you have honestly handed over to Jesus. They are gone, ancient history, let them go. If you still have things you are finding hard to forgive yourself for, maybe you need to confess them and ask for forgiveness. Then live in the power of Jesus.

December 27

"Therefore go and make disciples of all nations, baptizing them in the name of the Father and of the Son and of the Holy Spirit."(Matthew 28:19)

I have ridden on both sides of the biker world. In other words, I have not always been a Christian biker. There are things I have done that I will never mention. But now I am a born again Christ follower who rides for Jesus.

One night, at a biker event, a man asked me which bar I would be going to when I left the biker event? My reply was simple; none, because I had already visited four bars that day. The look on his face was truly comical. Being a Pastor, I felt I needed to explain...

Why does a Pastor visit four bars in one day? I go because our focus verse tells me to. I don't recommend that every Christian visit bars, but I have a calling to tell others about God. So I go where most Christians won't and don't go. Christians are called to spread the word and, for me, that means anywhere bikers hang out.

Jesus came to earth for sinners, which includes me, so that they could hear the Gospel. So if Christians don't "go" tell the world, how will they ever know? I like people and I want to be around people that I feel a common bond with. I want people to know that I like them, no matter their choices, what they ride, how they look or where they live or hang out. I make friends with bikers because I am a biker.

So, I go where God tells me to go, bars, bike nights, secular events, festivals, hospitals, the streets, wherever to tell people about Jesus. It is just what I do, and to be honest, I enjoy it. I enjoy doing what I know God wants me to do and I get a blessing when I am accepted for who I am and what I believe in. I have found that most people don't care what I know as a Pastor, they just want to know that I care about them, and I do. The one thing that is the most important thing to me is being real. I am a biker that got saved and I want others to know that they too can find the love of Christ and still keep riding.

So if you are ever in a bar and you see me walk in, don't get alarmed, I am not there to hit you on the head with my bible, I am only there to check on you. I like people, especially bikers and I am concerned about my brothers' and sisters' salvation. Your eternal salvation is my heartfelt concern, and I don't mind talking to anyone, anytime, anywhere about the saving grace of Jesus Christ.

December 28

"Those who turn away from you will be written in the dust because they have forsaken the LORD, the spring of living water." (Jeremiah 17:13)

Ever heard of a watering hole? It's a place where people go to feel comfortable, to get a drink of what they think they need or want. It is a place to replenish. Most towns have a watering hole or two and it usually doesn't take one much time to find them. The problem with these watering holes and the refreshment they offer is normally you just get thirsty again and it is just a short run down the road.

These places existed in biblical times as well. Normally they were public wells, a place to get a drink or to water their animals. This was also a place where travelers could stop to get some refreshment. Hang around a watering hole long enough and something unusual may happen.

In John 4, Jesus stops off at a watering hole in a place called Samaria. Jews weren't likely to visit such a place, but then Jesus isn't the normal Jew. As innocent as it sounds, one must think there was another purpose for His visit. Maybe He had a plan.

Jesus used the importance of water in an arid environment to illustrate what He offered. He knows the people knew how important it was to go to the well daily, to draw the one thing in a desert that was crucial to life, water. He speaks of *"living water"*, something people could relate to. The Old Testament spoke of this water, Jesus just reminded people of its importance, and that its source was Him.

As you travel the roads of your journey, where are your watering holes? Do you rely on the "water" of this world or are you seeking the *"living water"* that quenches your soul and lasts a lifetime? Are you seeking a quick moment of refreshment or are you seeking something more lasting? Jesus offers us a spiritual thirst quencher that not only lasts a worldly life, but an eternal life.

The watering holes we should be seeking are those that have eternal thirst quenching capabilities. The next time your journey gets you tired and thirsty, stop off at God's watering hole and get the refreshment that lasts forever. Ask Him to fill you with that *"living water"*, the water that lasts forever. And the next time you meet a stranger at one of those watering holes, be careful, it just may be someone that is offering you the same thing Jesus offered the woman at the well...lasting refreshment that can only come from Him!

December 29

"Not everyone who says to me, 'Lord, Lord,' will enter the kingdom of heaven, but only the one who does the will of my Father who is in heaven.
(Matthew 7:21)

Have you ever been on a team where one kid just doesn't make the cut? He wore the uniform, he came to the practices, yet he just didn't have what it took to get out on the field. The church has a few of these.

Many people say they believe in God. They say they have given their heart to Jesus. They attend church, yet they go on living as if nothing ever changed. They have head knowledge, but no heart knowledge of what a real relationship with God is like. God wants people that make the cut. People who live changed lives and are obedient to His teachings.

One can believe, go to church, do good things, but that doesn't necessarily guarantee them a spot in Heaven. Jesus said many times that getting into heaven, living an eternal life with Him and the Father was hard and not everyone would make it. He spoke of a narrow road in which only a few would travel.

Jesus said that it takes more to make the cut than simply going through the motions. We must *"Make every effort to enter through the narrow door, because many, I tell you, will try to enter and will not be able to."* (Luke 13:24) In order to make it through that narrow gate or door we must not only believe, we must follow, obey, live changed lives and be "Christ-like" as we are called to do so many times in the bible.

James gave some good advice when he wrote *"You believe that there is one God. Good! Even the demons believe that and shudder."* (James 2:19) Satan and his followers believe in God, but we know they will never enter into the gates of Heaven. The same can be said for those good people who say they believe. Being good and believing doesn't earn you a place in Heaven. Relook at Matthew 7:21-23 and understand that although Heaven is available to all, it is, in fact, a very exclusive club and membership comes at a cost. One must sacrifice their life for the life Christ wants them to lead. One must put God and His will before their own will. One must love others as Christ does. One must not only ask for forgiveness, but forgive as well. As hard as it may be, it is available to each and every one of us, if we want it. Will you make the team?

December 30

"These twelve Jesus sent out with the following instructions: "Do not go among the Gentiles or enter any town of the Samaritans. Go rather to the lost sheep of Israel. As you go, proclaim this message: 'The kingdom of heaven has come near.' Heal the sick, raise the dead, cleanse those who have leprosy, drive out demons. Freely you have received; freely give."
(Matthew 10:5-8)

Our focus verse sounds like an episode right out of Mission Impossible. Can you see Jesus recording this on a mini-cassette, the disciples listening and then the tape self-destructing? Can you see the disciple's faces as they think about the task at hand? Who me? Heal sick people, raise dead people, cleanse the lepers, and drive out demons? How? Has Jesus sent the disciples and us today on an impossible mission?

Few of us today have experienced healing, seeing dead people rise to life, cleansing and exorcisms. How can we declare what we haven't seen? No, we are called to declare what we do know. The disciples saw and were present to see the miracles, the dead rise, the leper cleansed, so they were to share their direct experiences. We are to do the same. This is every Christian's calling. Have you seen Jesus heal? Then declare His healing. Have you seen Him deliver? Then declare His deliverance. Have you seen Him release captives? Then declare His freedom. Whatever He has done for you, you are to do for others.

He intends not only to care for us in a way that we become like Him. Those of us, who have been forgiven, forgive. If your debts have been cancelled, cancel someone else's debt. If you have been given ample resources, then give to others. We are to minister to others as Jesus ministered to us. His blessings are the means for us to bless others. In the same ways we have experienced the kingdom of heaven, we are to share it. If we follow this principle, the mission is easy.

"Christianity is one beggar telling another beggar where he found bread." D.T. Niles

December 31

"Therefore anyone who sets aside one of the least of these commands and teaches others accordingly will be called least in the kingdom of heaven, but whoever practices and teaches these commands will be called great in the kingdom of heaven." (Matthew 5:19)

To be a follower of Jesus means to obey ALL of His commands, with no exceptions, no compromise and no reservation. We should do or say nothing that goes against any biblical teachings that could lead you or someone else to sin willingly. But, let me warn you, to live this lifestyle means that you may not fit in with the group you hang with. Being different will make you feel like an outcast.

Also, to hold other believers accountable for their actions may even be seen as offensive, brain washing or judging. Jesus taught while He walked this earth that His followers would feel this way. He warned that people would hate us because of Him. He also warned us that there would be those among us that would look and sound like us on the surface, but *"...are ferocious wolves."* (Matt 7:15) If you are a fully devoted follower of Jesus Christ, not just a casual believer, and everyone likes you, then you probably aren't doing something right.

A new Contemporary Christian artist, Kerry Roberts has a song entitled *"Outcast"* and her lyrics speak of this very thing. She sings: *"But let me tell you what, I know who I am, so just throw me out for not fitting in, I will stand my ground and be an outcast... No matter what it costs, I'll be an outcast."*

So in a world where everyone just wants to fit in, get along and do what everyone else is doing, living a life devoted to following Jesus may make you feel like an outcast. But stand your ground; the end result far outweighs the here and now. The Apostle Paul knew this world would be tough, that is why he told us to keep our eye on the prize. *"I press on toward the goal to win the prize for which God has called me heavenward in Christ Jesus."* (Philippians 3:14)

The prize for standing firm in your belief, standing firm when the world would have you bend, is an eternity in heaven. So being an outcast in this world isn't so bad. Living a life devoted to Jesus and being called an outcast in this world may be the biggest compliment you could ever receive. Be an outcast that leads you to heaven, God will be pleased.